LOOK TO THE TEMPLE

FINDING JOY IN YOUR TEMPLE WORSHIP

ALSO BY ED J. PINEGAR AND RICHARD J. ALLEN:

Teachings and Commentaries on the New Testament
Living by the Word
Teachings and Commentaries on the Book of Mormon
Teachings and Commentaries on the Doctrine and Covenants
(with Karl R. Anderson)
Teachings and Commentaries on the Old Testament
Your Patriarchal Blessing
Come unto Me
Press Forward, Saints
Choose Ye This Day
Words of Wisdom for Missionaries

ALSO BY ED J. PINEGAR

Latter-day Commentary on the New Testament: The Four Gospels
(with K. Douglas Bassett and Ted L. Earl)
The Ultimate Missionary Companion
A Prophet's Voice

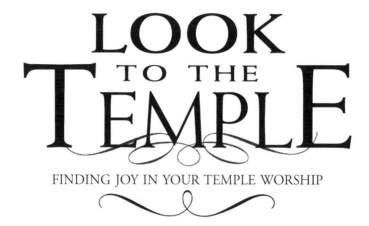

FINDING JOY IN YOUR TEMPLE WORSHIP

Ed J. Pinegar
and
Richard J. Allen

Covenant Communications, Inc.

Cover image: *Timpanogos Temple* © Val Brinkerhoff

Cover design copyrighted 2007 by Covenant Communications, Inc.

Published by Covenant Communications, Inc.
American Fork, Utah

Copyright © 2007 by Ed J. Pinegar and Richard J. Allen
All rights reserved. No part of this book may be reproduced in any format or in any medium without the written permission of the publisher, Covenant Communications, Inc., P.O. Box 416, American Fork, UT 84003. This work is not an official publication of The Church of Jesus Christ of Latter-day Saints. The views expressed within this work are the sole responsibility of the authors and do not necessarily reflect the position of The Church of Jesus Christ of Latter-day Saints, Covenant Communications, Inc., or any other entity.

Printed in the United States of America
First Printing: February 2007

17 16 15   10 9 8 7 6

ISBN 978-1-59811-247-4

Acknowledgments

We wish to express our sincere thanks to the editors and design staff of Covenant Communications for their outstanding professional service in bringing forth this publication. In particular we recognize the committed service of Kathryn Jenkins, managing editor, and Kathryn Gille, project editor. In addition, may we express our appreciation to our wives, Patricia P. Pinegar and Carol Lynn Allen, and other family members for their devoted support and encouragement in the completion of this work.

Ed J. Pinegar
Richard J. Allen

ABBREVIATIONS

CR — Conference Report. Salt Lake City: The Church of Jesus Christ of Latter-day Saints.

Discourses — John A. Widtsoe, sel. *Discourses of Brigham Young.* Salt Lake City: Deseret Book, 1954.

DS — Joseph Fielding Smith, *Doctrines of Salvation.* Ed. Bruce R. McConkie. 3 vols. Salt Lake City: Bookcraft, 1954–56.

Gospel Doctrine — Joseph F. Smith. *Gospel Doctrine: Selections from the Sermons and Writings of Joseph F. Smith.* Comp. John A. Widtsoe. Salt Lake City: Bookcraft, 1998.

Gospel Ideals — David O. McKay. *Gospel Ideals: Selections from the Discourses of David O. McKay.* Salt Lake City: Improvement Era, 1953.

Gospel Kingdom — John Taylor. *The Gospel Kingdom: Selections from the Writings and Discourses of John Taylor.* Comp. G. Homer Durham. Salt Lake City: Bookcraft, 1964.

HC — Joseph Smith. *History of the Church of Jesus Christ of Latter-day Saints.* Ed. B. H. Roberts. 7 vols. Salt Lake City: The Church of Jesus Christ of Latter-day Saints, 1932–51.

TETB — Ezra Taft Benson. *The Teachings of Ezra Taft Benson.* Salt Lake City: Bookcraft, 1988.

TGAS — George Albert Smith. *The Teachings of George Albert Smith.* Ed. Robert McIntosh and Susan McIntosh. Salt Lake City: Bookcraft, 1996.

TGBH — Gordon B. Hinckley. *Teachings of Gordon B. Hinckley.* Salt Lake City: Deseret Book, 1997.

THBL   Harold B. Lee. *The Teachings of Harold B. Lee.* Ed. Clyde J. Williams. Salt Lake City: Bookcraft, 1996.

THWH   Howard W. Hunter. *The Teachings of Howard W. Hunter.* Ed. Clyde J. Williams. Salt Lake City: Bookcraft, 1997.

TLS   Lorenzo Snow. *The Teachings of Lorenzo Snow.* Ed. Clyde J. Williams. Salt Lake City: Bookcraft, 1984.

TSWK   Spencer W. Kimball. *The Teachings of Spencer W. Kimball.* Ed. Edward L. Kimball. Salt Lake City: Bookcraft, 1982.

TABLE OF CONTENTS

INTRODUCTION 1

PART ONE
Preparing to Enter the Temple 9

    CHAPTER 1
    The Vision of the Temple 11

    CHAPTER 2
    The Purpose of the Temple 35

    CHAPTER 3
    The Pathway to the Temple—Taking on the Divine Nature 43

    CHAPTER 4
    A House of Faith 51

    CHAPTER 5
    A House of Virtue 67

    CHAPTER 6
    A House of Knowledge 81

    CHAPTER 7
    A House of Temperance 93

    CHAPTER 8
    A House of Patience 103

    CHAPTER 9
    A House of Brotherly Kindness 109

    CHAPTER 10
    A House of Godliness 121

CHAPTER 11
A House of Charity 131

CHAPTER 12
A House of Humility 139

CHAPTER 13
A House of Diligence 147

PART TWO
Entering the Temple 159

CHAPTER 14
Obtaining a Temple Recommend 161

CHAPTER 15
Understanding the Symbolism of the Temple 175

CHAPTER 16
Participating in Temple Ordinances 183

CHAPTER 17
Temple Covenants 199

PART THREE
Temple Service for a Lifetime 213

CHAPTER 18
The Eternal Family—The Joy of Family History Work 215

CHAPTER 19
Enduring to the End with the Temple in View 229

CHAPTER 20
Looking Forward with Hope—The Glory and Blessings of the Fullness of the Gospel 245

Introduction

When the aging King Benjamin summoned his people to the temple at Zarahemla to bestow upon them his final words of inspired counsel, they organized themselves as family units in preparation for the message: "And they pitched their tents round about the temple, every man having his tent with the door thereof towards the temple, that thereby they might remain in their tents and hear the words which king Benjamin should speak unto them" (Mosiah 2:6). Therein lies a pattern for us all to follow: If we pitch our tents toward the temple of God, we avail ourselves of divine inspiration to lift and bless our families with the exalting truths of the everlasting gospel of peace and rest. By way of contrast, Abraham's nephew Lot, subsequent to the flight from Ur to Canaan, was charmed by the extravagant enticements of the cities of the plain, "and pitched his tent toward Sodom" (Gen. 13:12). That tendency toward worldliness did not serve him well, for it took the intervention of angelic messengers to draw him away from those wicked venues just prior to God pouring out His judgments in mighty destructive force upon them (see Gen. 19:24–25).

In the stark contrast of these two dispositions—pitching our tents toward the temple on the one hand, or toward Sodom on the other—we have the ultimate manifestation of the consequences of the use of agency. It is given unto us to make the key decisions of life: "Wherefore, men are free according to the flesh; and all things are given them which are expedient unto man. And they are free to choose liberty and eternal life, through the great Mediator of all men, or to choose captivity and death" (2 Ne. 2:27).

The moral of the story is the consummate wisdom of coming unto Christ by denying ourselves "of all ungodliness" (Moro. 10:32) and aligning ourselves valiantly with the principles and doctrines of the gospel of salvation.

Look to the Lord and Be Healed

When Nicodemus, a leading member of the Sanhedrin, came to Jesus by night to inquire of the Savior's mission, Jesus taught him concerning the need to be born again in order to enter the kingdom of God (see John 3:1–7). To support this doctrine, the Savior cited the testimony of Moses concerning the incident involving the serpent of brass during the period when the children of Israel wandered in the wilderness. When this symbolic serpent was lifted up before the murmuring Israelites, and they looked upon it, their lives were preserved from the attacks of poisonous snakes sent in response to their disobedience (see Num. 21:4–9). The Savior explained to Nicodemus the significance of the symbolism: "And as Moses lifted up the serpent in the wilderness, even so must the Son of man be lifted up: That whosoever believeth in him should not perish, but have eternal life" (John 3:14–15).

The prophets of the Book of Mormon emphasized again and again the need to look upon the Savior as the source for all healing. Nephi responded to the mocking derision of his rebellious brothers by reminding them of God's mercy, despite our pride and disobedience:

> And he loveth those who will have him to be their God. Behold, he loved our fathers, and he covenanted with them, yea, even Abraham, Isaac, and Jacob; and he remembered the covenants which he had made; wherefore, he did bring them out of the land of Egypt. And he did straiten them in the wilderness with his rod; for they hardened their hearts, even as ye have; and the Lord straitened them because of their iniquity. He sent fiery flying serpents among them; and after they were bitten he prepared a way

> that they might be healed; and the labor which they had to perform was to look; and because of the simpleness of the way, or the easiness of it, there were many who perished. And they did harden their hearts from time to time, and they did revile against Moses, and also against God; nevertheless, ye know that they were led forth by his matchless power into the land of promise. (1 Ne. 17:40–42; see also 2 Ne. 25:20–21)

By simply looking to the Savior and following in His footsteps with devotion, we can be assured of preservation in the face of all adversity and tribulation.

Alma taught the same doctrine to the Zoramites following his matchless discourse on having faith in the Savior (see Alma 32):

> Behold, he was spoken of by Moses; yea, and behold a type was raised up in the wilderness, that whosoever would look upon it might live. And many did look and live. But few understood the meaning of those things, and this because of the hardness of their hearts. But there were many who were so hardened that they would not look, therefore they perished. Now the reason they would not look is because they did not believe that it would heal them. O my brethren, if ye could be healed by merely casting about your eyes that ye might be healed, would ye not behold quickly, or would ye rather harden your hearts in unbelief, and be slothful, that ye would not cast about your eyes, that ye might perish? (Alma 33:19–21)

And Nephi, the son of Helaman, also referred to this concept while teaching the people about the Atonement: "Yea, did he [Moses] not bear record that the Son of God should come? And as he lifted up the brazen serpent in the wilderness, even so shall he be lifted up who should come. And as many as should look upon that serpent should live, even so as many as should look upon the Son of God with faith, having a contrite spirit, might live, even unto that life which is eternal" (Hel. 8:14–15).

Based on this interrelated array of scriptures, we can better understand the memorable counsel that Alma gave to his righteous son Shiblon concerning looking to Christ: "And now, my son, I trust that I shall have great joy in you, because of your steadiness and your faithfulness unto God; for as you have commenced in your youth to look to the Lord your God, even so I hope that you will continue in keeping his commandments; for blessed is he that endureth to the end" (Alma 38:2).

The beautiful and simple gospel teaching that we should "look to the Lord and live" is at the heart of all spiritual development in our quest to become more like the Savior. "Therefore, what manner of men ought ye to be?" asked the Savior of His devoted followers surrounding the temple at Bountiful. The answer He gave them continues to resound through the generations of time: "Verily I say unto you, even as I am" (3 Ne. 27:27).

Look to the Temple and Live

The decision to become even as the Savior leads us upward along the pathway of faith, repentance, baptism for the remission of sins, and the reception of the gift of the Holy Ghost. Through the Spirit we are guided in all light and truth: "For behold, again I say unto you that if ye will enter in by the way, and receive the Holy Ghost, it will show unto you all things what ye should do" (2 Ne. 32:5). Subsequent to our becoming members of the fold of Christ among the most edifying of all inducements of the Holy Ghost—"the enticings of the Holy Spirit" as King Benjamin described them (Mosiah 3:19)—is the desire, the motivation, the aspiration, the yearning, and the commitment to go to the temple and receive there the appointed blessings of heaven. After baptism and becoming "fellowcitizens with the saints, and of the household of God" (Eph. 2:19), going to the temple is the next step in the process of perfection. As we follow the natural progression of steps in the plan of redemption and exaltation, looking always to the Savior for all spiritual healing and vitality, we will be guided to look to the temple and live.

The pathway to exaltation and eternal life passes through the house of the Lord—the holy temple of the Almighty. He has ordained that it will be so. There are no byways, no circuitous detours or alternate routes. All heaven-bound Saints—the faithful and the valiant, the humble and the noble—ply the same straight and narrow gospel course leading directly homeward via the temples of God. In those sacred halls that rise on the foothills of eternity are to be found the essential truths and covenant ordinances to ensure that the journey can be completed with success—all the way to its final destination—according to the designs of a loving and merciful God.

The institution of the temple, organized by the power of God and governed through the keys of the holy priesthood, is a divine gift of incomparable and inestimable value. It is an essential dimension of the kingdom of God in any dispensation but particularly in the dispensation of the fullness of times, in which the Lord "will gather together in one all things, both which are in heaven, and which are on earth" (D&C 27:13). How grateful we should be for the temple, which encompasses all glory and truth, for the blessings of hope and love that abound there, and for the sacred opportunity to participate in the work of the temple for the purpose of ensuring our eventual return, and that of our families, into the presence of our Heavenly Father and His Only Begotten Son.

Those who make the commitment to "come unto Christ" (Jacob 1:7; Omni 1:26; Moro. 10:30; D&C 20:59) likewise commit to a process of becoming perfected to the degree that they can enter the temple and partake of its magnificent blessings. In the final verses of the Book of Mormon, Moroni characterized this process with the following invitation: "Yea, come unto Christ, and be perfected in him, and deny yourselves of all ungodliness; and if ye shall deny yourselves of all ungodliness, and love God with all your might, mind and strength, then is his grace sufficient for you, that by his grace ye may be perfect in Christ; and if by the grace of God ye are perfect in Christ, ye can in nowise deny the power of God" (Moro. 10:32).

To love God with complete and sincere devotion and to aspire in obedience to merit the requisite endowment of His redeeming grace—"after all we can do" (2 Ne. 25:23)—is to take the first steps toward preparing to enter the temple as worthy and faithful disciples of Jesus Christ. The temple beckons with the irresistible majesty of heaven's power. Its blessings are singularly compelling and abundant. The temple is a lighthouse of refuge on cliffs besieged by the raging tempests of worldly influences; it is a haven of security from the onslaughts of the adversary and his minions; it is an accessible archive of divine truth that supersedes and transcends the shallow superficiality of all prideful mortal campaigns. Those who worship and serve in the temples of God receive His choicest gifts. There is nothing in all the world to exceed the spiritual splendor of these hallowed precincts, which are veritably windows of opportunity offering "greater views" (D&C 10:45) of the things of heaven.

Admittance into the temple of God, as we shall see, is accorded all members who have reached the required age, who desire to go, and who willingly cultivate the simple qualities of goodness that flow naturally from the "godly walk and conversation" (D&C 20:69) characteristic of those who seek to become even as the Savior. Those qualities include faith, virtue, knowledge, temperance, patience, brotherly kindness, godliness, charity, humility, and diligence—elements of the divine nature in all of us (see 2 Pet. 1:3–8; D&C 4).

Temple attendance is a central part of our quest to become better, to become more like the Savior. It is the crowning blessing of our membership in the Church and a fundamental aspect of our worship. For these reasons, looking to the temple and its transcendent gifts of peace and hope is something we should all strive for with diligence and conviction. The Lord's chosen servants have continually emphasized the importance of the temple. President Gordon B. Hinckley has observed:

> These unique and wonderful buildings, and the ordinances administered therein, represent the ultimate in our worship. These ordinances become the most profound expressions of our theology. I urge our people everywhere, with all of the persuasiveness of which I am capable, to live worthy to hold a temple recommend, to secure one and

regard it as a precious asset, and to make a greater effort to go to the house of the Lord and partake of the spirit and the blessings to be had therein. I am satisfied that every man or woman who goes to the temple in a spirit of sincerity and faith leaves the house of the Lord a better man or woman. There is need for constant improvement in all of our lives. There is need occasionally to leave the noise and the tumult of the world and step within the walls of a sacred house of God, there to feel His spirit in an environment of holiness and peace. (*Ensign,* Nov. 1995, 51)

President Howard W. Hunter has also encouraged us to "look to the temple of the Lord as the great symbol of your membership" (*THWH,* 238). To be worthy to enter the house of the Lord—even if circumstances and distances preclude attending as frequently as one might desire—and to savor the peace and inspiration prevailing within those holy walls is a choice and unique opportunity to be lifted and edified, and to render loving service to those who have gone beyond the veil, as President Hunter confirmed:

Truly, the Lord desires that His people be a temple-motivated people. It would be the deepest desire of my heart to have every member of the Church be temple worthy. I would hope that every adult member would be worthy of—and carry—a current temple recommend, even if proximity to a temple does not allow immediate or frequent use of it. Let us be a temple-attending and a temple-loving people. Let us hasten to the temple as frequently as time and means and personal circumstances allow. Let us go not only for our kindred dead, but let us also go for the personal blessing of temple worship, for the sanctity and safety which is provided within those hallowed and consecrated walls. The temple is a place of beauty, it is a place of revelation, it is a place of peace. It is the house of the Lord. It is holy unto the Lord. It should be holy unto us. (*Ensign,* Oct. 1994, 2)

In that spirit, this book is a systematic treatment of how to prepare for the temple by purifying attitudes, thoughts, and deeds—whether one is going for the first time or returning continually in faith and devotion to honor covenant obligations. Going to the temple takes careful spiritual preparation—every time we go. We will explore ways to cultivate a fuller understanding of the principles and doctrines that pertain to the house of the Lord and recommend a step-by-step method to bring our attitudes and actions into alignment with the standards set forth by the Lord and His chosen prophets as befitting those with the desire and commitment to gather to the temples of Zion. The goal is to "look to the temple and live." The blessings awaiting us there are precious: peace, joy, inspiration, revelation, wisdom, instructions for eternal progression, sacred covenants and promises of everlasting consequence, bonding of family members now and forever, and the comfort and assurance that come only through the illumination of the Holy Spirit. We commend all those who embark on the temple journey—and express our best wishes for a fulfilling and edifying experience within the halls of glory that prepare us for exaltation in the celestial kingdom.

PART ONE
PREPARING TO ENTER THE TEMPLE

Guiding Principle: We are drawn to the temple as the gateway to exaltation, as the essential passageway to receive the highest blessings of the Almighty through our diligence and covenant faithfulness.

> *Endowments [are] essential for exaltation hereafter. These blessings insure to us, through our faithfulness, the pearl of great price the Lord has offered us for* these are the greatest blessings we can receive in this life. *It is a wonderful thing to come into the Church, but you cannot receive an exaltation until you have made covenants in the house of the Lord and received the keys and authorities that are there bestowed and which cannot be given in any other place on the earth today.*
> —JOSEPH FIELDING SMITH, DOCTRINES OF SALVATION, 2:253; EMPHASIS IN ORIGINAL.

CHAPTER 1
THE VISION OF THE TEMPLE

Guiding Principle: Within the walls of the house of the Lord we are privileged to view our destiny from the divine perspective—to understand the majestic scope of the Lord's design for our immortality and eternal life and to perceive ourselves in the context of our personal relationship with our Heavenly Father and His Only Begotten Son.

> *Temple work . . . gives a wonderful opportunity for keeping alive our spiritual knowledge and strength. The mighty perspective of eternity is unraveled before us in the holy temples; we see time from its infinite beginning to its endless end; and the drama of eternal life is unfolded before us. Then I see more clearly my place amidst the things of the universe, my place among the purposes of God; I am better able to place myself where I belong, and I am better able to value and to weigh, to separate and to organize the common, ordinary duties of my life, so that the little things shall not oppress me or take away my vision of the greater things that God has given us.*
> —JOHN A. WIDTSOE, CONFERENCE REPORT, APR. 1922, 97–98.

"Holiness to the Lord"

There are countless ways to sing praises to God for His protecting hand and merciful blessings. Some express their thankful praise through the medium of painting or sculpture; some through poetry or discourse; some in the pages of books; some through quiet acts of selfless service when they "succor the weak, lift up the hands which hang down, and strengthen the feeble knees" (D&C 81:5). Elder Theodore M. Burton told of his Grandfather Moyle, who had been a skilled craftsman in his day. The gentleman had lost his leg on a farm in Alpine, Utah, after being kicked by a cow and had great difficulty moving about thereafter. But he nevertheless traveled twenty-eight miles each day to reach the construction site of the Salt Lake Temple, where his appointed mission was to chisel in the walls of granite the phrase "Holiness to the Lord." That is a form of praise and honor that has inspired countless thousands who visit the temple and its sacred grounds.

Genuine praise for God, in all of its forms, is a means to lift the one who praises, to edify the community of thanksgivers, and to magnify the joy we find in the gospel. It is a way to give utterance to the transcendent concept of "Holiness to the Lord"—and to open the vision of those with eyes fixed on the temple as a tactile and enduring symbol of how the heavens can touch the earth with grace and benevolence.

In many respects we are all engaged in the process of chiseling or engraving the words "Holiness to the Lord" on temple walls—namely, on the walls of our own (physical) spiritual frames, which Paul designated thus: "Know ye not that ye are the temple of God, and that the Spirit of God dwelleth in you? If any man defile the temple of God, him shall God destroy; for the temple of God is holy, which temple ye are" (1 Cor. 3:16–17). We engrave upon our hearts and minds the sacred truths of our covenants with God. In this regard, the prophet Jeremiah predicted: "Behold, the days come, saith the Lord, that I will make a new covenant with the house of Israel, and with the house of Judah: . . . I will put my law in their inward parts, and write it in their hearts; and will be their God, and they shall be my people" (Jer. 31:31, 33). We write the ingredients of salvation upon the "fleshy tables of the heart" (2 Cor. 3:3), preparing the way for us to become holy, even as the Lord Jesus Christ is holy. "Therefore I would that ye should be perfect," He commanded, "even as I, or your Father who is in heaven is perfect" (3 Ne. 12:48).

Above all, a disposition to cultivate "Holiness to the Lord" within our patterns of living is one of discernment—seeing more clearly the pathway that lies ahead, perceiving the hand of God in all of our wholesome and enlightening experiences in life, enjoying "great views of that which is to come" (Mosiah 5:3).

To look upon the spired temples of God—the radiant edifices each known as His house—is to enjoy "great views of that which is to come," because the temple is the revelatory manifestation of the eternities that lie before us and the outward expression of our divine heritage and potential as "heirs of God, and joint-heirs with Christ" (Rom. 8:17). We see the temple as the veritable gateway to the throne of God, the final ascent to our ultimate destination, the greatest motivating influence for good in our lives. President David O. McKay observed the following on the occasion of the dedication of the Los Angeles Temple:

> There are few, even temple workers, who comprehend the full meaning and power of the temple endowment. Seen for what it is, it is the step-by-step ascent into the Eternal presence. If our young people could but glimpse it, it would be the most powerful spiritual motivation of their lives. (As reported by J. Richard Clarke in "Celestial Pursuit," Brigham Young University—Idaho Devotional, Sept. 23, 2003)

Essential to our personal preparation for entering the temple is catching this "glimpse" of the glory of the temple as the ascent into the presence of God. The temple is His holy house—the sacred edifice where priesthood covenants and sealing blessings are made available to those who heed the Lord's commandment to come unto Him and be sanctified and prepared to enter His presence. "Why do we build temples?" asked President Joseph Fielding Smith. "It is because the Lord commands it. For what purpose are they built? In order that sacred ordinances and covenants necessary to the exaltation in the celestial kingdom may be bestowed upon all those who are *worthy* of the exaltation" (*DS,* 2:243; emphasis in original).

The vision of the temple of God is the crowning experience of seeing our way forward, drawn on by the power of the Atonement and the glorious principles of the gospel of Jesus Christ in its fullness. There is joy in the fruits of faith and repentance; there is deep satisfaction from entering into the fold of Christ through baptism and the gift of the Holy Ghost. But there is joy beyond measure when one is able to magnify the blessings of membership in the Lord's Church through the sublime experience of attending the temple regularly and worthily.

The Destiny of Mankind

Preparing to enter the temple is the same thing as preparing for the fulfillment of one's divine destiny. The temple enables individuals and families to extend their reach beyond the confines of the mortal experience and into the eternities. The most profound questions of life are not answered through the wisdom of mortals or the philosophies of the world—rather they are considered and answered only in the temples of the Lord, where our true identity as sons and daughters of God is illuminated in the light of revealed truth.

Many years ago, as a member of the Quorum of the Twelve, President Gordon B. Hinckley expounded upon this theme:

> Was there ever a man who, in a time of quiet introspection, has not pondered the solemn mysteries of life? Has he not asked himself: "where did I come from? Why am I here? Where am I going? What is my relationship to my Maker? Will death rob me of the treasured associations of life? What of my wife and children? Will there be another existence after this, and, if so, will we know one another there?"
>
> The answers to these questions are not found in the wisdom of men. They are found only in the revealed word

of God. Temples of The Church of Jesus Christ of Latter-day Saints are sacred structures in which these and other eternal questions are answered. Each is dedicated as a house of the Lord, a place of holiness and peace, shut apart from the world, where truths are taught and ordinances are performed that bring knowledge of things eternal and motivate the participant to live with understanding of his divine inheritance as a child of God and an awareness of his potential as an eternal being. (*Ensign,* Aug. 1974, 37)

The Lord revealed to the prophet Moses the all-encompassing truth: "For behold, this is my work and my glory—to bring to pass the immortality and eternal life of man" (Moses 1:39). The Lord has also revealed to us what it is that constitutes our own work and glory: "Behold, this is your work, to keep my commandments, yea, with all your might, mind and strength" (D&C 11:20). One of the Lord's central commandments is expressed in this passage: "Behold, it is my will, that all they who call on my name, and worship me according to mine everlasting gospel, should gather together, and stand in holy places" (D&C 101:22; see also D&C 45:32; 87:8; 101:64; 124:39). Such holy places include the congregations of the Saints in the stakes of Zion, the blessed homes of the families of Zion, and—in particular—the sacred temples of the Lord.

Temples are built by the commandment of God. We are called to temples by His commandment. How earnestly and devoutly we should prepare for the fulfillment of this sublime obligation and opportunity. King Benjamin declared: "And behold, all that he requires of you is to keep his commandments; and he has promised you that if ye would keep his commandments ye should prosper in the land; and he never doth vary from that which he hath said; therefore, if ye do keep his commandments he doth bless you and prosper you" (Mosiah 2:22).

To the world in general, the commandments of God appear as harsh and inflexible restrictions on agency. To the faithful they are instruments that liberate and disentangle the soul from the tethers of sin that would hold us back and prevent our ascent to higher levels of spirituality.

Are we grateful for the commandments? A sure test of our devotion is our attitude toward the commandments. Let us teach ourselves and our children to see the commandments as blessings from the God of salvation. Let us echo the words of the Psalmist: "O how love I thy law! it is my meditation all the day. Thou through thy commandments hast made me wiser than mine enemies" (Ps. 119:97–98). And furthermore: "Thy testimonies [commandments] are wonderful: therefore doth my soul keep them" (Ps. 119:129).

By fulfilling the commandment of the Lord to visit Him in His temples, we are on track to achieve our divine potential as sons and daughters of God. The gospel of Jesus Christ reveals to individuals who they are—children of God—what their destiny and potential is—to be heirs of all that God has and to return to His presence one day—and how they can achieve this supernal mission through faith and obedience. And nowhere is this knowledge more clearly and fully revealed than in God's holy temples.

The temple is the icon of the eternities. Within its holy precincts we set aside the concerns of daily living and align ourselves with the majestic panorama of God's plan of happiness. We come to understand more fully the part we are to play within the family of God and the obligations we take upon ourselves to rise to our potential according to the divine seed of perfectibility within us. Such a vista takes preparation—and obedience. We purify ourselves in preparation for crossing the threshold of the house of the Lord. We make ourselves worthy of the blessings that await us there. Concerning our obligation of obedience with regard to the temple, President Gordon B. Hinckley has stated:

> Everything that occurs in the temple is eternal in its consequences. We there deal with matters of immortality, with things of eternity, with things of man and his relationship to his Divine Parent and his Redeemer. Hands must be clean and hearts must be pure and thoughts concerned with the solemnities of eternity when in these sacred premises. Here is taught the great plan of man's eternal journey. Here are solemnized covenants sacred and everlasting. Entering

the temple is a privilege to be earned and not a right that automatically goes with Church membership. How does one earn that privilege? By obedience to the laws and ordinances of the gospel. (*Ensign,* May 1990, 51)

A Crowning Blessing from God

The temple is a supreme and ennobling blessing from Heavenly Father to each of His faithful sons and daughters. The endowment and sealing powers of the holy priesthood confer upon us and our families unique honors and benefits that convey to us the eventual privileged access to the most holy of destinations: the very presence of the Father and of the Son. In his inspired dedicatory prayer for the Kirtland Temple on March 27, 1836, the Prophet Joseph Smith expressed the fervent desire "that this house may be a house of prayer, a house of fasting, a house of faith, a house of glory and of God, even thy house" (D&C 109:16). Truly the temple is the house of God—that singularly sacred place on the earth ordained of God for conferring His holiest of blessings upon the faithful and obedient of His fold.

Of course, a chapel is also the "house of God"—and we love to gather there to renew our covenants and be instructed in gospel doctrines and teachings. Great blessings come to us in the chapels of Zion—but the blessings given in temples are of a different and higher order. In those unique and holy edifices we are privileged to take part in sacred ceremonies, organized and administered according to the sealing keys of the priesthood of God and designed to prepare and equip the faithful Saints for exaltation in the mansions on high. President Joseph Fielding Smith made this clear:

> What is a Temple? *Temples, according to the revelations of the Lord, are sanctuaries specially dedicated for sacred rites and ceremonies pertaining to exaltation in the celestial kingdom of God. They are separate and distinct in their purpose from the ordinary houses of worship.* A church building, no matter how magnificent and costly, if its purpose is for the general gatherings of the people, is not a temple. *Temples are sanctified for the purpose of performing*

> *rites for and making covenants with the pure in heart, who have proved themselves by faithful service worthy of the blessings of exaltation.* (*DS*, 2:231; emphasis in original)

The Lord desires that we have a fullness of blessings from His benevolent and merciful hand. He wants us to return home from our mortal journey cleansed and sanctified and worthy to enter into His rest, "which rest is the fulness of his glory" (D&C 84:24). Such glory is revealed only in His very presence, as the linguistic source of the word *glory* in our scriptures implies. That source is the Hebrew word *kabod,* translated as "glory" in the Old Testament and having to do with the aura of light and radiance associated with God's presence. In this sense, those who are preparing to enter the temples of God are preparing for a blessing of divine light to flood in upon their lives. Truly, the proceedings within the temple constitute a grand rehearsal for the occasion when we will, in very deed, be welcomed into the presence of God and partake of the blessings of light and glory that await us there. In this regard, the Lord commanded us through the Prophet Joseph Smith to have the following goal: "And seek the face of the Lord always, that in patience ye may possess your souls, and ye shall have eternal life" (D&C 101:38).

In ancient times, the Lord commanded Moses to prepare the people to behold His face and receive His glory on Mount Sinai. Israel had been suffering in the bondage of slavery for four hundred years; but now the Lord extended the supreme opportunity for them to become royal subjects before His hallowed throne—transformed by His divine power from slaves to kings and queens, from bondspersons to princes and princesses. But the people shrank back in fear before the glory (*kabod*) of Deity and preferred to hide behind the intermediary representation of the prophet. In His anger—or "provocation" (see Heb. 3:8, 15; Jacob 1:7; Alma 12:36)—the Lord withdrew the privilege of His presence and bestowed upon the people the lesser endowment of schoolmasterly ordinances and procedures (the law of Moses) designed to point them systematically toward an understanding of the redeeming mission of the Savior and His atoning sacrifice on their behalf. Thereafter only the priestly officers of the kingdom were permitted in the tabernacle—the unique portable temple of God—

and only the high priest was permitted to enter the Holy of Holies, the most sacred of the tabernacle chambers, and even he only one time per year, on the Day of Atonement (see Ex. 30:10).

No such restrictions apply in the dispensation of the fullness of times. All who are worthy can be admitted into the temple of the Lord and into the celestial room of sublime peace and rest. That is the ultimate blessing that comes from God—the universal access to the center of sacredness representing, in effect, the throne room of God. What an extraordinary privilege! What a remarkable blessing! A fullness of privileges through the holy priesthood is available in the temple to every worthy individual of age who responds with complete devotion to the invitation to come unto God. It is not the office and calling of the individual that accords him or her the license to enter and participate; it is not the position or official rank among God's workers that qualifies him or her to walk through the hallowed doors. Rather, it is being an obedient son or daughter of God—humble and teachable, meek and contrite—that is the primary precondition for being recommended to the temple.

President Joseph Fielding Smith expressed it this way:

> Do not think because anybody has a higher office in this Church than you have, that you are barred from blessings, because you can go into the temple of the Lord and get all the blessings there are that have been revealed, if you are faithful, have them sealed upon you as an elder of this Church, and then you have all that any man can get. There have to be offices in the Church, and we are not all called to the same calling, but you can get the fulness of the priesthood in the temple of the Lord by obeying this which I have read to you. I want to make this emphatic. (*Elijah the Prophet and His Mission* [Salt Lake City: Deseret Book, 1957], 46–47)

THE LIGHT OF ETERNITY

The temple radiates the light of eternity amidst the darkness of doubt and confusion rampant in the world. Service in the Lord's house provides a protective cover against the forces of pride and evil that can act against us. President Boyd K. Packer has stated it this way: "Our labors in the temple cover us with a shield and a protection, both individually and as a people" (Boyd K. Packer, *The Holy Temple* [Salt Lake City: Bookcraft, 1980], 265). In addition, temple service extends the Lord's blessings to us across the full spectrum of our experiences along the pathway of mortal life, as President Packer has likewise confirmed: "The Lord will bless us as we attend to the sacred ordinance work of the temples. Blessings there will not be limited to our temple service. We will be blessed in all of our affairs. We will be eligible to have the Lord take an interest in our affairs both spiritual and temporal" (*The Holy Temple,* 182.)

Indeed, the Lord does take an interest in our lives. We know we are highly favored of the Lord because the truths pertaining to the fullness of the gospel have been given to us. In his day, Alma taught: "And they are made known unto us in plain terms, that we may understand, that we cannot err; and this because of our being wanderers in a strange land; therefore, we are thus highly favored, for we have these glad tidings declared unto us in all parts of our vineyard" (Alma 13:23; see also 1 Ne. 1:1; Alma 9:20). We can magnify our position of being favored recipients of the truth inasmuch as we are humble (see Alma 48:20), keep the Lord's commandments (see Mosiah 10:13), restrain ourselves from murmuring (see 1 Ne. 3:6), maintain a lifestyle of righteousness (see 1 Ne. 17:35), and honor our covenants (see Alma 27:30). Being favored of the Lord means that we merit the light of eternity as bestowed in the holy temples of God. Being favored of the Lord means that we are invited to gather and "stand in holy places" (D&C 101:22), where the Spirit illuminates our beings with understanding and vision so that we are prepared to receive all that is requisite for our salvation and exaltation. The Prophet Joseph Smith petitioned the Lord on our behalf during his dedicatory prayer for the Kirtland Temple, the first temple of the new dispensation: "And do thou grant, Holy Father, that all those who shall worship in this house may be taught words of wisdom out of the best books, and that they may seek learning even by study, and also by faith, as thou hast said; And that they may grow up in thee, and receive a fulness of the Holy Ghost, and be organized according to thy laws, and be prepared to obtain every needful thing" (D&C 109:14–15).

What is the nature of the light and truth dispensed through the ordinances and teachings of the temple? Brigham Young gave us this introductory view:

> It is absolutely necessary that the Saints should receive the further ordinances of the house of God before this short existence shall come to a close, that they may be prepared and fully able to pass all the sentinels leading into the celestial kingdom and into the presence of God. . . . Then go on and build the temples of the Lord, that you may receive the endowments in store for you, and possess the keys of the eternal Priesthood, that you may receive every word, sign, and token, and be made acquainted with the laws of angels, and of the kingdom of our Father and our God, and know how to pass from one degree to another, and enter fully into the joy of your Lord. (*Discourses,* 395–96)

Clearly the light of the temple marks the way home—the way back to the presence of God. What greater beam of illumination could there be than one that reaches from our present location to the distant mansions of God prepared for our future bliss and joy? How keenly we should be engaged in the process of preparing ourselves in every needful way to complete this journey of self-mastery and sanctification after the pattern of the Savior!

The Temple through the Ages

Those who are preparing to enter the temple can benefit from an understanding of the antiquity and universality of the temple experience throughout the dispensations of time. Wherever the Saints of God are gathered under the auspices of the holy priesthood, there you will find the temple (see D&C 124:39). The temple principle—using priesthood power and ordinances to capacitate God's people to return to His presence—has been in force and activated in every dispensation of the gospel. In periods where the building of temple structures was beyond the capacity of the Lord's people, mountaintops were used. But in our day, when temples are being proliferated across the globe, it is only in those dedicated places where the covenant blessings pertaining to exaltation are bestowed. President Joseph Fielding Smith emphasized this point:

> You cannot receive the fulness of the priesthood unless you go into the temple of the Lord and receive these ordinances of which the prophet speaks. No man can get the fulness of the priesthood outside of the temple of the Lord. There was a time when that could be done, for the Lord could give these things on the mountain tops—no doubt that is where Moses got it, that is no doubt where Elijah got it—and the Lord said that in the days of poverty, when there was no house prepared in which to receive these things, that they can be received on the mountain tops. But now we have temples, and you cannot get these blessings on the mountain tops, you will have to go into the house of the Lord, and you cannot get the fulness of the priesthood unless you go there. (*Elijah the Prophet and His Mission*, 46)

After the exodus of Israel from Egyptian bondage around 1547 BC, and following the promulgation of the Ten Commandments from Mount Sinai (serving as a kind of natural temple), the Lord provided arrangements for the establishment of the tabernacle—a portable temple sanctuary in which the holiest of religious artifacts could be stored and sacred rites of priestly worship could be carried out. Israel participated in temple-related worship from without the central chambers of the tabernacle when prompted by signals given by the priestly officers within (smoke from the burning incense, musical intonation, etc.). However, as far as we have been told, it was not until the erection of the temple of Solomon (approximately a thousand years before the birth of Christ [see 1 Kgs. 6:37–38; 8:1–2, 65–66; 2 Chr. 7:9–10]), that a permanent structure for sacred rites and ceremonies was established among God's people. The temple of Solomon was destroyed during the Babylonian conquest under King Nebuchadnezzar around 600 BC (see 2 Kgs. 25:9).

A second temple was built under Zerubbabel, the governor of Palestine appointed by Cyrus the Great of Persia (see Ezra 1:8), and was dedicated in the year 516 BC (see Ezra 6:15–16). After the temple of Zerubbabel had fallen into disrepair and declined in sanctity over the generations, King Herod sought to gain favor among the Jewish people by inaugurating a campaign to restore the second temple, section by section, beginning in 17 BC. It was in the various courts of this restored temple complex that the Savior was to carry on His ministry from time to time (see Mark 12:41; John 8:20; 10:22). The temple of Herod was destroyed by the Romans in AD 70. During the period of the Great Apostasy, following the end of the apostolic period in the meridian of time, authorized temple work was no longer carried out in the Holy Land. Only at the time of the Second Coming will authorized temple work be restored in that part of the kingdom of God.

In the New World, the faithful priesthood leadership carried on the institution of the temple. Shortly after Nephi and his loyal group separated themselves from the rebellious older brothers following the death of Lehi, we find this account in the Book of Mormon: "And I, Nephi, did build a temple; and I did construct it after the manner of the temple of Solomon save it were not built of so many precious things; for they were not to be found upon the land, wherefore, it could not be built like unto Solomon's temple. But the manner of the construction was like unto the temple of Solomon; and the workmanship thereof was exceedingly fine" (2 Ne. 5:16). Later, it was from the temple site at Zarahemla that King Benjamin delivered his stirring sermon about the gospel of Jesus Christ (see Mosiah 1:18; 2:1, 5–7; 7:17). And it was at the temple site in Bountiful that the resurrected Savior ministered unto the people of ancient America, revealing the glorious truths of the gospel to a people hungering for enlightenment, comfort, and divine blessings (see 3 Ne. 11:1).

After the decline of the Nephite nation, temple work was suspended until the Restoration of the fullness of the gospel in the latter days. "The priesthood, which is essential to temple ordinances, did not exist upon the earth," explained President Howard W. Hunter. "After the Restoration of the gospel through a prophet of the Lord, raised up for that very purpose, and the establishment of The Church of Jesus Christ of Latter-day Saints, temples were again erected according to divine commandment" (*Ensign,* Oct. 1994, 2).

The first such temple in the latter days was built in Kirtland, Ohio, through the sacrifice and diligence of the early Saints. It was dedicated on March 27, 1836, by the Prophet Joseph Smith (see D&C 109) and became the scene of the Lord's miraculous visitation on April 3, 1836. On the same occasion, Moses appeared and restored the keys of the gathering of Israel from the four parts of the earth. Elias, too, appeared and delivered the keys of the dispensation of Abraham, and was followed by Elijah, who brought again the sealing keys whereby temple ordinances on earth are recognized in heaven (see D&C 110). Several years later the temple at Nauvoo, Illinois, was erected to continue the work of the Lord in behalf of His faithful sons and daughters.

Authorized and recognized temple work is carried on solely under the auspices of those holding the keys of the priesthood of God. The temple is a manifest confirmation that the work of the kingdom of God is taking place and that revelation from the Almighty is flowing to His chosen servants on earth—those who are called to administer the sacred and holy ordinances that can occur only in the house of the Lord by virtue of the authority and sealing keys restored for this very purpose. Declared Elder David B. Haight: "Without revelation, temples can neither be built nor properly used. They are one of the evidences of the divinity of our Lord's true gospel. In our day, the Lord has said: 'How shall your washings be acceptable unto me, except ye perform them in a house which you have built to my name? . . . that . . . ordinances might be revealed which had been hid from . . . the world.' (D&C 124:37–38)" (*Ensign,* Nov. 1990, 59).

This same principle was emphasized by President Joseph Fielding Smith:

> It makes no difference how great an office you have, what position in the Church you hold, you cannot officiate

unless the keys, the sealing power, is there back of it. That is the thing that counts; and that is why Elijah came, that is why Moses came—for he also held keys of the priesthood—and that is why they conferred upon the head of Peter, James and John in that dispensation these privileges or these powers, these keys, that they might go forth and perform this labor; and that is why they came to the Prophet Joseph Smith. (*Elijah the Prophet and His Mission,* 13–14)

What a glorious privilege it is to live in a time of the world's history where the fullness of the gospel has been restored, including all of the principles and ordinances pertaining to salvation and exaltation in the celestial kingdom. Once more the sacred blessings of the temple are made available to the faithful of the Lord's flock. Once more the requisite covenant rites are accessible in the house of the Lord to prepare the Lord's people to return to His presence, endowed with power from on high and ennobled as "a chosen generation, a royal priesthood, an holy nation" (1 Pet. 2:9). President Howard W. Hunter has declared: "The gospel proclaimed to the world by the Latter-day Saints is the gospel of Jesus Christ as restored to the earth in this dispensation and is for the redemption of all mankind. The Lord Himself has revealed what is essential for the salvation and exaltation of His children. One of these essentials is that temples are to be erected for the performance of ordinances that cannot be performed in any other place" (*Liahona,* Mar. 2004, 40).

The Temple: Symbol of the Enabling and Ennobling Power of God on the Earth

On January 21, 1836, the Prophet Joseph Smith was privileged to receive a vision in the temple at Kirtland on the occasion of "the administration of the ordinances of the endowment as far as they had then been revealed." As recorded in section 137 of the Doctrine and Covenants, the prophet beheld the following: "The heavens were opened upon us, and I beheld the celestial kingdom of God, and the glory thereof, whether in the body or out I cannot tell. I saw the transcendent beauty of the gate through which the heirs of that kingdom will enter, which was like unto circling flames of fire; Also the blazing throne of God, whereon was seated the Father and the Son. I saw the beautiful streets of that kingdom, which had the appearance of being paved with gold" (D&C 137:1–4).

The magnificent vision of the heavenly temple in the midst of the celestial kingdom, with its "blazing throne of God," offers a compelling view of the pathway the faithful will tread as they are permitted, in due time, to enter the abode of Deity and come before the Father and the Son, having become worthy of this august audience through the sanctifying power of eternal truth and covenant sealings in earthly temples. Temples, no matter where they are located throughout the world, are dynamic symbols of the enabling and ennobling power of God at work for the blessing of His sons and daughters on the earth. The temple—with its pure doctrine and sacred covenants—is the channel connecting the earthly and the heavenly realms. When the Savior appeared to Joseph Smith and Oliver Cowdery in the Kirtland Temple on April 3, 1836, He fulfilled the prophetic announcement that He would come suddenly to His temple (see Mal. 3:1):

> The veil was taken from our minds, and the eyes of our understanding were opened. We saw the Lord standing upon the breastwork of the pulpit, before us; and under his feet was a paved work of pure gold, in color like amber. His eyes were as a flame of fire; the hair of his head was white like the pure snow; his countenance shone above the brightness of the sun; and his voice was as the sound of the rushing of great waters, even the voice of Jehovah, saying: I am the first and the last; I am he who liveth, I am he who was slain; I am your advocate with the Father. Behold, your sins are forgiven you; you are clean before me; therefore, lift up your heads and rejoice. Let the hearts of your brethren rejoice, and let the hearts of all my people rejoice, who have, with their might, built this house to my name. For behold, I have accepted this house, and my name shall be here; and I will manifest myself to my people in mercy

in this house. Yea, I will appear unto my servants, and speak unto them with mine own voice, if my people will keep my commandments, and do not pollute this holy house. Yea the hearts of thousands and tens of thousands shall greatly rejoice in consequence of the blessings which shall be poured out, and the endowment with which my servants have been endowed in this house. And the fame of this house shall spread to foreign lands; and this is the beginning of the blessing which shall be poured out upon the heads of my people. Even so. Amen. (D&C 110:1–10)

What the Prophet Joseph and his companion saw on that historic day is what every temple-goer is yearning to see in the due time of the Lord, for the temple is designed to prepare the devout and righteous to see the face of the Lord and enjoy His glorious presence. The Lord has organized and empowered the process whereby His faithful sons and daughters can be prepared to come before Him, see His face, and carry on His work of salvation in the eternities. That process of the administration of the power of godliness through priesthood ordinances and covenants belongs to the holy temple:

And this greater priesthood administereth the gospel and holdeth the key of the mysteries of the kingdom, even the key of the knowledge of God. Therefore, in the ordinances thereof, the power of godliness is manifest. And without the ordinances thereof, and the authority of the priesthood, the power of godliness is not manifest unto men in the flesh; For without this no man can see the face of God, even the Father, and live. (D&C 84:19–22)

The blessings of the eternities await the faithful who enter the temple as worthy sons and daughters of God. There they can joyfully partake of the abundant truth that they are on the correct course back into the presence of their Maker. There they can fully orient themselves toward God with the assurance that they have a noble and sacred heritage; that He lives; that His Son is the Redeemer of the world; that families can be forever; and that love, light, and covenant valor are the essence of our discipleship as Latter-day Saints. In this regard, President Gordon B. Hinckley reminded us:

> I hope you are using the temple constantly, because you will gain blessings there that you cannot gain anywhere else on the face of the whole earth. The temple stands as a monument for all to see. It stands as a statement that we as a people believe in the immortality of the human soul. Everything that occurs in that temple is of an uplifting and ennobling kind. It speaks of life here and life beyond the grave. It speaks of the importance of the individual as a child of God. It speaks of the importance of the family as a creation of the Almighty. It speaks of the eternity of the marriage relationship. It speaks of going on to greater glory. It is a place of light, a place of peace, a place of love where we deal with the things of eternity. If there is any man here tonight who is not worthy to go into that holy house, I urge you to put your life in order so that you may go there and partake of the unique and wonderful blessings that we have there. (*TGBH,* 623–24)

The work of the temple is the instrument that binds generations together so that God's eternal purposes can be enabled and carried out. President John Taylor, upon the completion of the temple in Logan, Utah, explained how the temple establishes the seamless connection with the eternities:

> What Are Temples For?—We have now finished this temple, and some people inquire, what is it for? For many things: that our sealings and ordinances may be performed in a manner that will be acceptable before God and the holy angels; that whatsoever is bound on the earth according to the laws of the eternal priesthood shall be bound in the heavens; that there may be a connecting link between the living and the dead, between those who have lived, all those ancient fathers of which I have spoken who are interested in the welfare of their posterity; that there may be a royal

> priesthood, a holy people, a pure people, a virtuous people on the earth to officiate and operate in the interests of the living and the dead; not looking so much after themselves, but after God, after the work of God, and after the accomplishment of those things which God has designed to be carried out in the dispensation of the fulness of times when all things are to be united in one, and that they may be prepared to operate with the priesthood in the heavens in the redemption of the inhabitants of this world from the days of Adam unto the present time. (*Gospel Kingdom*, 290)

In our day, as in times past, the chosen servants of the Lord continually emphasize temple service as the culminating manifestation of our progress toward a higher level of essential preparation to return home to the presence of the Lord. The temple is a monument to the atoning sacrifice of the Savior, for the work of the temple confirms and extends the redemptive power of the Atonement to willing and accepting individuals in all generations of time—whether alive or deceased. Elder Russell M. Nelson has reminded us of these points and the need to prepare carefully and thoroughly for the privilege of receiving temple blessings:

> The temple is the house of the Lord. The basis for every temple ordinance and covenant—the heart of the plan of salvation—is the Atonement of Jesus Christ. Every activity, every lesson, all we do in the Church, point to the Lord and His holy house. Our efforts to proclaim the gospel, perfect the Saints, and redeem the dead all lead to the temple. Each holy temple stands as a symbol of our membership in the Church, as a sign of our faith in life after death, and as a sacred step toward eternal glory for us and our families. . . . To enter the temple is a tremendous blessing. But first we must be worthy. We should not be rushed. We cannot cut corners of preparation and risk the breaking of covenants we were not prepared to make. That would be worse than not making them at all. (*Ensign,* May 2001, 32)

Sustaining the Vision of the Temple in the Home

It is in the homes of the faithful Saints that the primary preparation for temple work takes place. The homes of Zion are schools where eternal truths about the continuity of life beyond the veil are first taught. It was in our heavenly home, prior to the advent of our mortal sojourn, that we received our "first lessons in the world of spirits and were prepared to come forth in the due time of the Lord to labor in his vineyard for the salvation of the souls of men" (D&C 138:56). In like manner, we are receiving in our earthly homes our first lessons of preparation for returning to the presence of God when our mortal journey is over: "Wherefore, the course of the Lord is one eternal round" (1 Ne. 10:19).

How can we ensure that our homes are truly annexes to the holy temples of the Lord? One simple way would be to adorn our homes with imagery of the temple as a reminder to keep the highest principles of exaltation before us. On this point, President Spencer W. Kimball counseled as follows:

> Having in mind the importance of temple work, wouldn't it be wonderful if every Latter-day Saint home had in the bedroom of each boy and each girl, or on the mantle of the living room, a fairly good-sized picture of a temple which would help them recall, frequently, the purpose of these beautiful edifices. I believe there would be far more marriages in the temple than there are today, because the children would have as a part of their growing experience the picture of one of our temples constantly before them as a reminder and a goal. I recommend that to the Saints. It is almost costless and certainly would help develop the thinking processes of little minds that are growing, as the temple and its meaning is contemplated and is discussed in the family home evening. (*Ensign,* Jan. 1977, 3)

We can all improve the spiritual elements of our home decor and environment in order to invite the Spirit of our Father in Heaven into our family circles. Having a temple-reflecting environment in the home reinforces the plan to fill that environment with temple-ready discourse and practices. One sister observed:

> Constructing a positive environment that incorporates all these elements helps us furnish a virtuous home, in which we can practice godliness. We can learn eventually to respond in a godly manner. We can learn godly attributes and incorporate them into our lives. In the Old Testament, the high priest wore on his head a hammered gold crown on which was engraved, "Holiness to the Lord." On each of our temples there also is a sign proclaiming, "Holiness to the Lord." It is a promise to put that on a building. I wonder if we could, at least in our minds, have that kind of promise on our homes. "Holiness to the Lord"—in this place there will be only those things conducive to the presence of the Lord's Spirit. While this is a lofty ideal, we can work to make our homes holy places. (Ann N. Madsen, in *As Women of Faith: Talks Selected from the BYU Women's Conferences* [Salt Lake City: Deseret Book, 1989], 152–153)

"Holiness to the Lord" is an appropriate motto for any home within the kingdom of God. As we practice virtue before the Lord and counsel one another in the principles of saving grace, we will unfold within our mind's eye the vision of the temple and keep that vision before us in compelling vividness as the defining framework of our existence.

Time to Meditate and Ponder

1. What can we do to inscribe the motto "Holiness to the Lord" indelibly upon our hearts and keep the vision of the temple dynamically alive in our minds?

2. How does the temple help us answer life's most challenging questions: Where did I come from? Why am I here? Where am I going? What is my relationship to my Maker?

3. The Lord revealed to the prophet Moses the all-encompassing truth: "For behold, this is my work and my glory—to bring to pass the immortality and eternal life of man" (Moses 1:39). If that is the Lord's work, then what is *our* work? (See D&C 11:20.)

4. How could we explain to someone not of our faith the essential difference between chapels and temples?

5. The Lord has commanded us to be "perfect," even as He and His Father are perfect (see 3 Ne. 12:48). How does preparing to enter the temple—whether for the first time or for subsequent visits—contribute to that process?

6. The Lord commanded us through the Prophet Joseph Smith to have the following goal: "And seek the face of the Lord always, that in patience ye may possess your souls, and ye shall have eternal life" (D&C 101:38). How does preparing to go to the temple take patience?

7. How can we be assured that we are "favored" of the Lord as we prepare for the temple? (See 1 Ne. 1:1; 3:6; 17:35; Mosiah 10:13; Alma 9:20; 13:23; 27:30; 48:20.)

8. How can we demonstrate that temple work is a pervasive dimension of the gospel of Jesus Christ down through the ages?

9. How are God's children blessed today more than in previous dispensations in regard to temple work?

10. In what ways are temples dynamic symbols of the enabling and ennobling power of God at work for the blessing of His sons and daughters on the earth?

11. We are told in the Doctrine and Covenants that in the ordinances of the higher priesthood "the power of godliness is manifest. And without the ordinances thereof, and the authority of the priesthood,

the power of godliness is not manifest unto men in the flesh; For without this no man can see the face of God, even the Father, and live" (D&C 84:20–22). How does this statement help us understand the importance of temple work as a means to prepare to see God by accepting the sacred ordinances and covenants of the temple?

12. We all face the inevitability of death. How does the temple give us hope and faith that we will ultimately triumph over death through the power of the Atonement of Jesus Christ?

13. What can we do to sustain the importance of the temple in our homes?

CHAPTER 2
THE PURPOSE OF THE TEMPLE

Guiding Principle: Temple work is a sacred partnership with God as we follow in the footsteps of the Redeemer to serve our families and our kindred ancestors as saviors on Mount Zion.

> *Saviors on Mount Zion—We have a work to do just as important in its sphere as the Savior's work was in its sphere. Our fathers cannot be made perfect without us; we cannot be made perfect without them. They have done their work and now sleep. We are now called upon to do ours; which is to be the greatest work man ever performed on the earth. Millions of our fellow creatures who have lived upon the earth and died without a knowledge of the Gospel must be officiated for in order that they may inherit eternal life (that is, all that would have received the Gospel). And we are called upon to enter into this work.*
> —JOHN A. WIDTSOE, SEL., *DISCOURSES OF BRIGHAM YOUNG*, 406.

The purpose of life is to receive a physical tabernacle—man being "the tabernacle of God" (D&C 93:35)—and then prove ourselves worthy of the highest blessings of eternal happiness and exaltation in the presence of God by virtue of the Atonement and the redeeming grace of Jesus Christ. As the divine leadership in the premortal realm declared: "And we will prove them herewith, to see if they will do all things whatsoever the Lord their God shall command them" (Abr. 3:25). The purpose of the temple is to ensure that we are empowered—under covenant—and enlightened—through the endowment of priesthood blessings—to be able to return to our heavenly home as eternal families in dignity and worthiness, having fulfilled the measure of our creation and answered the ends of the law through obedience and the mercy of salvation. In perhaps the most celebrated statement concerning this divine process, Brigham Young declared: "Your endowment is, to receive all those ordinances in the house of the Lord, which are necessary for you, after you have departed this life, to enable you to walk back to the presence of the Father, passing the angels who stand as sentinels, being enabled to give them the key words, the signs and tokens, pertaining to the holy Priesthood, and gain your eternal exaltation in spite of earth and hell" (*Discourses,* 416).

That a merciful Heavenly Father and His Only Begotten Son have communicated to us through chosen prophets all the essential protocols and principles for this temple "journey" is evidence of Their abiding love and Their enduring commitment to bring about the immortality and eternal life of man (see Moses 1:39). That the priesthood keys and authority to carry on temple work have been restored in this, the final dispensation, is further evidence of the inexorable power of divine guidance at work in behalf of all mankind. In turn, our obligation under the auspices of priesthood covenants is to obey all of God's commandments "with all [our] might, mind and strength" (D&C 11:20), including preparing for and participating in the ordinances of the house of God—and then doing all in our power to assist others, both the living and the dead, to have the same privilege. In short, we are to look to the temple and live.

The final words of the Old Testament resound with awesome significance: "Behold, I will send you Elijah the prophet before the coming of the great and dreadful day of the Lord: And he shall turn the heart of the fathers to the children, and the heart of the children to their fathers, lest I come and smite the earth with a curse" (Mal. 4:5–6).

The keys to preserving the lives of God's progeny lie in the sealing powers of the priesthood operating in the temples to bind generations and unite all the family of God. When Elijah appeared in the Kirtland Temple on April 3, 1836, in fulfillment of his commission to restore the keys of temple work to righteous disciples of Jesus Christ, he declared to the Prophet Joseph Smith and Oliver Cowdery the following words: "Behold, the time has fully come, which was spoken of by the mouth of Malachi—testifying that he [Elijah] should be sent, before the great and dreadful day of the Lord come—To turn the hearts of the fathers to the children, and the children to the fathers, lest the whole earth be smitten with a curse—Therefore, the keys of this dispensation are committed into your hands; and by this ye may know that the great and dreadful day of the Lord is near, even at the doors" (D&C 110:14–16). It was thus, in accordance with divine decree, that temple work was inaugurated in the latter days, never to be taken from the earth again.

Saviors on Mount Zion

When we participate in the magnificent program of temple work, we assist in the process of turning the hearts of the fathers to their children and the hearts of the children to their fathers. It is an enterprise of the highest spiritual order. Each individual first prepares himself or herself to receive the endowment blessings of the temple, and then, in turn, becomes fully committed to the task of ensuring that all forebears as well as all posterity have the same opportunity for salvation and exaltation. It is an extraordinary partnership with God to bring to pass the program of eternal life for all mankind. We further God's eternal designs by becoming "saviours" on "mount Zion," as the prophet Obadiah expressed it (Obad. 1:21). This means that we participate willingly and worthily in the saving protocols and ordinances of the temple for ourselves as well as for our kindred dead.

The Prophet Joseph Smith explained this office and calling in a discourse given on the Nauvoo Temple grounds in January 1844:

> The Bible says, "I will send you Elijah the Prophet before the coming of the great and dreadful day of the Lord; and he shall turn the hearts of the fathers to the children, and the hearts of the children to the fathers, lest I come and smite the earth with a curse."
>
> Now, the word turn here should be translated bind, or seal. But what is the object of this important mission? or how is it to be fulfilled? The keys are to be delivered, the spirit of Elijah is to come, the Gospel to be established, the Saints of God gathered, Zion built up, and the Saints to come up as saviors on Mount Zion.
>
> But how are they to become saviors on Mount Zion? By building their temples, erecting their baptismal fonts, and going forth and receiving all the ordinances, baptisms, confirmations, washings, anointings, ordinations and sealing powers upon their heads, in behalf of all their progenitors who are dead, and redeem them that they may come forth in the first Resurrection and be exalted to thrones of glory with them; and herein is the chain that binds the hearts of the fathers to the children, and the children to the fathers, which fulfills the mission of Elijah. And I would to God that this temple [in Nauvoo] was now done, that we might go into it, and go to work and improve our time, and make use of the seals while they are on earth.
>
> The Saints have not too much time to save and redeem their dead, and gather together their living relatives, that they may be saved also, before the earth will be smitten, and the consumption decreed falls upon the world.
>
> I would advise all the Saints to go to with their might and gather together all their living relatives to this place, that they may be sealed and saved, that they may be prepared against the day that the destroying angel goes

forth; and if the whole Church should go to with all their might to save their dead, seal their posterity, and gather their living friends, and spend none of their time in behalf of the world, they would hardly get through before night would come, when no man can work; and my only trouble at the present time is concerning ourselves, that the Saints *will be divided, broken up, and scattered,* before we get our salvation secure; for there are so many fools in the world for the devil to operate upon, it gives him the advantage oftentimes. (*HC,* 6:183–84; emphasis in original)

Brigham Young confirmed this doctrine once again a few years later:

We are called, as it has been told you, to redeem the nations of the earth. The fathers cannot be made perfect without us; we cannot be made perfect without the fathers. There must be this chain in the holy Priesthood; it must be welded together from the latest generation that lives on the earth back to Father Adam, to bring back all that can be saved and placed where they can receive salvation and a glory in some kingdom. This Priesthood has to do it; this Priesthood is for this purpose.

Can the fathers be saved without us? No. Can we be saved without them? No, and if we do not wake up and cease to long after the things of this earth, we will find that we as individuals will go down to hell, although the Lord will preserve a people unto himself. (*Discourses,* 407)

Every prophet since then has testified continually of the sacred responsibility placed upon the shoulders of the Saints to become saviors on Mount Zion by fulfilling the purpose of the temples of God in extending the blessings of eternity to all of mankind. In this same spirit, President Harold B. Lee proclaimed:

We can be saviors for the dead. This work for the dead, performed in holy temples by members of the Church, does in reality make of them who do this work "saviors" to those who have died without a knowledge of the gospel, for thereby they may claim the complete gift of the Savior promised to all mankind through His atonement.

It might be said of all who engage in this great work of salvation that they are "saviours on mount Zion" (see Obad. 1:21)—building temples, erecting baptismal fonts, and receiving all the ordinances in behalf of their progenitors who are dead, redeeming them that they might come forth in the morning of the first resurrection. May we all, by engaging in this work, be as saviors on Mount Zion. (*THBL,* 569; emphasis in original)

How to Prepare to Be Saviors on Mount Zion

To serve faithfully as saviors on Mount Zion and return as families to the presence of God, we are to follow the guidelines set forth in the scriptures and in the pronouncements of His chosen prophets. We are to be servants of the Most High in furthering the mission of the Church, including carrying out the provisions of the Abrahamic covenant to convey saving truths of the gospel—culminating in the indispensable blessings of temple work—to all quarters of the world (see Abr. 2:10–11). As President Howard W. Hunter confirmed: "The temple is at the center of the mission of the Church. All of our efforts in proclaiming the gospel, perfecting the Saints, and redeeming the dead lead to the holy temple. This is because the temple ordinances are absolutely crucial; we cannot return to God's presence without them" (*THWH,* 244).

The fundamental key for our preparation is to seek to become more like the Savior day by day, allowing Him to lift us, bless us, and transform us through the "mighty change in [our] hearts" (Alma 5:14; see also Mosiah 5:2), thus imparting to us a measure of His divine nature that operates on the power of vicarious service. We do those things for others that they are not able to do for themselves, just as the Savior did for us what was not in our power to transact on our own behalf. The venue of vicarious charity is the temple, and the program of such charity consists of the proxy administration of ordinances for those who have gone before us into the world of spirits. We receive our own endowment in the temple, together with the sealing blessings to ensure that our families can be eternal, and then we repeat the process as saviors on Mount Zion to provide saving ordinances for our departed.

> For we without them cannot be made perfect; neither can they without us be made perfect. Neither can they nor we be made perfect without those who have died in the gospel also; for it is necessary in the ushering in of the dispensation of the fulness of times, which dispensation is now beginning to usher in, that a whole and complete and perfect union, and welding together of dispensations, and keys, and powers, and glories should take place, and be revealed from the days of Adam even to the present time. And not only this, but those things which never have been revealed from the foundation of the world, but have been kept hid from the wise and prudent, shall be revealed unto babes and sucklings in this, the dispensation of the fulness of times. (D&C 128:18)

How great is the opportunity we have to prepare ourselves for the unique and divine service that transpires in the temples of the Lord, and we need to prepare ourselves carefully and humbly as worthy servants and saviors on Mount Zion. The Lord has laid down the markers of qualification and the milestones of preparation for our temple journey. In the next chapter we will consider the road map for the journey in more detail.

Time to Meditate and Ponder

1. What was Brigham Young referring to when he spoke about what "is to be the greatest work man ever performed on the earth"?

2. What is the purpose for our life upon the earth?

3. How does the temple relate to such a purpose?

4. What did Brigham Young refer to when he talked about that which would "enable you to walk back to the presence of the Father" (*Discourses,* 416)?

5. What is the power of Elijah, and how does it relate to temple work?

6. What does it mean to become "saviours" on "mount Zion" (Obad. 1:21)?

7. What did Joseph Smith mean when he said, "The Saints have not too much time to save and redeem their dead" (*HC,* 6:183–84)?

8. Comment on this passage of scripture: "For we without them cannot be made perfect; neither can they without us be made perfect" (D&C 128:18).

9. How can we best prepare to become "saviours" on "mount Zion" (Obad. 1:21)?

CHAPTER 3
THE PATHWAY TO THE TEMPLE—TAKING ON THE DIVINE NATURE

Guiding Principle: The Lord has commanded, "Be ye therefore perfect, as your Father which is in heaven is perfect" (Matt. 5:48). In order to receive all of the blessings God has in store for us, we must constantly strive to become as He is—to take on the divine nature.

> *Let us study the Master's every teaching and devote ourselves more fully to his example. He has given us "all things that pertain unto life and godliness." He has "called us to glory and virtue" and has "given unto us exceeding great and precious promises: that by these [we] might be partakers of the divine nature" (2 Pet. 1:3–4).*
>
> *I believe in those "exceeding great and precious promises," and I invite all within the sound of my voice to claim them. We should strive to "be partakers of the divine nature." Only then may we truly hope for "peace in this world, and eternal life in the world to come" (D&C 59:23).*
> —HOWARD W. HUNTER, "FOLLOWING THE MASTER: TEACHINGS OF PRESIDENT HOWARD W. HUNTER," *ENSIGN*, APR. 1995, 21.

Many of us have had occasion, at one time or another, to walk beside a stream of pure water as it descends with irrepressible energy from some higher elevation to a valley below. There is something renewing and refreshing about the dynamic movement of such a stream as it flows from one pool to the next, bringing moisture to the trees and wildflowers along the embankments and ultimately delivering vitality to the communities below as it gathers momentum and breadth, often becoming a river of some scope and magnitude.

The metaphor of the fertile stream is often used in prophetic expression. "The Lord is my shepherd; I shall not want," sang the Psalmist. "He maketh me to lie down in green pastures: he leadeth me beside the still waters" (Ps. 23:1–2). Jeremiah uttered the memorable phrase: "Blessed is the man that trusteth in the Lord, and whose hope the Lord is. For he shall be as a tree planted by the waters, and that spreadeth out her roots by the river, and shall not see when heat cometh, but her leaf shall be green; and shall not be careful in the year of drought, neither shall cease from yielding fruit" (Jer. 17:7–8). In our day, the Lord has promised: "Verily I say unto you, all among them who know their hearts are honest, and are broken, and their spirits contrite, and are willing to observe their covenants by sacrifice—yea, every sacrifice which I, the Lord, shall command—they are accepted of me. For I, the Lord, will cause them to bring forth as a very fruitful tree which is planted in a goodly land, by a pure stream, that yieldeth much precious fruit" (D&C 97:8–9).

In many ways, preparing to enter the temple is analogous to an invigorating and pleasant walk upwards along a stream-aligned pathway. Where does the pathway lead? How high does it go? What is the source or origin of the stream beside which we are walking?

President John Taylor used the analogy of the stream to teach a compelling lesson about the Savior and His mission in reference to the statement by Jacob, "Wherefore, it must needs be an infinite atonement" (2 Ne. 9:7):

> Why did it need an infinite atonement? For the simple reason that a stream can never rise higher than its fountain; and man having assumed a fleshly body and become of the

earth earthy, and through the violation of a law having cut himself off from his association with his Father, and become subject to death; in this condition, as the mortal life of man was short, and in and of himself he could have no hope of benefiting himself, or redeeming himself from his fallen condition, or of bringing himself back to the presence of his Father, some superior agency was needed to elevate him above his low and degraded position. This superior agency was the Son of God, who had not, as man had, violated a law of His Father, but was yet one with His Father, possessing His glory, His power, His authority, His dominion. . . . A man, as a man, could arrive at all the dignity that a man was capable of obtaining or receiving; but it needed a God to raise him to the dignity of a God. For this cause it is written, "Now are we the sons of God; and it doth not yet appear what we shall be: but we know that, when he shall appear we shall be like him." (*Mediation and Atonement of Our Lord and Savior Jesus Christ* [Salt Lake City: Deseret News, 1882], 145)

The verity that only a God can raise man to the dignity of a God is the essence of the institution of the temple. There are temples aplenty in the culture of our day—temples of entertainment, temples of commerce, temples of athletics, temples of beauty, and so forth. Within such man-made temples, with time and effort, one can predictably rise to the lofty stature of the mortal exemplars that set the defining standards for such institutions—*but no higher*. Within the house of the Lord it is different: therein men and women have the sacred opportunity to rise to the stature of the divine Exemplar who is our Redeemer and Savior, even the Son of God. We can rise beyond the mortal bar of excellence to realize our God-given potential as sons and daughters of Deity. Through the Atonement of Christ, and through the sealing powers of the priesthood administered within the temple walls, we can rise to a heavenly altitude—even to the level of the Creator of all things (see Acts 17:29; Rom. 8:16; Heb. 12:9). Such is the promise of our Father in Heaven; such is the purpose of the gospel of Jesus Christ; such is the mission of the temple of the Lord.

Ezekiel was privileged to have a vision of the magnificent heavenly temple of God. He saw, flowing from beneath the temple complex, a stream of water that brought vital strength to the land through which it flowed:

> Now when I had returned, behold, at the bank of the river were very many trees on the one side and on the other. Then said he [the presenter] unto me, These waters issue out toward the east country, and go down into the desert, and go into the sea: which being brought forth into the sea, the waters shall be healed. And it shall come to pass, that every thing that liveth, which moveth, whithersoever the rivers shall come, shall live: . . . and every thing shall live whither the river cometh. (Ezek. 47:7–9)

By analogy, everyone that is refreshed by the living waters of the temple of God shall live and shall be healed. We go to the temple not because we are perfect, but because we are aspiring to be "perfect in Christ" (Moro. 10:32), having prepared ourselves to the utmost by striving to take upon ourselves the divine nature of Christ, thus allowing Him to lift us up to the source of all divine vitality through His grace and power. Indeed, from the temple of God issues forth the stream of living water essential for our salvation and exaltation (see Jer. 17:13; John 4:10–11; 7:38; 1 Ne. 11:25). That is why we can look to the temple and live, and why we can find joy therein.

John the Revelator was privileged to receive a visionary view of the domain of our Heavenly Father and His Son in the supernal realms of heaven, surrounded by countless Saints of valor and nobility:

> After this I beheld, and, lo, a great multitude, which no man could number, of all nations, and kindreds, and people, and tongues, stood before the throne, and before the Lamb, clothed with white robes, and palms in their hands; And cried with a loud voice, saying, Salvation to our God which sitteth upon the throne, and unto the Lamb. And all the angels stood round about the throne,

and about the elders and the four beasts, and fell before the throne on their faces, and worshipped God, Saying, Amen: Blessing, and glory, and wisdom, and thanksgiving, and honour, and power, and might, be unto our God for ever and ever. Amen. And one of the elders answered, saying unto me, What are these which are arrayed in white robes? and whence came they? And I said unto him, Sir, thou knowest. And he said to me, These are they which came out of great tribulation, and have washed their robes, and made them white in the blood of the Lamb. Therefore are they before the throne of God, and serve him day and night in his temple: and he that sitteth on the throne shall dwell among them. They shall hunger no more, neither thirst any more; neither shall the sun light on them, nor any heat. For the Lamb which is in the midst of the throne shall feed them, and shall lead them unto living fountains of waters: and God shall wipe away all tears from their eyes. (Rev. 7:9–17)

To be led by the Lamb "unto living fountains of waters" is the mission of the temple. It is there that all the tears of mortal anguish and sorrow shall be wiped away and all the burdens of earthly travail shall be replaced with the much lighter burdens of the Lord: "Come unto me, all ye that labour and are heavy laden, and I will give you rest. Take my yoke upon you, and learn of me; for I am meek and lowly in heart: and ye shall find rest unto your souls. For my yoke is easy, and my burden is light" (Matt. 11:28–30).

Only those who are holy can be admitted into the presence of Holiness. Only those who choose to become like the Savior and who are willing to learn the process of perfection through humble submission to heavenly principles can be admitted into the presence of Holiness. What a unique privilege it is to visit the house of the Lord and partake there of the refreshing spiritual gifts with which the Saints of God are endowed through the ordinances of the holy priesthood. To seek for pure knowledge on how to enter the presence of God—something that is taught in the temple in all essential detail—is to manifest a willingness to take on the divine nature.

Taking on the Divine Nature

Preparing to enter the temple of the Lord—whether initially or upon any subsequent visit—is an exercise in systematically taking upon ourselves what Peter called the "divine nature" (2 Pet. 1:4), consisting of such spiritual qualities as diligence, faith, virtue, knowledge, temperance, patience, godliness, brotherly kindness, and charity (see 2 Pet. 1:5–8). In our day, the Lord has confirmed through the Prophet Joseph Smith in the fourth section of the Doctrine and Covenants, these eternal qualities of preparation, where humility is referenced in addition to the other qualities just listed. Cultivating these qualities constitutes the pathway leading upward to the temple. The next sequence of chapters will address each of these ten preparatory qualities and how they relate to temple work.

Modern prophets have given us wonderful counsel on the process of taking on the divine nature that lies within us as a seed waiting to sprout and emerge in word and deed as the manifestation of our innate goodness. President Gordon B. Hinckley, who has led an unprecedented and inspired campaign for expanding temple accessibility throughout the world, has reminded us of our great potential to be more like the Savior and acquire the qualities that defined His mission and character:

> I challenge every one of you who can hear me to rise to the divinity within you. Do we really realize what it means to be a child of God, to have within us something of the divine nature?
>
> I believe with all my heart that the Latter-day Saints, generally speaking, are good people. If we live by the principles of the gospel, we must be good people, for we will be generous and kind, thoughtful and tolerant, helpful and outreaching to those in distress. We can either subdue the divine nature and hide it so that it finds no expression in our lives, or we can bring it to the front and let it shine through all that we do. (*Ensign,* Nov. 2002, 99)

In preparing to go to the temple, we have the singular privilege of increasing our understanding concerning the nature and work of Deity. The temple is a place of learning where we can come to know the Father and the Son—not know *about* Them, but know *Them* more directly and intimately through the sacred ordinances of the temple and the inspiration of the Holy Ghost. The temple teaches us how to take upon ourselves the divine nature and follow the pathway leading back into the presence of God. Elder Joseph B. Wirthlin of the Quorum of the Twelve has confirmed this truth as follows:

> Considering all that Jesus is and all he does for us, what should we be doing to show our appreciation? We should go far beyond knowing *about* Jesus and *about* his attributes and mission. We should come to "know . . . the only true God, and Jesus Christ, whom thou hast sent" (John 17:3). "It is one thing to know about God and another to know him. . . . To know God is to think what he thinks, to feel what he feels, to have the power he possesses, to comprehend the truths he understands, and to do what he does. Those who know God become like him, and have his kind of life, which is eternal life." In other words, to possess a knowledge of Christ, we must become as he is. We become "partakers of the divine nature" (2 Pet. 1:4). (*Ensign,* Nov. 1993, 5; emphasis in original)

Finally, we are thankful to know that the light of the gospel is universally available. Everyone is invited to leave the shadows of uncertainty and come unto Christ in order to receive the illumination of saving truth as it fills the soul with hope and courage to go forward on the errand of the Lord. President James E. Faust has said: "There is no need for anyone to remain in darkness; the light of the everlasting gospel is here; and every sincere investigator on earth can gain a personal witness from the Holy Spirit of the truth and divine nature of the Lord's work" (*Ensign,* Jan. 1999, 2).

The Lord has commanded us to gather and stand in holy places (see D&C 101:22–23; see also D&C 87:8; 101:64; 124:39). This pertains in particular to the temples of the Almighty, where "Holiness to the Lord" is the prevailing ambiance and culture. The scriptures are replete with counsel on the concept of holiness (see the Topical Guide). We can read all such references with great personal profit in our process of preparing for the temple. In the chapters to follow, we will consider the attributes and qualities of the divine nature, laying out in some detail the defining essence of the pathway that leads to the temples of God.

Time to Meditate and Ponder

1. We are promised, as partakers of the divine nature—reflected in the qualities of diligence, faith, virtue, knowledge, temperance, patience, godliness, brotherly kindness, charity, and humility (see D&C 4:6)—that we will "neither be barren nor unfruitful in the knowledge of our Lord Jesus Christ" (2 Pet. 1:8). In which of these qualities do we need most to improve as a means to prepare for the temple and strengthen our testimony "in the knowledge of our Lord"?

2. Why do the scriptural metaphors of the fertile stream and the "living waters" resonate so well with most people?

3. Explain the reasoning of President John Taylor in the statement "Why did it need an infinite atonement? For the simple reason that a stream can never rise higher than its fountain" (*Mediation and Atonement,* 143).

4. What does it mean that we do not go "perfect" to the temple but rather in the aspiration to be "perfect in Christ" (Moro. 10:32)?

5. What does this reference to those assembled in the temple in heaven mean to you: "And God shall wipe away all tears from their eyes" (Rev. 7:17)?

6. The pathway to the temple is defined by the qualities comprising the divine nature of Christ. Which of these qualities can you remember?

CHAPTER 4
A HOUSE OF FAITH

Guiding Principle: The temples of the Church are unique and distinguishing icons of hope and faith confirming the certainty of God's eternal plan of happiness for mankind and the eternal commission given to His sons and daughters to prepare themselves through sealing ordinances to return to His presence as eternal families.

> *With us, there is no building as sacred as a dedicated house of God. Only in Latter-day Saint temples are preserved in an indissoluble union for all eternity the precious associations of mortality. Among many things of a doctrinal nature that distinguish this Church from all others is the work that occurs in the house of the Lord under divine priesthood authority.*
>
> *Every temple throughout the world stands as a visible monument to the faith of this people in the certainty of immortality and the continuation of sacred bonds in that immortal realm (Temple groundbreaking, Sacramento, California, Aug. 22, 2004).*
> —GORDON B. HINCKLEY, "INSPIRATIONAL THOUGHTS," *ENSIGN,* MAR. 2006, 3.

Faith is a central element of the divine nature. The pathway to the temple is paved with the timeless faith of those who love the Lord and honor His eternal plan of life and exaltation. To step onto that pathway fills the soul with the magnificent vision of the divine destiny of God's children—to rise in worthiness and perfection through the blessings of the Atonement and learn how to return home again to the presence of our Father in Heaven, sealed to that end by the power of the priesthood and lifted by the grace of God according to our obedience and valor. It takes faith to step onto that pathway—but the blessings far exceed the measure of our sacrifice and personal investment of time, energy, and devotion in doing so. "In the strength of the Lord" (Alma 20:4) we can accomplish all things in faith and obedience to the commandments.

The faith that leads us to the temple embraces five interrelated categories:

Faith in our Heavenly Father and our Savior—the Creator, the "author of eternal salvation" (Heb. 5:9), the "finisher of our faith" (Heb. 12:2; see also Moro. 6:4).

Faith in eternity—the continuity of life after death and the efficacy of temple ordinances that extend beyond the veil.

Faith in the temple builders—the prophets who envision, the laborers who construct, the tithe payers who fund, and the Saints who operate the temples day and night.

Faith in ourselves—our ability to learn, progress, sacrifice, and guide our families to the temple, despite all tribulations and trials.

Faith in promised blessings—we will find peace, joy, and glory in temple activity and ultimately return to the presence of God.

Let us consider in turn each of these five categories of faith, seeking added wisdom and understanding from the scriptures and from the counsel of the Lord's chosen leaders.

Faith in Our Heavenly Father and Our Savior

The Apostle Paul taught, "Now faith is the substance of things hoped for, the evidence of things not seen" (Heb. 11:1). The prophet Alma declared: "And now as I said concerning faith—faith is not to have a perfect knowledge of things; therefore if ye have faith ye hope for things which are not seen, which are true" (Alma 32:21). When we go to the temple, we hope for things divine that we do not yet see with full clarity, and we process evidence of God's presence in our lives that is not yet manifested unto us in full measure. Our testimony of faith draws us to the house of the Lord, for we believe with all our hearts that there we will find knowledge to strengthen our conviction of God's mercy. As we pass through the doors marked "Holiness to the Lord," we find that the temple is a sanctuary of faith, a place where faith is enhanced, confirmed, sanctified, energized, and converted to a commitment of charitable action for our colleagues in this life and our fellow beings who have passed through the veil.

Joseph B. Wirthlin confirmed these principles as follows:

> The ideals of faith, hope, and charity are most evident in the holy temples. There we learn the purpose of life, strengthen our commitment as disciples of Christ by entering into sacred covenants with Him, and seal our families together for eternity across generations. Receiving our own endowment in a temple and returning frequently to perform sacred ordinances for our kindred dead increases our faith, strengthens our hope, and deepens our charity. We receive our own endowment with faith and hope that we will understand the Lord's plan for His children, will recognize the divine potential within each of us as children of our Heavenly Father, and will be faithful to the end in keeping the covenants we make. Performing temple ordinances for the dead is a manifestation of charity, offering essential blessings to those who have preceded us, blessings that were not available to them during their mortal lives. We have the privilege of doing for them what they are unable to do for themselves. (*Ensign,* Nov. 1998, 25)

Above all, the temple increases our faith in the Atonement of the Lord Jesus Christ. We are assured in the scriptures that we can do all things in the strength of the Lord (Alma 26:12). Through His redeeming love we can be united in the conviction of faith that the gospel is true and that the Savior is indeed the Head of His Church. President Gordon B. Hinckley has stated: "Participating in these dedicatory services, one senses the true strength of the Church. That strength is in the hearts of the people, who are united by a bond of recognition of God as our Eternal Father and Jesus Christ as our Savior. Their individual testimonies are firmly established on a foundation of faith concerning things divine" (*Ensign,* Nov. 1984, 50).

Faith in Eternity

When we go to the temple of the Lord, we pass through the gates of eternity. The temple is a symbol of the continuity of life after death, of the perpetuation of the eternal family. Our faith in everlasting life is that power that draws us to the temple. The Spirit of Elijah is what turns (or seals) the hearts of the fathers and mothers to their children and the hearts of the children to their fathers and mothers (see Mal. 4:5–6). We have an abiding faith that the love we feel for one another here in this sphere of existence will be preserved and glorified in the hereafter. What a choice exercise in faith it is to go to the house of the Lord and celebrate through solemn vows and covenants the sanctity of life in the eternities. As such, we come to appreciate the temple as the culminating experience in gospel living, the grand symbol of what the Apostle Paul prophesied: "That in the dispensation of the fulness of times he might gather together in one all things in Christ, both which are in heaven, and which are on earth; even in him" (Eph. 1:10; see also D&C 27:13). Everything points to the temple. Our vision is focused on the temple as the sure pathway leading us back into the presence of God.

Russell M. Nelson has confirmed these truths in the following words:

> Each temple is symbolic of our faith in God and an evidence of our faith in life after death. The temple is the object of every activity, every lesson, every progressive step in the Church. All of our efforts in proclaiming the gospel, perfecting the Saints, and redeeming the dead lead to the

holy temple. . . . Ordinances of the temple are absolutely crucial. We cannot return to God's glory without them. . . .

Each temple stands as a symbol of our membership in the Church, as a sign of our faith in life after death, and as a stepping-stone to eternal glory for us and our family. (*Ensign,* Mar. 2002, 17)

The temple is divine evidence that the Resurrection is a reality. Paul declared: "Else what shall they do which are baptized for the dead, if the dead rise not at all? why are they then baptized for the dead?" (1 Cor. 15:29). Because the Savior "finished [His] preparations unto the children of men" (D&C 19:19) and brought about the Atonement, all mankind is granted the blessing of immortality—to rise in the Resurrection in triumph over the power of death, the Savior Himself being "the firstfruits of them that slept" (1 Cor. 15:20). Because of the eternal gift of the Resurrection, as Paul pointed out, there is compelling reason to do temple work, including proxy baptisms and other temple ordinances on behalf of deceased persons, who can then exercise their agency to accept the vicarious work performed on their behalf. Going to the temple is the active equivalent of bearing our testimony, for temple attendance confirms our faith in the hereafter, our certainty about the resurrection of the body and the perpetuity of life, and our conviction about the eternal nature of the family. Elder Dallin H. Oaks stated: "Our temples are living, working testimonies to our faith in the reality of the resurrection. They provide the sacred settings where living proxies can perform all of the necessary ordinances of mortal life in behalf of those who live in the world of the spirits. None of this would be meaningful if we did not have the assurance of universal immortality and the opportunity for eternal life because of the Resurrection of our Lord and Savior, Jesus Christ" (*Ensign,* May 2000, 14).

In his later years, the Prophet Joseph Smith was fully absorbed in the urgent need to lay an enduring foundation for temple work in this dispensation. In an epistle to the Saints dated September 6, 1842, he stated: "It may seem to some to be a very bold doctrine that we talk of—a power which records or binds on earth and binds in heaven. Nevertheless, in all ages of the world, whenever the Lord has given a dispensation of the priesthood to any man by actual revelation, . . . this power has always been given" (D&C 128:9). Further, he wrote concerning proxy work for the dead that "they without us cannot be made perfect—neither can we without our dead be made perfect" (D&C 128:15). Joseph did not live long enough to witness the physical completion of the Nauvoo Temple, but he fulfilled his divine commission to lay the groundwork for the continuing operation of temples in the dispensation of the fullness of times, bestowed upon the Twelve Apostles the keys and enlightenment pertaining to the work of these sacred houses of the Lord, and sealed his life with the everlasting witness that temples are the gateway to eternal life and exaltation for the faithful and the obedient children of God.

Faith in the Temple Builders

It is well, when we go to the temple, to remember in gratitude the faith and contributions of all who have labored to make the temple a reality. We should ponder the sacrifice of those who laid the foundation of temple work as a central part of the Restoration of the gospel in this latter-day dispensation of the fullness of times. In his remarkable vision of the spirit world and the coming forth of the leadership of the Restoration, President Joseph F. Smith made reference to the temple builders of our times:

> The Prophet Joseph Smith, and my father, Hyrum Smith, Brigham Young, John Taylor, Wilford Woodruff, and other choice spirits who were reserved to come forth in the fulness of times to take part in laying the foundations of the great latter-day work, Including the building of the temples and the performance of ordinances therein for the redemption of the dead, were also in the spirit world. I observed that they were also among the noble and great ones who were chosen in the beginning to be rulers in the Church of God. Even before they were born, they, with many others, received their first lessons in the world of

spirits and were prepared to come forth in the due time of the Lord to labor in his vineyard for the salvation of the souls of men. (D&C 138:53–56)

In their poverty, the Saints at Kirtland erected a magnificent temple to the Lord, investing all their earthly possessions therein and guarding its construction with their lives. We learn from the *History of the Church* in the entry for Wednesday, January 8, 1834, that "guards are placed to protect the Kirtland temple as a result of persecution by detractors and the threat of violence at the hands of a gathering mob. Some workmen are seen armed with a hammer in one hand and a rifle in the other." Of this period, Heber C. Kimball wrote in the *Times and Seasons*: "We had to guard ourselves night after night, and for weeks were not permitted to take off our clothes, and were obliged to lay with our fire locks [rifles] in our arms" (*HC,* 2:2).

By contrast, the temple sites of today are peaceful and serene. What a blessing! As we prepare to go to the temple, are we willing to stand up for righteous principles and guard the things of God with our lives as did our pioneer forebears? Are we prepared to don in faith the armor of God to repel all influences that would keep us from the temple?

The temples are enduring monuments to the faith, courage, stamina, diligence, and obedience of those who have shown us the way to serve God with full conviction and who embody the principles of enduring faith in the purpose of temple work as the key to the redemption of God's sons and daughters. Speaking of the Salt Lake Temple, Elder David B. Haight declared: "One hundred years after its dedication, it proudly stands as a regal monument of the faith, industry, and vision of the Saints of God who built it. . . . But even more majestic than the temple itself is the vision of the purpose of temples which guided the builders. That purpose is to redeem all mankind who are obedient to the laws and commandments of God" (*Ensign,* May 1993, 23).

Temple builders are disciples of the Savior in very deed, for they invest their lives in His sacred work with a full measure of trust and covenant valor. They are on the Lord's errand to extend the reach of temple work to all quarters of the earth, that all may embrace the saving principles available to those who come unto Christ, in faith and obedience, and make themselves worthy of His holy house. Elder John K. Carmack discussed this obedience and faith as follows: "Increasing our faith requires trusting the Lord with our whole souls and striving to act as He would in all circumstances." As an example, he cited the faith of President Gordon B. Hinckley, who represents the vanguard of temple expansion in our time:

> When President Hinckley announced his goal of providing 100 temples by the year 2000, he acted by faith. He didn't build any of the temples using his own construction skills. He acted by the word of faith, and that faith unlocked the energy of thousands of others who physically planned and built those temples. He also exercised the priesthood keys that he and only he held. This was a miracle just as surely as if he had removed a mountain. Faith has thus brought about the miracle of more than 100 temples. . . . This example helps us understand more fully what Jesus suggested to His Apostles in answering their request for increased faith. (*Ensign,* Mar. 2002, 53)

In this context, let us remember the stalwart faith of the Saints of Zion in paying their tithes and offerings to support temple construction and temple work worldwide. Sacrifice is an act of faith; consecration of one's means for the building up of the kingdom of God is an expression of love for the Lord and reverential recognition of His majestic atoning sacrifice. President Thomas S. Monson has stated: "Temples . . . are built with stone, glass, wood, and metal. But they are also a product of faith and an example of sacrifice. The funds to build temples come from all tithe payers and consist of the widow's mite, children's pennies, and workmen's dollars—all sanctified by faith." As an illustration, President Monson related the following inspiring story:

> Whenever I attend a temple dedication, I think of Brother and Sister Gustav and Margarete Wacker of Kingston, Ontario. He was once the branch president of the Kingston

Branch. He was from the old country. He spoke English with a thick accent. He never owned or drove a car. He plied the trade of a barber. He made but little money cutting hair near an army base at Kingston. How he loved the missionaries! The highlight of his day would be when he had the privilege to cut the hair of a missionary. Never would there be a charge. When they would make a feeble attempt to pay him, he would say, "Oh no; it is a joy to cut the hair of a servant of the Lord." Indeed, he would reach deep into his pockets and give the missionaries all of his tips for the day. If it were raining, as it often does in Kingston, President Wacker would call a taxi and send the missionaries to their apartment by cab, while he, himself, at day's end would lock the small shop and walk home—alone in the driving rain.

I first met Gustav Wacker when I noticed that his tithing was far in excess of that expected from his potential income. My efforts to explain to him that the Lord required no more than a tenth fell on attentive but unconvinced ears. He simply responded that he loved to pay all he could to the Lord. It amounted to about a third of his income. His dear wife felt exactly as he did. Their unique manner of tithing payment continued.

Gustav and Margarete Wacker established a home that was a heaven. They were not blessed with children but mothered and fathered their many Church visitors. A sophisticated and learned Church leader from Ottawa told me, "I like to visit the Wacker home. I come away refreshed in spirit and determined to ever live close to the Lord."

Did our Heavenly Father honor such abiding faith? The branch prospered. The membership outgrew the rented Slovakian Hall where they met and moved into a modern and lovely chapel of their own to which the branch members had contributed their share and more, that it might grace the city of Kingston. President and Sister Wacker had their prayers answered by serving a proselyting mission to their native Germany and later a temple mission to that beautiful temple in Washington, D.C. Then, in

1983, his mission in mortality concluded, Gustav Wacker peacefully passed away while being held in the loving arms of his eternal companion, dressed in his white temple suit, there in the Washington Temple. (*Ensign,* Nov. 1990, 67)

Let us give our own offering in faith each time we prepare to go to the temple. Let us look upon tithes and offerings as opportunities to demonstrate our love for God by returning to Him willingly a portion of His abundant blessings so that the work of the kingdom can go forward. Let us leave a legacy of faith for our children and later generations so that they, too, can inherit the torch of glory that constitutes temple work—the eternal design of Father and Son to embrace those who come forward with broken hearts and contrite spirits—with the exalting principles of everlasting life. Elder Robert D. Hales has provided us with these inspiring words on this theme:

> Tithing has been established in these latter days as an essential law for members of the Lord's restored Church. It is one of the basic ways we witness our faith in Him and our obedience to His laws and commandments. Tithing is one of the commandments that qualifies us, by our faith, to enter the temple—the house of the Lord. . . . The strict observance of the law of tithing not only qualifies us to receive the higher, saving ordinances of the temple, it allows us to receive them on behalf of our ancestors. . . . Tithing develops and tests our faith. . . . Our faith in Him makes it possible to keep temple covenants and receive eternal temple blessings. . . . What a marvelous opportunity this is to plant the seed of faith in the hearts of your children. You will start them on a path that leads to the temple. The generations of your ancestors before you and your posterity after you will rise up and call you blessed, for you will have prepared your children to perform saving ordinances on their behalf. . . . Keeping the commandments, which includes paying our tithing, will qualify us to enter those temples, be sealed to our families, and receive eternal blessings. (*Ensign,* Nov. 2002, 26)

Finally, let us remember the faith of all those devoted servants of the Lord who labor day and night to keep the temples going and to prepare the way for us to enter and partake of our temple blessings. President James E. Faust tells with admiration about a faithful man he observed one day walking toward the temple at Papeete, Tahiti, in the wee hours of the morning to prepare for his service there. "I marveled at the faith of that man, who is willing to forgo his sleep and other activities in order to meditate and contemplate. . . . It is important for us to nurture such a simple, untroubled faith. I urge complete acceptance of the absolutes of our own faith. . . . In our belief, it is possible to be even a helper of the Father and of the Son and to be under their personal tutelage" (*Ensign,* Mar. 1988, 69).

FAITH IN OURSELVES

Going to the temple of God requires faith in ourselves—faith that we can learn and progress under the Spirit, that we can come to understand the beauties and symbolism of temple worship, that we can begin to unfold our divine potential under the guidance of a wise and loving Creator. As visitors within the sacred walls of the temple, we are faithful builders of the kingdom of God, of eternal families, and of our own character as heirs of salvation and as "children of the covenant" (3 Ne. 20:26). Said Elder Russell M. Nelson in this regard:

> We are to be creators in our own right—builders of an individual faith in God, faith in the Lord Jesus Christ, and faith in His Church. We are to build families and be sealed in holy temples. We are to build the Church and kingdom of God upon the earth. We are to prepare for our own divine destiny—glory, immortality, and eternal lives. These supernal blessings can all be ours, through our faithfulness. (*Ensign,* May 2000, 84)

In all of this, we are to view ourselves in faith, as from a higher perspective—moving upwards, advancing along the pathway to eternal life, passing the milestones of our spiritual development, coming closer to our destination of the heavenly home from which we departed but a lifetime ago.

By cultivating faith in ourselves, we will build up the strength to make the needed sacrifices of time and effort that are associated with temple service. Ardeth G. Kapp, former Young Women general president, observed:

> Knowing and remembering who we are and whose we are, we become guided by a force affecting our attitude and our conduct. We draw close to our Father in Heaven through sacred ordinances and covenants available only through His restored church.
>
> I had the privilege of visiting with a faithful family of Latter-day Saints in a small nipa hut in the Philippines. In this humble setting a beautiful young woman, fourteen years old, listened intently while her father explained that by saving all the money they could and selling everything they owned, the family would one day have enough to go to the temple where they could be sealed as a family forever.
>
> It is our faith in the importance of making covenants with God and coming to understand our immense possibilities that the temple, the house of the Lord, becomes the focus for all that really matters. In the temple we participate in ordinances and covenants that span the distance between heaven and earth. They prepare us to one day return to God's presence and enjoy the blessings of eternal families and eternal life. (*Ensign,* May 1992, 78)

Similarly, our personal faith ensures that we can endure the tribulations of life, especially as we are endowed in the temples of the Lord with the wisdom and fortitude accessible to the obedient. Elder Robert D. Hales has stated this truth as follows:

> In our day, the steadying arm of the Lord reaches us through the ordinances of His holy temples. Said the Prophet Joseph to the early Saints in Nauvoo, "You need an endowment, brethren, in order that you may be

prepared and able to overcome all things." How right he was! Being blessed with the temple covenants and endowed with power made it possible for the Latter-day Saints to endure tribulation with faith. At the end of her own pioneer journey, Sarah Rich recorded, "If it had not been for the faith and knowledge that was bestowed upon us in that temple . . . our journey would have been like . . . taking a leap in the dark." (*Ensign*, May 2003, 15)

Through faith we can look to God and live. We can look to the house of the Lord and find joy therein. We can guide our children in the pathways of truth and ensure that they, too, will have the blessings of the temple to enrich and edify their lives.

Faith in Promised Blessings

On behalf of his beloved colleagues, the Apostle Paul prayed:

> That he would grant you, according to the riches of his glory, to be strengthened with might by his Spirit in the inner man; That Christ may dwell in your hearts by faith; that ye, being rooted and grounded in love, May be able to comprehend with all saints what is the breadth, and length, and depth, and height; And to know the love of Christ, which passeth knowledge, that ye might be filled with all the fulness of God. (Eph. 3:16–19)

To have Christ abide with us by virtue of His grace—and through the exercise of our faith as enlightened by His Spirit—is a transcendent blessing associated with temple work, for the temple is the appointed venue where we learn the deeper truths about our relationship with our Father and His Son. It is there also that we gain wisdom concerning how to resolve the pressing challenges of life, how to secure access to blessings of peace and hope, and how to become worthy and empowered to return to God's glorious presence one day. Of this surpassing promise, Elder John A. Widtsoe said:

> Though he may not be here in person, he is here by his Holy Spirit and by earthly men holding the priesthood. By that Spirit they direct the Lord's work here on earth. Every person who enters this sacred place in faith and prayer will find help in solving life's problems.
>
> It is good to be in the temple, the house of the Lord, a place of priesthood instruction, of peace, of covenants, of blessings, and of revelation. Gratitude for this privilege and an eager desire to possess the spirit of the occasion should overflow in our hearts. (*Ensign,* Jan. 1972, 56)

The pathway to the temple is the pathway of faith in covenant promises. We will, through our obedience and through the majesty of temple blessings, see the Lord in person one day. A visiting teaching message several years ago confirmed this truth as follows: "Anna, a faithful woman 'of a great age' and a widow in Jerusalem, served in the temple with fasting and daily prayer. After many years, her faith was rewarded when she saw the infant Jesus in the temple and recognized him as the Redeemer (see Luke 2:36–38)" (*Ensign,* Mar. 1995, 70). The temple is a house of divine promises. In the sacred precincts of the house of the Lord are bestowed blessings of unfathomable importance to our lives and the lives of our families. President Gordon B. Hinckley has stated: "I make you a promise that if you will go to the house of the Lord, you will be blessed, life will be better for you. . . . Avail yourselves of the great opportunity to go to the Lord's house and thereby partake of all of the marvelous blessings that are yours to be received there" (*Ensign,* July 1997, 73).

The full scope of truth and light associated with the temple is not to be fathomed in a single visit. Going to the temple is a process, a never-ending process of learning the things of God line upon line, precept upon precept. When we receive the truths of the temple in a spirit of thanksgiving and add them, brick by brick, to the foundation of our lives, we build unto the Lord an edifice of solidarity and honor, rising upon the rock of the Redeemer: "Therefore thus saith the Lord God, Behold, I lay in Zion for a foundation a stone, a tried stone, a precious corner stone, a sure foundation" (Isa. 28:16). As Alma taught:

"He that will not harden his heart, to him is given the greater portion of the word, until it is given unto him to know the mysteries of God until he know them in full" (Alma 12:10). What a privilege it is to return to the temple often and add to our store of truth yet another portion of pure knowledge that flows from God.

In counseling people as they prepare for the temple, Elder L. Aldin Porter, former president of the Salt Lake Temple, taught these truths in candor and love:

> I hope they come to the temple in faith. They will not understand all at first, nor would they in any other activity with deep meaning. But they will learn more as they return to the Lord's temples.
>
> The Lord honors those who respect His sacred gifts. Those who don't respect them lose them. They drift away from the mind and heart, and the temple and its blessings are soon forgotten. On the other hand, those who honor the Lord's gifts will find greater joy and understanding that cannot be found in any other way in mortality.
>
> If young adults make and keep sacred covenants, they will, in time, experience a fulfillment of the Apostle Paul's words: "Eye hath not seen, nor ear heard, neither have entered into the heart of man, the things which God hath prepared for them that love him" (1 Cor. 2:9). (*New Era*, Oct. 2004, 8)

It takes faith to look forward and view the fulfillment of those grand promises associated with the sacred temples of the Lord. The temple inspires and strengthens our faith. With faith, all things are possible. With faith, we can complete our preparations to be worthy of the temple. With faith we can come to understand the essence of the temple experience—even though much will be new to us. With faith, our prayers will be answered as we prepare humbly and systematically to enter the temple. With faith we can discern opportunities for future service. With faith, we can look forward to returning again to the presence of God.

Time to Meditate and Ponder

1. In what ways are the temples of the Lord monuments to faith?

2. How can the temple experience strengthen our faith in God and in the Atonement of the Savior?

3. In what way is the temple a validation of the joyous doctrine of the Resurrection and the immortality of man?

4. How does the temple provide compelling evidence of the faith of our forebears?

5. In what special way does each of us today contribute to the expansion and operation of the holy temples around the globe?

6. The remarkable legacy of President Gordon B. Hinckley includes the unprecedented expansion of temple accessibility in the world. What is the inevitable impact of this movement on the faith of Church members everywhere?

7. How can we ensure that we have gratitude in our hearts for the many temple workers who give so abundantly and faithfully of their time and energy to serve us in the house of the Lord? How can we express that gratitude?

8. How can we cultivate deeper faith in ourselves as sons and daughters of God with a divine destiny and promise to be "joint-heirs with Christ" (Rom. 8:17) of all eternal blessings?

9. How is the temple a source of faith and power to help us overcome life's tribulations and trials?

10. How will the temple strengthen our faith in the fulfillment of this commandment: "And seek the face of the Lord always, that in patience ye may possess your souls, and ye shall have eternal life" (D&C 101:38).

CHAPTER 5
A HOUSE OF VIRTUE

Guiding Principle: The temple is a house of chastity, a place that extends a haven of rest and comfort to those who aspire to endure in virtue and righteousness.

> *I believe we find the beauty and sanctity of "his holy place" as we enter the magnificent temples of God. . . . In the temples of the Lord, we learn obedience. We learn sacrifice. We make the vows of chastity and have our lives consecrated to holy purposes. It is possible for us to be purged and purified and to have our sins washed away so that we may come before the Lord as clean, white, and spotless as the newly fallen snow. . . .*
> *"Who shall ascend into the hill of the Lord? or who shall stand in his holy place? He that hath clean hands, and a pure heart; who hath not lifted up his soul unto vanity, nor sworn deceitfully" (Ps. 24:3–4). For "holiness becometh thine house, O Lord, for ever" (Ps. 93:5).*
> —JAMES E. FAUST, "WHO SHALL ASCEND INTO THE HILL OF THE LORD?" *ENSIGN*, AUG. 2001, 2.

The Savior taught, "Blessed are the pure in heart: for they shall see God" (Matt. 5:8). Paul enjoined us to fill our hearts and minds with virtuous and comely thoughts and aspirations: "Finally, brethren, whatsoever things are true, whatsoever things are honest, whatsoever things are just, whatsoever things are pure, whatsoever things are lovely, whatsoever things are of good report; if there be any virtue, and if there be any praise, think on these things" (Philip. 4:8; see also Articles of Faith 1:13). In this regard, President David O. McKay counseled us as follows: "That is the mission of every man, from the President of the Church down to the latest convert in the Church. Every officer holds his position to build up, to bless; and, as President Joseph F. Smith has said, to establish righteousness, purity, and virtue among mankind" (*Gospel Ideals,* 143).

When the Prophet Joseph Smith offered the inspired dedicatory prayer for the Kirtland Temple on March 27, 1836, he importuned the Lord to bless the Saints "that all people who shall enter upon the threshold of the Lord's house may feel thy power, and feel constrained to acknowledge that thou hast sanctified it, and that it is thy house, a place of thy holiness" (D&C 109:13). Virtue is a governing principle within the temple. Purity is a precondition for access to the house of the Lord, since "no unclean thing can dwell with God" (1 Ne. 10:21) and "no unclean thing shall be permitted to come into [His] house to pollute it" (D&C 109:20).

The prophet Isaiah proclaimed the solemn commandment of God: "Be ye clean, that bear the vessels of the Lord" (Isa. 52:11). We might ask what is meant by the reference to "vessels" in this passage of scripture. In ancient Israel certain vessels (such as bowls, cups, and basins) were used in the performance of sacred temple rites. Similar instruments were used for ritual purification in the homes of the people. But the principal vessels of temple service are not things but rather the Saints who labor there—the workers and patrons who frequent the halls of light found in the temple. The vessels of the Lord are the people of the Lord, sanctified by their endurance—through faith, repentance, baptism, and the gift of the Holy Ghost—to pass through the gates of the temple and carry on the work of glory that is accomplished there. Elder Jeffrey R. Holland explained the implications of the scriptural references to such vessels in this way: "The message is that as priesthood bearers not only are we to *handle* sacred vessels and emblems of God's power—think of preparing, blessing, and passing the sacrament, for example—but we are also to *be* a sanctified instrument as well. Partly because of what we are to *do* but more importantly because of what we are to *be,* the prophets and apostles tell us to . . . call on the Lord out of a pure heart. They tell us to be clean" (*Ensign,* Nov. 2000, 38; emphasis in original).

Those who are preparing to enter the temple may rightfully regard themselves as "vessels of the Lord"—His servants and disciples who are following in His footsteps. The Apostle Paul wrote the following to his young companion Timothy: "If a man therefore purge himself from these [aspects of unworthiness], he shall be a vessel unto honour, sanctified, and meet for the master's use, and prepared unto every good work. Flee also youthful lusts: but follow righteousness, faith, charity, peace, with them that call on the Lord out of a pure heart" (2 Tim. 2:21–22).

The Lord characterized the converted Saul of Tarsus—despite this man's history of evil persecutions against the Church—as "a chosen vessel unto me" (Acts 9:15). The Lord reached out and touched the life of this remarkable individual and guided him to become one of the greatest missionaries of the gospel in the meridian of time. In a similar way, the Lord reached out earlier through the ministering of an angel to touch the lives of Alma and his youthful companions, the sons of Mosiah, turning them from their aberrant ways and onto the pathway of righteousness and service for countless thousands of Saints. Mormon confirmed the role of angelic messengers to declare "the word of Christ unto the chosen vessels of the Lord, that they may bear testimony of him" (Moro. 7:31).

All are appointed to be chosen vessels of the Lord. All deserve our service and guidance in fulfilling this divine mandate. Blessings await us in abundance as we reach out and help our fellow Saints to rise to their potential as sons and daughters of God, recipients of all the promised blessings of the Lord. President James E. Faust counsels us,

"Somehow we must reach the one—every single one—for they are 'chosen vessels' unto the Lord" (*Ensign,* July 1973, 86). In this light, those who are preparing for the blessings of the temple have the opportunity to bring themselves to a higher level of moral purity where they can continue to be touched by the Lord and invited to enter His house worthily. In addition, all such individuals have the privilege and commission to work with those in their circle of influence by assisting them also to be "chosen vessels of the Lord," prepared and willing to labor in the building up of His kingdom. Through the power of the Atonement, the Savior has brought about "means unto men that they may have faith unto repentance" (Alma 34:15). Through this process, all members of the Church can prepare themselves, sustained by the blessings of the Holy Ghost, to enter the house of the Lord in purity and righteousness.

How can we honor ourselves as eternal vessels of God? How can we preserve our dignity and maintain our capacity to emanate the light of the gospel of Jesus Christ in all we do? By remaining faithful to our covenant of purity and holiness before the Lord. Elder David A. Bednar stressed the urgency and importance of honoring ourselves as temples of God:

> Brothers and sisters, both the Church's temples and our personal temples must be used to accomplish the righteous purposes for which they were created. Our physical body is a marvelous blessing and a timeless trust. The most sacred of all our divine powers is to become a co-creator with Heavenly Father in providing physical bodies for His spirit sons and daughters and in establishing a righteous and Christ-centered family. Nothing is more holy; nothing deserves more reverence; nothing is more central to the plan of happiness. And our very souls are at stake. . . .
>
> The choices we make about the use of our physical temples will affect us throughout eternity. (*Ensign,* Sept. 2001, 14)

Meeting the Standards of Virtue

Those who enter the sacred premises of the temple should be clean in thought, word, and deed. Through the power of the Spirit, they have deflected or overcome the stain of worldly entanglements that would degrade the body with harmful substances (such as alcohol, tobacco, and illicit drugs) and pollute the mind with impure thoughts and imagery that all too persistently lead to sinful practices. They have prevailed over the forces of evil rampant in the world, and they have qualified themselves in every way to meet the standards of righteousness that are enumerated in the temple recommend interview. Elder L. Aldin Porter, while serving as president of the Salt Lake Temple, explained the purpose of the uncompromisingly high standards of purity that pertain to the house of the Lord: "To protect His holy house and those who enter it, the Lord has given certain requirements. The questions a bishop asks us as we obtain a recommend will help us to be spiritually prepared to make temple covenants. Our Heavenly Father has set these standards of worthiness to bless His children. They are not to keep people out of the temple unless they are unprepared" (*New Era,* Oct. 2004, 8).

Purity is the essence of family relationships. Virtue is the bond that preserves the spirit of togetherness and enduring affection between husband and wife. Uncompromising moral cleanliness fortifies the family against the onslaught of darkness and degradation that flows relentlessly up against the outer walls of the home from evil influences in society. President James E. Faust has stated the sacred importance of moral purity as follows:

> We believe in being chaste. There is no different or double standard for moral cleanliness for men and women in the Church. In fact, I believe holders of the priesthood have a greater responsibility to maintain standards of chastity before marriage and fidelity after marriage. The Lord has said, "Be ye clean that bear the vessels of the Lord." This means being pure in thought as well as in deed. The Prophet Joseph Smith stated, "If we would come before God, we must keep ourselves pure, as He is pure." If

husband and wife will remain pure and chaste, completely devoted to each other during the storms and sunshine of life, their love for one another will deepen into something of supernal fulfillment. An early LDS Apostle, Parley P. Pratt, said, "From this union of affection, springs all the other relationships, social joys and affections diffused through *every* branch of human existence." (*Ensign*, May 1998, 43; emphasis in original)

Before leaving on missions, the valiant youth of Zion have the opportunity to attend the temple and receive the sacred endowment of truth bestowed there as a blessing from the Lord. They prepare themselves carefully for this magnificent experience by repelling from their lives every aspect of impurity, whether in the form of harmful substances or degrading influences that could beckon the unprincipled to venture down hidden pathways. President Ezra Taft Benson had this counsel for those who have chosen to serve missions for the Church and are thus preparing to receive their endowment in the temple:

> A two-year mission today requires good physical health. It requires that you keep your body clean. In your early teenage years, when temptations come to you to take things into your body which are unsuitable, have the courage to resist. Live the Word of Wisdom—no smoking, no drinking of any alcoholic beverages, and no drugs. Keep your body pure—a pure vessel for the Lord.
>
> Stay morally clean. This means that you keep a clean mind. Your thoughts will determine your actions, and so they must be controlled. It's difficult to control those thoughts if you submit yourself to temptation. So you will have to carefully select your reading material, the movies you see, and the other forms of entertainment in order to have good thoughts rather than unwholesome desires. (*Ensign*, May 1985, 36)

In our modern culture there is a pervasive surfeit of immoral enticements to draw God's children away from the pathway of eternal principles and onto the byways of profligate and impure activities. Especially foreboding is the tsunami of illicit and perverse imagery flowing from the media and the Internet. President Gordon B. Hinckley has warned repeatedly of the perils of partaking of such things:

> Declared the Lord in 1831: "Go ye out from among the wicked. Save yourselves. Be ye clean that bear the vessels of the Lord." (D&C 38:42.)
>
> There is an ever-growing plague of pornography swirling about us. The producers and purveyors of smut are assiduously working a mine that yields them many millions in profit. Some of their products are artfully beguiling. They are designed to titillate and stimulate the baser instincts. Many a man who has partaken of forbidden fruit and then discovered that he has destroyed his marriage, lost his self-respect, and broken his companion's heart, has come to realize that the booby-trapped jungle trail he has followed began with the reading or viewing of pornographic material. . . . I am suggesting a personal avoidance of such things. There is so much of the good and the beautiful and the uplifting in literature and art and life itself that there should be no time for any man who holds the priesthood of God to patronize, to watch, to buy that which only "carefully leads him down to hell." (*Ensign*, Nov. 1983, 44)

Maintaining the highest moral standards of purity and holiness is paramount for all who call themselves Saints of the Most High—but in particular for all those who enter the temples of the Lord. In the temples of God we have the opportunity to renew our commitment to live the standards of the Church from the depths of our being. We prepare ourselves to enter the temple by choosing to move beyond token compliance to a condition of life where we subscribe fully to the mission of taking upon ourselves the divine nature, where we willingly do all in our power to embody the very qualities we find displayed so masterfully in Christ's mission. President Spencer W. Kimball explained this remarkable transition from an outward and shallow commitment to one that is authentic and all-consuming, one that opens to our view the majesty of the eternities and the glory of exaltation as eternal families in the kingdom of heaven:

> But all these ordinances are futile unless with them there is a great righteousness. . . . So we go out into every field to perfect our lives. It is not enough to pay tithing and live the Word of Wisdom. We must be chaste in mind and in body. We must be neighborly, kind, and clean of heart. Sometimes people feel if they have complied with the more mechanical things that they are in line. And yet perhaps their hearts are not always pure. . . . With hearts that are absolutely purged and cleaned, and living the more mechanical things, we are prepared to come into the holy temple, . . . where perfection should be found. Here we receive extension of our glimpses we have had of the eternities. In our lives we have had little glimpses when the curtain has been moved a little. And here our vision will be extended until our knowledge and understanding will be greatly increased.
>
> As we come here we will want to be sure that we are prepared for this great experience. Self-mastery is another name for the gospel of Jesus Christ. . . . When all of these ordinances are performed, then the self-mastery must accompany them. No one can be exalted in the kingdom of our Father without the ordinances. Neither can they be exalted without the righteousness; and sometimes people receive these ordinances unworthily, and at the least jeopardize their eternities. And then, as you know, in the world many people feel if they are just good they will receive all the blessings of eternity. Neither is complete in and of itself. They are joined together in one union which makes perfection; and to that end temples are built so that these final ordinances may be performed for the children of our Heavenly Father. (*TSWK,* 537)

THE GRAND HARVEST OF THE VIRTUOUS LIFE

Why would the Lord have us be virtuous and pure? Because in His eternal wisdom He knows that such a disciplined and chaste state of existence leads to blessings of unspeakable peace, joy, happiness, glory, and spiritual fulfillment that are only available under these conditions:

> Let thy bowels also be full of charity towards all men, and to the household of faith, and let virtue garnish thy thoughts unceasingly; then shall thy confidence wax strong in the presence of God; and the doctrine of the priesthood shall distil upon thy soul as the dews from heaven. The Holy Ghost shall be thy constant companion, and thy scepter an unchanging scepter of righteousness and truth; and thy dominion shall be an everlasting dominion, and without compulsory means it shall flow unto thee forever and ever. (D&C 121:45–46)

Virtue and purity provide the mantle of worthiness that will induce feelings of comfort and ease in the minds and hearts of the penitent and faithful who serve the Lord in His holy house. What a great blessing it is to wear such a mantle and receive the sublime blessings of temple worship and service.

The opportunity to go to the temple provides powerful momentum in our quest to achieve lives of integrity and commitment. Temple worthiness is anchored in uncompromising devotion to the principles of righteousness and covenant valor. President Howard W. Hunter explained the importance of the attribute of integrity that applies to us all as we prepare to enter the temple:

> The ability to stand by one's principles, to live with integrity and faith according to one's belief—that is what matters. That devotion to true principle—in our individual lives, in our homes and families, and in all places that we meet and influence other people—that devotion is what God is ultimately requesting of us. It requires commitment—whole-souled, deeply held, eternally cherished commitment to the principles we know to be true in the commandments

God has given. If we will be true and faithful to the Lord's principles, then we will always be temple worthy, and the Lord and His holy temples will be the great symbols of our discipleship with Him. (*Ensign,* Oct. 1994, 5)

Living up to those standards of worthiness prepares one to see God in the temple—not as yet with the real eye, but with the inner eye of spiritual vision. As the Lord Himself promised:

> And inasmuch as my people build a house unto me in the name of the Lord, and do not suffer any unclean thing to come into it, that it be not defiled, my glory shall rest upon it; Yea, and my presence shall be there, for I will come into it, and all the pure in heart that shall come into it shall see God. But if it be defiled I will not come into it, and my glory shall not be there; for I will not come into unholy temples. (D&C 97:15–17)

Looking up to God through the experience of His holy temple leads to an abundant harvest of divine blessings. The temple focuses our vision on the eternities and promotes within us an abiding sensitivity to the promptings of the Spirit, even the Comforter "whom the Father will send in my name, he shall teach you all things, and bring all things to your remembrance, whatsoever I have said unto you" (John 14:26). The temple enlivens the word of God within us. It lifts our view to the heavens and capacitates us to discern the signs of the Divine all about us in our lives. President Thomas S. Monson recalled sentiments of this nature following the dedication of the Toronto Temple:

> When I prepared to leave Toronto following the concluding dedicatory session, I gazed upward toward heaven, that I might offer a silent prayer of gratitude to God for His watchful care, His bounteous blessings and for "days never to be forgotten." High above the gleaming white temple, which personifies purity and reflects righteousness, is the gold-leafed statue of the Angel Moroni. I remembered being told that from that height of 105 feet, on a clear day

one can see all the way to Cumorah. I noted that in Moroni's hand was his familiar trumpet. He was gazing homeward—homeward to Cumorah. The beautiful Toronto Temple prepares all who enter to return homeward—homeward to heaven, homeward to family, homeward to God. (*Ensign,* Nov. 1990, 67)

Those who receive the marvelous and all-encompassing blessings of the temple feel inspired to introduce their family members to such blessings. Like Lehi of old, they want to guide their loved ones to the tree of life, that they might partake of the fruit thereof and have enduring joy (see 1 Ne. 8:12). Like Enos, those who have filled their lives with the purity and holiness that belong to the house of God wish with all their hearts to bring their colleagues into the circle of peace and glory within the temple. Such is the operation of the Spirit. In this regard, Elder David B. Haight had this wise counsel:

> Help your sons and daughters to understand that we marry in the temple. We live to be worthy to go there. Teach your children to take a firm stand regarding sexual purity. We have a great song: "Who's on the Lord's side? Who? Now is the time to show." Teach your children to be on the Lord's side of morality. The would-be destroyers of our youth who are pushing sex for pleasure only or cheap entertainment have not reckoned with the intense spirit of the Mormon woman who has a glimpse of the eternities.
>
> Our family affections and desires are prepared to endure through all eternity. The Latter-day Saint woman who has this lofty concept will influence her husband and children to realize this blessing. It is yours to be accomplished. (*Ensign,* Apr. 1976, 66)

The temple is a house of virtue, a house of purity, a house of cleanliness, a house of holiness. We go in holiness to the temple to perfect our spiritual vision, as the Savior declared: "Blessed are the pure in heart: for they shall see God" (Matt. 5:8). Though we live in an imperfect world as imperfect children of God, we as vessels of the Lord are striving to achieve the level of purity consonant with the principles of a Zion society: "Therefore, verily, thus saith the Lord, let Zion rejoice, for this is Zion—the pure in heart" (D&C 97:21). The temple instructs us in the divine doctrine of repentance and forgiveness and endows us with a blessing of strength to maintain virtue and holiness before the Lord. Between temple visits we remember to partake of the sacrament as a means for continually renewing our baptismal and temple covenants. We go clean to the temple, arrayed in our Sunday best as we present ourselves before the Lord. We dress ourselves in the white attire of the temple as we participate in the holy ordinances thereof. Within the temple, we enhance the spirit of joy and worthiness that accompanied us there, and we return to our homes and communities afterward to share that same spirit freely with others.

In this regard, President Gordon B. Hinckley has reminded us that "Those who come to these holy houses are arrayed in white as they participate therein. They come only on recommendation of their local ecclesiastical authorities, having been certified as to their worthiness. They are expected to come clean in thought, clean in body, and clean in dress to enter the temple of God. As they enter they are expected to leave the world behind them and concentrate on things divine" (*Ensign,* Aug. 1974, 37).

The journey to the temple proceeds apace upon the calm seas of purity. As seagoers on the voyage to the eternities, we are thankful that the Lord has given us sufficient wisdom and courage to reach our intended haven and present ourselves pure before the Lord. "May we be wise mariners as we go forth on such a voyage," counseled President Thomas S. Monson. "Let us be pure vessels before the Lord" (*Ensign,* May 2000, 46). It is our duty and privilege to worthily enter God's holy temples. He requires us to be clean in every way, to let "virtue garnish [our] thoughts unceasingly" (D&C 121:45), so that we might rid ourselves of spot and radiate the light of the gospel with brightness and hope. As President Faust has reminded us, "It is possible for us to be purged and purified and to have our sins washed away so that we may come before the Lord as clean, white, and spotless as the newly fallen snow" (*Ensign,* Aug. 2002, 2).

Time to Meditate and Ponder

1. What is the answer to the question of the Psalmist: "Who shall ascend into the hill of the Lord? or who shall stand in his holy place?" (Ps. 24:3)?

2. The Savior taught: "Blessed are the pure in heart: for they shall see God" (Matt. 5:8). How does this promise relate to the work of the temples?

3. The expression "Holiness to the Lord" is inscribed on every temple. How does the same expression apply to those who visit the temples?

4. What is meant by the word "vessels" in the commandment "Be ye clean, that bear the vessels of the Lord" (Isa. 52:11)?

5. Following his miraculous conversion, Paul, the erstwhile enemy of the Church, was designated by the Lord as "a chosen vessel unto me" (Acts 9:15). Similarly, Alma and the sons of Mosiah became pure and noble servants of God following their transformation from wickedness to righteousness. How do such stories give us the confidence and faith to ensure that our repentance is complete as we strive to achieve the level of virtue and holiness required to come into the temples of God?

6. How can we best help our loved ones follow the pathway of purity and virtue?

7. Concerning temple work, President Spencer W. Kimball explained: "But all these ordinances are futile unless with them there is a great righteousness" (*TSWK*, 537). How does this statement motivate us to prepare ourselves more fully as we go to the temples of God?

8. How does purity of mind and thought help us to understand more readily the doctrines of the gospel?

9. What are the blessings of a virtuous life?

10. What did the Lord mean when He said of the sanctity of His house, "Yea, and my presence shall be there, for I will come into it, and all the pure in heart that shall come into it shall see God" (D&C 97:16)?

CHAPTER 6
A HOUSE OF KNOWLEDGE

Guiding Principle: The temple experience, as administered through the sealing powers of the priesthood of God, is permeated by a spirit of "pure knowledge, which shall greatly enlarge the soul" (D&C 121:42). Such knowledge is a saving knowledge that renders clear and lucid the vision of our destiny as faithful and covenant-centered children of God, to return to His presence one day and partake of eternal glory.

> *In the temple we learn the things of eternity and make sacred covenants which, if fulfilled, will bring us back into the presence of the Lord. The knowledge we gain in this holy house helps us to see clearly our priorities in life and our place among the purposes of God.*
> —HOWARD W. HUNTER, *TEACHINGS OF HOWARD W. HUNTER*, 237.

The temple is a house of knowledge. Gospel knowledge as imparted in the temple has to do with eternal truths given by God to man as both an anchor and a beacon in the process of gaining immortality and eternal life. Unlike worldly knowledge, spiritual knowledge never changes but is the same yesterday, today, and forever. Spiritual knowledge is centered in the word of God as revealed through the scriptures, through the message of the Lord's chosen servants, and through the ongoing inspiration of the Holy Ghost. The temple is a haven for the Spirit and place of spiritual nurture where guidance is imparted in answer to humble prayer. Elder David E. Sorensen has emphasized, "The temple is a place of revelation, of inspiration, meditation, and peace—a place to restore ourselves, to clear our minds, to find answers to our prayers, and to enjoy the satisfaction of worship and service" (*Liahona*, Aug. 2002, 30).

When we gain a clear understanding of the doctrines, principles, concepts, and covenants pertaining to the gospel and the kingdom of God—particularly those concerning the temple—we possess knowledge of divine truth pertinent to our salvation. We are enlightened. We increase in our intelligence for we have acquired light and truth of an exalting kind. This pure knowledge comes by the power of the Holy Ghost. "And by the power of the Holy Ghost ye may know the truth of all things" (Moro. 10:5). We should avidly seek such knowledge in order to understand the nature of God and prepare ourselves to enter His presence as part of our postmortal inheritance of glory.

Let us remember that the acquisition of pure knowledge contributes to our taking upon ourselves the divine nature of Jesus Christ (see 2 Pet. 1:3–12; D&C 4). If we live according to these eternal truths, we will come to know God and Jesus Christ. This process of learning constitutes life eternal (see John 17:3), for "it is impossible for a man to be saved in ignorance" (D&C 131:6). We are commanded by the Lord to seek wisdom continually. The temple is the superlative venue for gaining knowledge of the eternities—a place where learning is a joy and study is a delight. As President Gordon B. Hinckley has taught, "There is . . . incumbent upon you, you who are members of The Church of Jesus Christ of Latter-day

Saints, the responsibility to observe the commandment to continue to study and to learn. Said the Lord: 'Seek ye out of the best books words of wisdom; seek learning, even by study and also by faith' (D&C 88:118)" (*TGBH*, 300).

Preparing by Prayer and Study

The pathway to the temple is the pathway of knowledge. Through study and prayer, we can prepare ourselves to receive the endowment of magnificent truth found only in the house of God. Our preparation can be shaped and honed in three ways: by cultivating a learning attitude, by going to the true and correct sources, and by organizing our learning blueprints.

Cultivate a learning attitude. Willingly accept God's commandment to seek learning: "Learn of me, and listen to my words; walk in the meekness of my Spirit, and you shall have peace in me" (D&C 19:23). We are to "live by every word that [proceeds] forth from the mouth of God" (D&C 84:44). We are to learn by faith (see James 1:5–6) and gratefully receive the greater truths that come from our Father in Heaven: "What we gain from the temple will depend to a large degree on what we take to the temple in the way of humility and reverence and a desire to learn. If we are teachable we will be taught by the Spirit, in the temple" (*Preparing to Enter the Holy Temple* [Church Booklet, 2002], 10).

Go to the true and correct sources. Pray to receive knowledge from the Lord, remembering that the Holy Ghost will reveal the truth of all things (see Moro. 10:5). Hearken to the words of the living prophets. Search the scriptures: "Thy word is a lamp unto my feet, and a light unto my path" (Ps. 119:105). Participate in the myriad opportunities for gospel instruction at church and at home.

Organize your learning blueprint. Set goals for seeking gospel knowledge diligently and with devotion. Be consistent in your study. Remember that we should never cease to learn, for "the glory of God is intelligence, or, in other words, light and truth" (D&C 93:36).

Using these three strategies, we can focus on enriching our understanding of gospel principles and temple work by systematically reading and pondering from dependable sources that include the following:

1. The scriptures. "Feast upon the words of Christ," Nephi taught, "for behold, the words of Christ will tell you all things what ye should do" (2 Ne. 32:3). Whenever we go to the font of truth and drink of the living waters of the gospel message, we are refreshed in our commitment to serve more faithfully, walk more steadfastly, and imbue our lives more fully with the "godly walk and conversation" (D&C 20:69) characteristic of the children of God. In 2005, President Gordon B. Hinckley appealed to the worldwide Church to focus on reading and rereading the Book of Mormon:

> I offer a challenge to members of the Church throughout the world and to our friends everywhere to read or reread the Book of Mormon. . . . Without reservation I promise you that if each of you will observe this simple program, regardless of how many times you previously may have read the Book of Mormon, there will come into your lives and into your homes an added measure of the Spirit of the Lord, a strengthened resolution to walk in obedience to His commandments, and a stronger testimony of the living reality of the Son of God. (*Ensign,* Aug. 2005, 3)

The blessings of responding to the prophet's challenge were enormous, as people from every region of the Church strengthened their testimonies and harvested a treasure of truth from this remarkable testament of Jesus Christ. All who are preparing to go to the temple can likewise be lifted in spirit and edified in understanding by making the Book of Mormon the subject of regular daily study. King Benjamin's timeless sermon given from the temple grounds at Zarahemla (see Mosiah 2–5) and the Savior's miraculous appearance and instruction, largely at the temple grounds in Bountiful (see 3 Ne. 11–28), are two of the unforgettable ways in which the Book of Mormon fulfills its mission of "convincing . . . the Jew and Gentile that Jesus is the Christ, the eternal God, manifesting himself unto all nations" (Book of Mormon title page).

In addition, the student of the temple can find enlightenment from specific passages of scripture in the standard works having to do with the purposes, powers, ordinances, and blessings of the temple. Here are but a few of the more familiar examples:

Power of godliness revealed through priesthood ordinances. D&C 84:19–22 ("Therefore, in the ordinances thereof, the power of godliness is manifest"—verse 20)

Endowment from on high. D&C 95:8–9 ("Build a house, in the which house I design to endow those whom I have chosen with power from on high"—verse 8)

The temple as a place of instruction. D&C 97:10–21 ("That they may be perfected in the understanding of their ministry, in theory, in principle, and in doctrine, in all things pertaining to the kingdom of God on the earth, the keys of which kingdom have been conferred upon you"—verse 14)

The temple as a place of holiness. D&C 109 ("Organize yourselves; prepare every needful thing, and establish a house, even a house of prayer, a house of fasting, a house of faith, a house of learning, a house of glory, a house of order, a house of God"—verse 8)

The appearance of the Savior in the temple. D&C 110 ("For behold, I have accepted this house, and my name shall be here; and I will manifest myself to my people in mercy in this house"—verse 7)

Washings, anointings, and other sacred ordinances in the temple. D&C 124:28–42 ("And verily I say unto you, let this house be built unto my name, that I may reveal mine ordinances therein unto my people"—verse 40)

Baptisms for the dead. D&C 128 ("For we without them cannot be made perfect; neither can they without us be made perfect"—verse 18)

Eternal marriage covenants of the temple. D&C 132:7–14 ("I am the Lord thy God; and I give unto you this commandment—that no man shall come unto the Father but by me or by my word, which is my law, saith the Lord"—verse 12)

Activity in the spirit world in support of temple work. D&C 138 ("[Prophets and leaders commissioned for] the building of the temples and the performance of ordinances therein for the redemption of the dead, were also in the spirit world"—verse 54)

Promulgation of the Ten Commandments from Mount Sinai (a natural temple). Exodus 20

Completion of the tabernacle (the portable temple of ancient Israel). Exodus 40

Dedication of the temple of Solomon. 2 Chronicles 6–7

Dedication of the temple of Zerubbabel. Ezra 6:15–16

Promised coming of Elijah with the keys of the sealing power. Malachi 4:5–6

Bestowing of keys on the Mount of Transfiguration. Matthew 17:1–13

The Topical Guide and Bible Dictionary can direct a student of the gospel to many other references concerning the themes and topics associated with temple work.

2. Pronouncements of latter-day prophets and leaders. There is a rich inventory of wisdom concerning temple work in the discourses and speeches of the latter-day prophets of God and other enlightened students of the gospel. Those preparing for the temple can refer to the *Ensign* and other official periodicals of the Church for guidance on this subject. Many of these articles are quoted in this book. In addition, the following books have become classics of literature concerning temple preparation:

James E. Talmage. *The House of the Lord.* Salt Lake City: Deseret Book, 1968 (and later editions).

Boyd K. Packer. *The Holy Temple.* Salt Lake City: Bookcraft, 1980.

3. Church materials and brochures. A number of helpful titles have been made available through Church Distribution, including the following:

Preparing to Enter the Holy Temple (item no. 36793)—adapted from *The Holy Temple* by Boyd K. Packer.

Temples of The Church of Jesus Christ of Latter-day Saints (item no. 35863).

A Member's Guide to Temple and Family History Work (item no. 34697).

The Temple as a Place of Revelation

By treasuring up in our hearts the words of truth as a means for preparing ourselves for the temple, we will find that our capacity to learn has been enhanced. As a result, our minds and hearts will be ready to receive additional—and higher—truth within the walls of the holy temple. Truth descends upon the softened heart "as the dews from heaven" (D&C 121:45).

The temple is a house of revelation, beginning with the ordained endowment of truth associated with the ordinances and covenants of the house of the Lord, but also including personal inspiration and revelation bestowed upon the honest in heart who go there seeking guidance from the Lord and answers to the challenges of life. John A. Widtsoe wrote:

> I believe that the busy person on the farm, in the shop, in the office, or in the household, who has his worries and troubles, can solve his problems better and more quickly in the house of the Lord than anywhere else. If he will . . . [do] the temple work for himself and for his dead, he will confer a mighty blessing upon those who have gone before, and . . . a blessing will come to him, for at the most unexpected moments, in or out of the temple will come to him, as a revelation, the solution of the problems that vex his life. That is the gift that comes to those who enter the temple properly. ("Temple Worship," *The Utah Genealogical and Historical Magazine,* Apr. 1921, 63–64)

The temple brings choice blessings of inspiration to those who are open to truths flowing from a benevolent and merciful God into the hearts of the receptive and teachable. What greater expression of thanks can there be than to act forthrightly and obediently in response to the whisperings of the Spirit. Elder David B. Haight has confirmed this principle: "The environment in the temple is intended to provide the worthy member of the Church with the power of enlightenment, of testimony, and of understanding. The temple endowment gives knowledge that, when acted upon, provides strength and conviction of truth" (*Ensign,* Nov. 1990, 59).

Truly the temple is a house of knowledge and glory where the prayerful and faithful obtain "great views of that which is to come" (Mosiah 5:3) and realign their lives to a state of harmony with the designs of heaven. In this thematic context, Elder Russell M. Nelson has taught:

> Scriptures describe the temple as "a house of prayer, a house of fasting, a house of faith, a house of learning, a house of glory, a house of order, a house of God."
>
> As a house of learning, the temple becomes "a school of instruction in the sweet and sacred things of God." Here we learn about "the odyssey of man's eternal journey from premortal existence through this life to the life beyond. (*Ensign,* Mar. 2002, 17)

Let us all pray with full conviction that we might prepare ourselves for a spiritual banquet every time we attend the temple. Let us soften our hearts to receive added wisdom from on high when we enter the sacred precincts of the house of the Lord—especially wisdom and knowledge concerning our Heavenly Father and His Son. Truman Madsen has observed:

> The temple is a house of learning. And it is intended that therein we not simply learn *of* or *about* Christ, but that we come to *know Him.* It has always impressed me that in the Joseph Smith Translation the classic passage about the hereafter when many will say, "Lord, Lord, did we not do this and that?" is rendered more fittingly. The King James Version says that Christ will respond, "I never knew you." The Joseph Smith Translation renders it, "You never knew me." (Matt. 7:23; JST Matt. 7:33.) (Truman G. Madsen, *The Radiant Life* [Salt Lake City: Bookcraft, 1994], 125; emphasis in original)

From the temple we gain knowledge of how to return to the presence of God. We go there with a prayer in our hearts to understand the things of eternity. We go there with the promise that the temple is a place of revelation—where pure knowledge can flow from God to our souls. We go there with the hope that we can receive guidance for solving problems and becoming more like our Savior. President Ezra Taft Benson observed: "In the peace of these lovely temples, sometimes we find solutions to the serious problems of life. Under the influence of the Spirit, sometimes pure knowledge flows to us there. Temples are places of personal revelation. When I have been weighed down by a problem or a difficulty, I have gone to the house of the Lord with a prayer in my heart for answers" (*Tambulilit,* June 1992, 2).

We go to the temple to be prompted by the whisperings of the Spirit bestowed upon the honest in heart. We go to the temple with the hope that the Lord will bless us there with an inner compass of inspiration to guide us through the complex and often perplexing landscape of our mortal experience. We go to the temple tuned to the impressions and promptings that surely distill upon the souls of the easily entreated "as the dews from heaven" (D&C 121:45). President Gordon B. Hinckley has enlarged upon this theme as follows:

> The temple is also a place of personal inspiration and revelation. Legion are those who in times of stress, when difficult decisions must be made and perplexing problems must be handled, have come to the temple in a spirit of fasting and prayer to seek divine direction. Many have testified that while voices of revelation were not heard, impressions concerning a course to follow were experienced at that time or later which became answers to their prayers. (*Ensign,* Mar. 1993, 6)

Finally, listen to the transporting and sublime words of the Savior Himself concerning the temple as a sanctuary of divine knowledge:

> Verily I say unto you, that it is my will that a house should be built unto me in the land of Zion, like unto the pattern which I have given you. Yea, let it be built speedily, by the tithing of my people. Behold, this is the tithing and the sacrifice which I, the Lord, require at their hands, that there may be a house built unto me for the salvation of

Zion—For a place of thanksgiving for all saints, and for a place of instruction for all those who are called to the work of the ministry in all their several callings and offices; That they may be perfected in the understanding of their ministry, in theory, in principle, and in doctrine, in all things pertaining to the kingdom of God on the earth, the keys of which kingdom have been conferred upon you. And inasmuch as my people build a house unto me in the name of the Lord, and do not suffer any unclean thing to come into it, that it be not defiled, my glory shall rest upon it; Yea, and my presence shall be there, for I will come into it, and all the pure in heart that shall come into it shall see God. (D&C 97:10–16)

Time to Meditate and Ponder

1. How does the temple help us to set our learning priorities for life?

2. How does knowledge gained through the gospel of Jesus Christ differ from knowledge gained through worldly sources?

3. The Savior said: "Learn of me, and listen to my words; walk in the meekness of my Spirit, and you shall have peace in me" (D&C 19:23). In what ways is this statement of promise a fitting guide for our preparation for the temple?

4. How will daily study of the Book of Mormon enhance our temple experience?

5. What are some of your favorite scriptural passages relating to the temple?

6. In what ways is the temple a house of revelation?

7. The Savior taught that the keys of temple work are conveyed to the Saints "that they may be perfected in the understanding of their ministry, in theory, in principle, and in doctrine, in all things

pertaining to the kingdom of God on the earth" (D&C 97:14). How does the promise of the Savior that we can be "perfected" in our knowledge of these things give us courage and confidence to prepare for the temple?

CHAPTER 7
A HOUSE OF TEMPERANCE

Guiding Principle: In the temple, the temperate are confirmed in their temperance, the modest are ennobled in their modesty, and the self-disciplined are edified in their conviction that they can, indeed, follow in the footsteps of the Master.

> *We endorse any movement looking to temperance, looking to virtue, tending to purity of life and to faith in God and obedience to his laws; and we are against evil of every description; and we are, in our faith and prayers, against evil-doers—not that we would pray for evil to come upon evil-doers, but that evil-doers might see the folly of their ways and the wickedness of their acts and repent of them and turn away from them.*
> —JOSEPH F. SMITH, *GOSPEL DOCTRINE,* 239–40.

The temple is a house of temperance. Temperance connotes self-control and self-discipline. It suggests modesty and kindness, reverence and humility, restraint and charity, and actions that accord with the priesthood injunction to extend our influence only "by persuasion, by long-suffering, by gentleness and meekness, and by love unfeigned" (D&C 121:41). In this regard, President Ezra Taft Benson taught:

> A priesthood holder is *temperate*. This means he is restrained in his emotions and verbal expressions. He does things in moderation and is not given to overindulgence. In a word, he has self-control. He is the master of his emotions, not the other way around. . . .
>
> If a man does not control his temper, it is a sad admission that he is not in control of his thoughts. He then becomes a victim of his own passions and emotions, which lead him to actions that are totally unfit for civilized behavior, let alone behavior for a priesthood holder. (*Ensign*, Nov. 1986, 45; emphasis in original)

Preparation to enter the house of the Lord includes improving one's ability to be temperate, for the temple is a place of reverence and modesty. Learning to control one's emotions and actions can be challenging, but the Holy Spirit will impart strength to do so—when we ask with a sincere desire for guidance and help. The test of life is to make the body subject to the spirit by following the principles of the gospel rather than being governed by appetite and emotion. Self-control is a vital part of self-mastery. We discipline ourselves to emulate the Savior and teach the same pattern of discipline and temperance to our children. Speaking of this principle, President James E. Faust made clear our responsibility as disciples of the Savior: "Self-discipline and self-control are consistent and permanent characteristics of the followers of Jesus" (James E. Faust, *To Reach Even unto You* [Salt Lake City: Deseret Book, 1980], 114).

How can we exercise more temperance and patience in our daily living as we prepare for the temple? Here are a few ideas.

Establish the right foundation. Build a strong foundation based on gospel principles. This will encourage positive action on our part, including the righteous exercise of moral agency and a clear understanding of liberating gospel doctrines, including the Atonement, love of God, and faith in Jesus Christ.

Understand the rewards and consequences. Cultivate temperance in order to gain self-respect and merit the respect and admiration of loved ones. Keep your eye on the goal. Never waver in your focus and determination. Recognize the harmful consequences deriving from a lack of self-control and discipline. Enjoy the blessings of patience and self-mastery. Reward your family with kindness and temperance.

Empower a team around you. Enlist the support of others. Tell them of your commitment to improve as you prepare to go to the temple. When you feel yourself slipping, enlist your team. Involve your family. Make it a goal to learn self-control as a family.

Make it a way of life. Give it time. Think of it as a process. Perfect self-control is rare at first. It takes time to develop the patterns and habits that buttress correct behavior. Do small things to build up your confidence. Learn that you can control yourself. You can train yourself to be obedient—thus increasing your self-control.

Pray for strength. Always pray for strength to uphold high standards and be true to your convictions. Remember what is taught in the Book of Mormon: "In the strength of the Lord thou canst do all things" (Alma 20:4).

THE BLESSINGS OF TEMPERANCE

The Apostle Paul taught: "And every man that striveth for the mastery is temperate in all things" (1 Cor. 9:25). The temple journey represents a sincere striving for mastery—mastery of the doctrines and principles of salvation and exaltation. Temperance is a quality reflecting submission to the will of the Father. When we submit to the will of the Father, then the blessings of salvation and exaltation are poured out without measure. Alma exhorted us to be "temperate in all things" (Alma 7:23; see also Alma 38:10) and continued: "And see that ye have faith, hope, and charity, and then ye will always abound in good works" (Alma 7:24).

Temperance of soul is consistent with the quiet grandeur and peace of the temple, for the temple is a place dedicated to the glory of the Lord and organized to honor and emulate His divine holiness in the spirit of reverence and composed service. President Gordon B. Hinckley reminded us of this blessing of peace:

> The temple must ever be a place of peace, a refuge from the turmoil of the world. All of us live in something of a jungle, if I may use that expression. We long for peace and quiet; we hunger for an opportunity to meditate and reflect on things spiritual and eternal in their nature. There must be no atmosphere of frenzy or hurry in the house of the Lord. It is to be a house of order. There must be an atmosphere that constantly proclaims, "Holiness to the Lord."
>
> We are dealing with the things of eternity. We need not rush. Of course there are ordinances to be performed. But this can be done in a manner that speaks of peace and the quiet assurance which dwells in the heart when there is an absence of pressure. (*TGBH,* 425)

The temple is a monument to reverence. It is an institution of reverence for things divine and a gathering place for those who are willing to follow Alma's injunction to be humble, submissive, gentle, patient, and temperate (see Alma 7:23). Reverence is an attitude that attends those who aspire to be in the presence of God. Elder L. Lionel Kendrick of the Seventy describes the worthy objective of cultivating temperance and reverence in preparation for visiting the temple:

> All who attend the temple should remember the counsel of the Lord when He said, "Reverence my sanctuary" (Lev. 19:30). Reverence is an expression of deep respect, honor, and adoration for the Lord. It is having reverence for His name, for His words, for His ordinances and covenants, for His servants, for His chapels, and for His temples.

> It is an outward indication of an inner feeling that we have for Him. We should always remember that it is by His invitation that we come to His holy house, the temple of the Lord. We should respond to His invitation by being worthy, by being prepared, and by having the temple as a priority in our lives. While in the temple we should act as if we are in His holy presence. . . .
>
> The temple is a place of holiness. It is the most sacred and holy place on earth and should be treated with the greatest degree of reverence and respect. Reverence in the temple is an expression to the Lord that we consider it to be sacred and that we recognize it to be, indeed, His holy house. (*Ensign,* May 2001, 78)

Preparation for the temple is an opportunity to remind ourselves of the counsel given in the scriptures to "cease from all your light speeches, from all laughter, from all your lustful desires, from all your pride and light-mindedness" (D&C 88:121) and to "lay aside the things of this world, and seek for the things of a better" (D&C 25:10). Temperance is the gateway to light and truth: "That which is of God is light; and he that receiveth light, and continueth in God, receiveth more light; and that light groweth brighter and brighter until the perfect day" (D&C 50:24). By fostering a lifestyle of temperance, modesty, humility, self-control, moderation, and submissiveness to the will of God, we come a long way toward taking upon ourselves the divine nature of Christ as a precondition for entering the house of the Lord.

THE HOLY GARMENT:
SYMBOL OF TEMPERANCE AND COMMITMENT

The holy garment ordained by God as an emblem of covenant vows made in the temple is a shield and protection for the faithful and a constant reminder of sacred obligations for righteous living. The garment is an icon of temperance and humility, a tangible reminder of covenant obligations we are to honor in perpetuity. Elder Russell M. Nelson has declared:

> Wearing the temple garment has deep symbolic significance. It represents a continuing commitment. Just as the Savior exemplified the need to endure to the end, we wear the garment faithfully as part of the enduring armor of God. Thus we demonstrate our faith in Him and in His eternal covenants with us. (*Ensign,* May 2001, 32)

The Lord assured that even though "the mountains shall depart, and the hills be removed; . . . my kindness shall not depart from thee, neither shall the covenant of my people be removed" (JST, Inspired Version, Isa. 54:10). Surely we would not ever want knowingly to discard from us an emblem of His everlasting covenant.

From time immemorial the Lord has ordained the use of special garments in remembrance of sacred covenants and duties. In the beginning, the Lord clothed Adam and Eve in "coats of skins" (Gen. 3:21) as He provided for them instructions concerning the Atonement and the principles of salvation. Those who officiated in the sacred rites of the tabernacle in ancient Israel were adorned with special vestments that reflected the honor and holiness of their office (see Ex. 28:1–3). The same practice was maintained in the temple of Solomon. Isaiah raised his voice in rejoicing, saying, "He hath clothed me with the garments of salvation, he hath covered me with the robe of righteousness" (Isa. 61:10; for additional commentary on the significance and history of the temple garment, see *Ensign,* Aug. 1997, 19).

In many respects, the temple garment belongs to the "armor of God" spoken of in the scriptures (see Eph. 6:13–17; D&C 27:15–18). To wear the garment of the holy priesthood is to carry the mantle of obedience to covenant promises and to clothe ourselves in temperance as to deportment and behavior. We fulfill the role of disciples of Christ. We remember our covenants. We reflect the attitudes and comportment of those who have "spiritually been born of God" and who have "received his image" in their countenances and "experienced this mighty change in [their] hearts" (Alma 5:14). Boyd K. Packer tells us that "the garment represents sacred covenants. It fosters modesty and becomes a shield and protection to the wearer" (*The Holy Temple,* 75).

In a statement to the Church, the First Presidency declared:

> Church members who have been clothed with the garment in the temple have made a covenant to wear it throughout their lives. This has been interpreted to mean that it is worn as underclothing both day and night. . . .
>
> The fundamental principle ought to be to wear the garment and not to find occasions to remove it. . . . When the garment must be removed, . . . it should be restored as soon as possible.
>
> The principles of modesty and keeping the body appropriately covered are implicit in the covenant and should govern the nature of all clothing worn. Endowed members of the Church wear the garment as a reminder of the sacred covenants they have made with the Lord and also as a protection against temptation and evil. How it is worn is an outward expression of an inward commitment to follow the Savior. (First Presidency Letter, 10 Oct. 1988)

Just as the scriptures "have enlarged the memory of this people, yea, and convinced many of the error of their ways, and brought them to the knowledge of their God unto the salvation of their souls" (Alma 37:8), the holy garment of the temple, by its pervasive presence in our lives, also serves to enlarge our memory of sacred covenants and remind us of our duty to follow the pathway of righteousness with exactness and true devotion and to keep our lives unspotted before the Lord. Elder Carlos E. Asay expressed the following memorable sentiments concerning the temple garment:

> I like to think of the garment as the Lord's way of letting us take part of the temple with us when we leave. It is true that we carry from the Lord's house inspired teachings and sacred covenants written in our minds and hearts. However, the one tangible remembrance we carry with us back into the world is the garment. And though we cannot always be in the temple, a part of it can always be with us to bless our lives.

> Don't forget that the word *garment* is used symbolically in the scriptures and gives expanded meaning to other words such as *white, clean, pure, righteous, modesty, covering, ceremonial, holy, priesthood, beautiful, perfection, salvation, undefiled, worthy, white raiment, shield, protection, spotless, blameless, armor, covenants, promises, blessings, respect, eternal life,* and so forth. All of these words occupy special places in the vocabularies of people sincerely essaying to become Saints. (*Ensign,* Aug. 1997, 19; emphasis in original)

In the book of Revelation, John the Apostle recorded, "He that overcometh, the same shall be clothed in white raiment; and I will not blot out his name out of the book of life, but I will confess his name before my Father, and before his angels" (Rev. 3:5). Going to the temple and participating in the sanctifying rites made available in that quiet and holy place is a central part of overcoming all that would hold us back from achieving our potential as sons and daughters of God. Temperance and modesty should attend those who attend the temple. The Advocate has promised that He will retain our names in the book of life and confess us acceptingly before the Father in the Day of Judgment—provided our garments are clean and our patterns of life are holy and saintly. May we prepare ourselves in temperance and faith for the sacred privilege of visiting the house of the Lord again and again as part of our journey to return to the presence of God.

Time to Meditate and Ponder

1. An important part of taking upon ourselves the divine nature of Christ is to cultivate temperance (see 2 Pet. 1:6; D&C 4:6). What qualities belong to the spirit of temperance?

2. How can we systematically foster a pattern of temperance in thought, word, and deed?

3. In what ways are temperance and reverence similar?

4. How does the holy garment serve as a symbol of our ongoing commitment to honor temple covenants with temperance and faithfulness?

5. In what ways may the temple garment be associated with the "armor of God" spoken of in the scriptures (see Eph. 6:13–17; D&C 27:15–18)?

6. In a statement to the Church, the First Presidency declared: "Church members who have been clothed with the garment in the temple have made a covenant to wear it throughout their lives" (First Presidency Letter, 10 Oct. 1988). What steps can be taken by those who are preparing for the temple to adjust their wardrobe, as needed, to ensure modesty and the appropriate covering of the garment?

CHAPTER 8
A HOUSE OF PATIENCE

Guiding Principle: The Savior taught: "In your patience possess ye your souls" (Luke 21:19). Surely the patient are reinforced in their patience as they wait upon the Lord in His holy house, earnest in their conviction to endure to the end.

> *The Lord has said: "And seek the face of the Lord always, that in patience ye may possess your souls, and ye shall have eternal life." (D&C 101:38. Emphasis added. See also Luke 21:19.) Could it be that only when our self-control has become total do we come into true possession of our own souls?*
> —NEAL A. MAXWELL, *NOTWITHSTANDING MY WEAKNESS* [SALT LAKE CITY: DESERET BOOK, 1981], 60.

The virtue of patience is of primary importance in preparing for the temple and becoming more like our Savior Jesus Christ. Patience is part of His divine nature. To emulate His example of patience is to make great progress in achieving spiritual success and establishing enduring positive relationships with family members, Church colleagues, and others. When we are patient, we can bless the lives of others. Those who are patient radiate a power of peace and tranquility that comes from an even temper, an understanding and tolerance of the situation at hand, and the demonstration of calmness under pressure. Everyone appreciates the patient person. Patience does not mean that we are permissive, easily manipulated, or weak. Rather, patience truly signifies a level of maturity that ennobles our character. Patience, like perseverance, is a governing virtue of success—success in all facets of life, especially in regard to our activities associated with the temples of the Lord.

For those who are preparing to enter the temple—or who make it part of their lives to return often to the temple—there is no more charming and edifying statement on patience (and the associated virtue of temperance) than this one from Alma: "And now I would that ye should be humble, and be submissive and gentle; easy to be entreated; full of patience and long-suffering; being temperate in all things; being diligent in keeping the commandments of God at all times; asking for whatsoever things ye stand in need, both spiritual and temporal; always returning thanks unto God for whatsoever things ye do receive" (Alma 7:23).

When we are patient, we practice self-mastery in disciplining our passions and emotions. We have understanding for the shortcomings of others as they strive to improve their lives. We await the blessings of the Lord, knowing that He will remember us in His "own due time," as the scriptures promise (1 Ne. 14:26; see also 2 Ne. 27:10; Morm. 5:12; Ether 3:27; D&C 117:16). President Ezra Taft Benson has counseled us as follows:

> A priesthood holder is to be *patient*. Patience is another form of self-control. It is the ability to postpone gratification and to bridle one's passions. In his relationships with loved

ones, a patient man does not engage in impetuous behavior that he will later regret. Patience is composure under stress. A patient man is understanding of others' faults.

A patient man also waits on the Lord. We sometimes read or hear of people who seek a blessing from the Lord, then grow impatient when it does not come swiftly. Part of the divine nature is to trust in the Lord enough to "be still and know that [he is] God" (D&C 101:16). (*Ensign,* Nov. 1986, 45; emphasis in original)

Here are several ideas to assist us in cultivating the divine attribute of patience as we foster a temple-ready pattern of living:

Plan for patience. Make it a goal to be patient. Look ahead—anticipate situations that will test your patience, and then change the environment or conditions to prevent any outburst or confrontation. Control your time—make time your ally by preparing well in advance so as not to allow a few minutes here or there to be so critical in your life.

Always observe from a higher perspective. Discern potential—see people not for what they are at this moment but for what they can become. Recognize that all are learning. Learn from adversity. Envision your legacy and how you wish to be remembered, then leave behind the seeds of harmony, peace, balance, and unity for the coming generations.

Use peacemaker strategies of leadership. Nurture family members—especially young people—in love. Work in teams by enlisting the support and cooperation of others. Commiserate with people. Be tolerant: the law of the harvest calls for us to practice patience as we nurture our crops and tend our herds.

Make time the common ally. Use the time-tested formula: "Let's give it a few more minutes (hours, days)." Patiently guide those you counsel through the exercise of seeing the ultimate consequence of their behavior.

Understand that patience is necessary to become more Christlike. Pray for patience. Make hope your governing principle—hope that is stronger than the forces of discouragement and anger.

Remember that we can become patient as we practice patience. Time is on our side.

Line upon Line

The temple is a house of patience. It represents and embodies the grand learning plan that God has ordained for our progress during mortality and beyond. He does not expect us to master the principles of salvation and exaltation all at once. He is patient. He is long-suffering. He is ever loving and merciful. He allows us to learn our duty one step at a time. Consider the wisdom in Nephi's words:

> For behold, thus saith the Lord God: I will give unto the children of men line upon line, precept upon precept, here a little and there a little; and blessed are those who hearken unto my precepts, and lend an ear unto my counsel, for they shall learn wisdom; for unto him that receiveth I will give more; and from them that shall say, We have enough, from them shall be taken away even that which they have. (2 Ne. 28:30; see also Isa. 28:13; Alma 12:9–11; D&C 98:11–13; 128:21)

Our spiritual progress in the temple conforms to the principle of "line upon line, precept upon precept." We do not fathom all at once the wealth of information, truth, symbolism, and wisdom that await us in the house of the Lord. The temple is less an event than a process—a never-ending process of becoming more like the Savior and learning how to rise in the majesty of our divine heritage and potential to achieve the blessings that have been promised to the faithful and the obedient. While in the temple, we should take note of important happenings and concepts concerning which we would appreciate greater understanding and then ponder and pray about such matters. On occasion, it is considered appropriate for us to consult quietly with associates in suitable places within the temple to gain greater understanding and wisdom. We can seek enlightenment through study, faith, and the blessings of the Holy Ghost.

The temple imparts exalting truths and equips us with the precious blessings and endowments that will enable us, if obedient and faithful, to pass by the angelic sentinels of God's domain and—through our patience and endurance—enter into His presence and rest, "which rest is the fulness of his glory" (D&C 84:24). J. Richard Clarke, for many years a counselor in the Presiding Bishopric and subsequently a member of the Presidency of the Seventy, has described the temple process of sanctification and enlightenment as follows:

> The Lord's temple is the symbol of all that is holy. It is the bridge between mortality and the celestial kingdom. We go there to receive the highest blessings of the Holy Priesthood to prepare us for the glory of the Father—indeed His fullness. It is in the ordinances of the Melchizedek Priesthood that the power of Godliness is manifested. In the temple we are invited to "grow up in the Lord" and receive a "fullness of the Holy Ghost." While the temple is a house of prayer, fasting, and glory, it is also a house of learning. But we must learn how to learn in the temple. Our tutor is the Holy Ghost. The sacred truths of the endowment can be learned only in the temple—line upon line, principle by principle. It is a lifetime pursuit. You can't take a college course or major in the endowment and other ordinances of the temple. They are carefully reserved for those who "hunger and thirst after righteousness" and they who do are "filled." ("Celestial Pursuit," Brigham Young University—Idaho Devotional, Sept. 23, 2003)

Every time we attend the temple, we learn more. We perceive things from a different perspective. We sense the whisperings of the Spirit to guide us to a fuller understanding of what is transpiring. It may seem like an overwhelming outpouring of new wisdom and insight—but it takes time to fathom more fully the message of the temple. It is the peace of the house of the Lord that gives us confidence to continue our learning—one precept at a time, here a little and there a little. Blessings from honoring temple covenants flow to us consistently—over the years of our progress in the schoolhouse of mortality. Let us be patient and receive all things in the "due time of the Lord" (1 Ne. 14:26; see also 2 Ne. 27:10).

Time to Meditate and Ponder

1. The Savior is patient. He is long-suffering. He is ever loving and merciful. How can we learn to become more like Him in this respect?

2. The temple experience is remarkable in its depth of meaning and all-encompassing truth. It takes patience to come to a fuller understanding of temple blessings and ordinances. In this regard, why is it essential to return to the temple as often as possible?

3. How does the concept of "line upon line, precept upon precept" operate in our lives? What lessons have required considerable time and experience to master?

4. The Lord has promised, "Unto him that receiveth I will give more" (2 Ne. 28:30). How does this promise help us in our preparations for temple activity?

CHAPTER 9
A HOUSE OF BROTHERLY KINDNESS

Guiding Principle: In the mirror of our own brotherly kindness we see the reflection of the mercy and loving-kindness of God, who gave us temples to lift our vision to heaven.

> *Wise men ought to have understanding enough to conquer men with kindness.*
>
> *"A soft answer turneth away wrath," says the wise man; and it will be greatly to the credit of the Latter-day Saints to show the love of God, by now kindly treating those who may have, in an unconscious moment, done wrong; for truly said Jesus, Pray for thine enemies.*
>
> *Humanity towards all, reason and refinement to enforce virtue, and good for evil are so eminently designed to cure more disorders of society than an appeal to arms, or even argument untempered with friendship, and the one thing needful that no vision for the future, guideboard for the distant, or expositor for the present, need trouble any one with what he ought to do.*
>
> —JOSEPH SMITH, *HISTORY OF THE CHURCH*, 6:219–20.

The temple is a house of brotherly and sisterly kindness, for kindness is an element of the divine nature. Heavenly Father is kind and merciful toward His children. The Savior is kind, for He exemplifies the supreme manifestation of brotherly compassion and service. Those who attend the temple strive to be forgiving, just as the Lord is forgiving of those who come unto Him with "a broken heart and a contrite spirit" (3 Ne. 12:19). They strive to have kind feelings toward everyone in the attitude of gratitude and reverence. The temple teaches us to be kinder and more forgiving, according to the gospel pattern. Kindness and peace of heart go hand in hand.

Who is admitted into the house of the Lord? Those who are gentle, thoughtful, sympathetic, cordial, pleasant, benevolent, and kind—for they have in their hearts the inner peace that harmonizes with the spirit of the temple. Kindness requires a character based on gospel principles. It becomes an outward expression of our love of God, a manifestation of a pure heart and genuine concern for others. Paul exhorted us: "And be ye kind one to another, tenderhearted, forgiving one another, even as God for Christ's sake hath forgiven you" (Eph. 4:32). The temple is a school of kindness, where we learn to associate with our brothers and sisters in harmony, being willing to forgive as the Savior forgives, being motivated by charity toward all in the manner of the Savior's redeeming love. Against the discord and hatred of the world, the temple rises as a monument to universal kindness. President Gordon B. Hinckley has taught: "Let us as Latter-day Saints cultivate a spirit of brotherhood in all of our associations. Let us be more charitable in our judgments, more sympathetic and understanding of those who err, more willing to forgive those who trespass against us. Let us not add to the measure of hatred that periodically sweeps across the world. Let us reach out in kindness to all men, even toward those who speak evil of us and who would, if they could, harm us" (*TGBH,* 661).

How can we be kinder in our daily living and thus take upon ourselves the merciful nature of the Savior and prepare to enter His house? We must understand the following principles:

Kindness operates on the basis of charitable principles. Kindness sees value and worth in all living things: people, animals, and the living environment of our world. Kindness is not preemptive but creates choices and options for people, honoring the principle that everyone is free to make informed and wise choices in life. Kindness is the mirror of the infinite, being the earthly embodiment of the eternal charity we see in the Creator. Thus, kindness operates on the principle that we must honor the highest potential within everyone to do good.

Kindness is a mirror that reflects the best human qualities. Practice tolerance, evenhandedness, authenticity, quietness, love, and gratitude—all of which reflect the essence of the temples of God.

Kindness has the power to transform. Kindness attracts kindness, for even the most hard-hearted person is disarmed in the presence of a kind soul. Kindness is the warm breeze that dispels the frost of anger, resentment, greed, and envy. Kindness recognizes graciously that everyone has weaknesses and imperfections but extends the hand of love and fellowship nevertheless. Such behavior causes sarcasm, mockery, scorn, and derision to flee in shame. Moreover, kindness quietly transforms the landscape of home, workplace, and community by lifting, strengthening, giving hope, and teaching the principles of self-improvement.

Kindness can be cultivated. Take the initiative. Look for ways to be thoughtful and gracious. Be genuine in your expressions. Make your demeanor reflect kindness, avoiding any display of boastfulness or self-aggrandizement. Do the simple things: remember that simple and small acts of kindness are often the most precious. Smile, diffuse difficult situations with a cordial and pleasant attitude, and perform random acts of kindness throughout the day.

Lessons on Kindness from Modern-Day Prophets

President Brigham Young, the incisive and bold pioneer leader, was also kind and forgiving. He taught the people as follows: "Be kind to all as our Father in Heaven is kind. He sends his rain upon the just and the unjust; and gives the sun to shine upon the evil and the good. So let our goodness extend to all the works of his hands, where we can; but do not yield to the spirit and influence of evil. Do not encourage wickedness in our midst. . . . Do I say, Love your enemies? Yes, upon certain principles. But you are not required to love their wickedness; you are only required to love them so far as concerns a desire and effort to turn them from their evil ways, that they may be saved through obedience to the Gospel" (*Discourses,* 272).

Should we not prepare for our temple visits by searching our hearts and exercising to a greater degree the kindness and forgiveness that the Spirit induces us to practice? We are not expected to love the unrighteous behavior that others may manifest in their lives—especially when it seems directed toward ourselves and our loved ones—but we do love the person just the same and strive to forgive them and serve as an example of kindness and upright behavior. Said the Savior, "A new commandment I give unto you, That ye love one another; as I have loved you, that ye also love one another" (John 13:34).

President Joseph F. Smith taught the following concerning kindness:

> Let it be the aim of the Saints to cultivate the spirit of generosity and good-will, such as was exemplified in the life of Christ, and proclaimed when the angels heralded abroad the message: "Peace on earth, to men good will," and which has been reiterated in the modern restoration of the gospel. Watch constantly for that which is worthy and noble in your fellowman. It makes a person better to see and speak of good in his neighbor; while there is unbounded delight in observing the effect that a few words of appreciation and encouragement have upon men, women, and children with whom we associate. Let those try it who really wish to get the genuine sweets out of life. (*Gospel Doctrine,* 112)

In this same spirit, President Joseph F. Smith also taught:

> If people were always as ready to administer kindness as they are indifferent to the pain of others—if they were as patient to heal as they are quick to wound—many an unkind word would never be spoken, many a slight would be avoided. The art of healing is really one of the highest

qualities and attributes of man; it is a characteristic of a great and noble soul; the sure indication of generous impulse. . . .

The cultivation of kindly thoughts and sentiments towards others is always helpful in the art of healing. . . . Constant consideration for the welfare and happiness of others, is every day imposed upon us by the divine injunction, "Thou shalt love thy neighbor as thyself." . . . The test, then, of our soul's greatness is rather to be sought in our ability to comfort and console, our ability to help others, rather than in our ability to help ourselves and crowd others down in the struggle of life. If the reader will stop a moment to reflect upon the healing qualities of Christ's life, he will understand that Christ was a Master in the art of healing, not alone of the wounds he made, but of self-inflicted wounds, and the wounds that others made. What a comfort his life is to those in sorrow! How instinctively our thoughts turn to him! How prone we are to go to him for consolation. He is truly the great Healer of the afflictions of others. (*Gospel Doctrine*, 264–65)

Should we not prepare for our temple visits by focusing on seeing the good in others, by recognizing and honoring their better qualities, and by projecting a spirit of encouragement and benevolence? Would that not help us, as President Smith promises, to "get the genuine sweets out of life" and to emulate the healing qualities of the Savior? The temple brings into our lives a continual reminder that all people are in the mind of the Lord, that He extends His arms of mercy and love toward all of His children—both living and deceased—and wants for them the choicest blessings that He can grant them in accordance with their desire to come to Him and keep His commandments. Should we not emulate His matchless example in our own relationships with family members and with all our fellow beings, in whatever circumstances they might be? We are all children of God and heirs to the promises of exaltation and eternal life confirmed in the temple. We are all beneficiaries of the gospel of love and kindness—to the extent we show love and kindness to others.

President George Albert Smith reflected on this theme as follows:

> *The gospel is a gospel of love and kindness.* I pray that the love of the gospel of our Lord will burn in our souls and enrich our lives, that it will cause husbands to be kinder to wives, and wives to be kinder to husbands, parents to children, and children to parents because of the gospel of Jesus Christ, which is a gospel of love and kindness. It will cause us, if we are living as we should, to love our neighbors as ourselves, and go out of our way, if possible, to help them understand better the purpose of life. These are some of our privileges.
>
> *We are all part of Heavenly Father's family.* As I think of my regard and my affection for my Father's family, the human family, I remember something my earthly father said, and I think probably I inherited that in part from him. He said, "I have never seen a child of God so deep in the gutter that I have not had the impulse to stoop down and lift him up and put him on his feet and start him again." I would like to say I have never seen one of my Father's children in my life that I have not realized he was my brother and that God loves every one of his children, but he does not love our wickedness and our infidelity. (*TGAS,* 136; emphasis in original)

In our preparations for the temple, should we not seek to ensure that our relationships with our family members and neighbors reflect the spirit of enduring kindness? Should we not regard going to the temple as the opportunity to enjoy a grand "family reunion" with our brothers and sisters in the gospel? We will, for the most part, be surrounded within the temple by those whom we may not know personally, but we can be assured that the spirit of brotherhood and sisterhood will abound within the family of God: "Now therefore ye are no more strangers and foreigners, but fellowcitizens with the saints, and of the household of God" (Eph. 2:19). Truly, participants within the temple constitute "the household of God," for this is His house and the place of His throne on earth.

One trip to the temple to show our devotion is a small act of kindness toward the Lord and His children. Each time we attend, we add to that measure of kindness. The fabric of our life is made up of tiny threads of kindness, one after the other blending to form the design of our character and the pattern of our existence. Each act for good dispenses a single beam of kindness into the world; our life as a whole is the aggregate of these sunny beams, reflecting in their totality the radiation of the gospel of Jesus Christ as it illuminates our life and extends to all whom we encounter along our mortal pathway. President David O. McKay, often recognized as the paragon of the kind and gracious leader, observed the following concerning what he called "little acts of kindness":

> There is no one great thing which we can do to obtain eternal life, and it seems to me that the great lesson to be learned in the world today is to apply in the little acts and duties of life the glorious principles of the gospel. Let us not think that because some of the things named this afternoon may seem small and trivial that they are unimportant. Life, after all, is made up of little things. Our life, our being, physically, is made up here of little heartbeats. Let that little heart stop beating, and life in this world ceases. The great sun is a mighty force in the universe, but we receive the blessings of its rays because they come to us as little beams, which, taken in the aggregate, fill the whole world with sunlight. The dark night is made pleasant by the glimmer of what seem to be little stars; and so the true Christian life is made up of little Christlike acts performed this hour, this minute, in the home, in the quorum, in the organization, in the town, wherever our life and acts may be cast. (*Gospel Ideals,* 151–52)

Should we not prepare for our temple visits by cultivating and displaying little acts of kindness day by day? Often our preparation can be centered in the little things of life, the simple expressions of love and kindness that are befitting an authentic disciple of Jesus

Christ. To be kind is to take on the divine nature, as Peter taught (see 2 Pet. 1:7).

An Illustration of Kindness

The kindness that prevails in the temple is an "infectious" quality that touches the lives of all who attend. We feel this peaceful influence upon entering, and we carry an abundant measure of temple kindness with us when we depart. Such is the spirit and power of rejuvenation—both for the living and the dead—that radiates from the temple. In this context, Elder Dean L. Larsen of the Presidency of the Seventy related the following testimony of temple attendance:

> We hurried from the parking lot at the temple to avoid becoming drenched by the rain. Immediately upon our entering the doors of the temple, the atmosphere changed. I sensed a spirit of warmth and peace. The countenances of the temple patrons were a marked contrast to those of the harried travelers whom I had left a short time before at the airport. In a very real sense, it seemed as though we had walked through the temple doors into a different world. I found myself smiling at the people in the foyer area. My spirits were lifted, and the concerns of the outside world melted away.
>
> I thought on this occasion, as I have often done upon entering the temple, of the words spoken by Joseph Smith in the dedicatory prayer offered at the Kirtland Temple in March 1836, when he asked of the Lord:
>
> "That thy glory may rest down upon thy people, and upon this thy house, . . . that it may be sanctified and consecrated to be holy, and that thy holy presence may be continually in this house;
>
> "And that all people who shall enter upon the threshold of the Lord's house may feel thy power, and feel constrained to acknowledge that thou hast sanctified it, and that it is thy house, a place of thy holiness." (D&C 109:12–13.)
>
> So often we relate the temples to the vicarious ordinances that are performed there for those who are deceased.

> Certainly this is a vital part of temple work. But there is another aspect of temple activity that has great importance for living members. I refer not only to the ordinances performed for the living but as well to the spiritually uplifting, strengthening influence in individual lives that results from regular temple attendance. (*Ensign,* Apr. 1993, 10)

Surely the quality of our service to fellow colleagues upon the pathway of life is a measure of our preparedness to go to the temple. We are kind to others, just as the Lord is kind to us all. We are gracious and accommodating to others, because that is our core desire—the spirit of fellowship being a reflection of the standard set for those who strive to make themselves worthy to go to the temple. President Ezra Taft Benson reminded us: "One who is kind is sympathetic and gentle with others. He is considerate of others' feelings and courteous in his behavior. He has a helpful nature. Kindness pardons others' weaknesses and faults. Kindness is extended to all—to the aged and the young, to animals, to those low of station as well as the high" (*Ensign,* Nov. 1986, 45).

Kindness is an essential ingredient of the abundant life. Sister Elaine L. Jack, former Relief Society general president, had this counsel for us about the particulars of "getting a life":

> To *get a life* is to be kind. Few things are as healing as simple kindnesses—a gentle touch, a pat on the arm, an encouraging word, patient silence, a probing question when something is obviously wrong, a withholding of judgment until all the facts are known. If we are sincere about being followers of Christ, if we really mean it when we partake of the sacrament on Sunday or attend a temple session, we will be kind. (*Ensign,* July 1995, 49; emphasis in original)

Let us in our preparations for attending the temple remember to be kind, to be gracious, and to be forgiving. When we look to the temple, we look to the emblem of kindness and gospel service. Those who complete their preparations to attend the temple are not perfect, but they can be perfectly attuned to the spirit of love shown by the Savior. Coming to the temple is a glorious part of our commitment to "come unto Christ, and be perfected in him" (Moro. 10:32). With this commitment in our hearts, we pass through the gateway of kindness and into the realm where small acts of love and charity toward others, being a little kinder and little more forgiving each day, will add up to a lifetime of improvement along the course of emulating the Savior. President Gordon B. Hinckley has consistently established the tone and measure of kindness as a divine quality that we should strive to practice more fully in our lives:

> Now, brethren and sisters, let us return to our homes with resolution in our hearts to do a little better than we have done in the past. We can all be a little kinder, a little more generous, a little more thoughtful of one another. We can be a little more tolerant and friendly to those not of our faith, going out of our way to show our respect for them. We cannot afford to be arrogant or self-righteous. It is our obligation to reach out in helpfulness, not only to our own but to all others as well. Their interest in and respect for this Church will increase as we do so. (*Ensign,* May 1999, 88)

TIME TO MEDITATE AND PONDER

1. The Prophet Joseph Smith enjoined us to "conquer men with kindness" and show "humanity to all" (*HC,* 6:219). How does this relate to our preparation for attending the temple?

2. How is the Lord the highest example of kindness?

3. In what ways is kindness a quality that transforms both the giver and the receiver?

4. How does the need to forgive others relate to our preparations for going to the house of the Lord?

5. President Joseph F. Smith encouraged us to show greater kindness and display a greater measure of encouragement to others in order to "get the genuine sweets out of life" (*Gospel Doctrine,* 112). What do you think he meant by that interesting expression?

6. The Savior was the Master of healing. How can we better emulate His example and thus prepare more fully to enter His house?

7. How are all those who are in attendance with us in the temple a part of our "families"?

8. How are the "little things"—the little acts of kindness and benevolence toward others—important in our preparations to go to the temple?

9. President Gordon B. Hinckley entreats us to be "a little kinder, a little more generous, a little more thoughtful of one another" (*Ensign,* May 1999, 88). How does this counsel relate to you personally as you prepare for the temple?

CHAPTER 10
A HOUSE OF GODLINESS

Guiding Principle: The temple is a house where God reveals to the faithful the depths and heights of His divine plan. It is the ordained place where He imparts to the Saints of Zion the inner mysteries of the sacred heavenly blueprint that enables mankind to build their lives after the manner of godliness, to prepare themselves, through the grace of God, to enter once again, worthily, into His presence.

> *The mysteries of godliness are taught in the temple. As early as 1841, the Lord revealed to Joseph Smith that "there is not a place found on earth that he may come to and restore again that which was lost unto you, or which he hath taken away, even the fulness of the priesthood. . . . For I deign to reveal unto my church things which have been kept hid from before the foundation of the world, things that pertain to the dispensation of the fulness of times." (D&C 124:28, 41.)*
>
> *These revelations, which are reserved for and taught only to the faithful Church members in sacred temples, constitute what are called the "mysteries of godliness." The Lord said He had given to Joseph "the keys of the mysteries, and the revelations which are sealed"*
> —HAROLD B. LEE, *THE TEACHINGS OF HAROLD B. LEE*, 574–75.

The temple is a house of godliness. Preparing for the temple means preparing to become more godlike in our thoughts and actions. Godliness implies those qualities associated with our Heavenly Father and our Savior Jesus Christ as part of the divine nature. If we aspire to godliness, then we are devout in our worship of God and seek to be Christlike in our everyday behavior. Indeed we seek to be even as the Father and the Son are. This is part of the process of taking upon ourselves the divine nature of Christ and of becoming as He is (see Moro. 7:48). Our life takes on a new vision. We have an eye single to His glory; we cultivate a perception born of love for all mankind. We feel an overwhelming desire to do good and to be good; in all things we seek to do as He would do. The temple kindles and reinforces that kind of desire.

Godliness has within it all the qualities and virtues of God. This should be our goal—in everything we do and in everything we say. Peter taught, "Seeing then that all these things shall be dissolved, what manner of persons ought ye to be in all holy conversation and godliness" (2 Pet. 3:11). Furthermore, from modern-day revelation we learn anew that godliness requires strict adherence to the principles and ordinances of the gospel: "Therefore, in the ordinances thereof, the power of godliness is manifest. And without the ordinances thereof, and the authority of the priesthood, the power of godliness is not manifest unto men in the flesh" (D&C 84:20–21). It is through experiencing the power of godliness inherent in the ordinances and services of the temple that we gain a higher measure of understanding about the purpose of life—where we originated, why we are here, and what our ultimate future may be. Elder John A. Widtsoe confirmed: "*The temple is a place where ceremonies pertaining to Godliness are presented.* The great mysteries of life, with man's unanswered questions, are here made clear: (1) Where did I come from? (2) Why am I here? (3) Where do I go when life is over? Here the needs of the spirit from which all other things of life issue are held of paramount importance" (*Ensign,* Jan. 1972, 56; emphasis in original).

How can we improve our attitude and behavior in the quest to make godliness a central focus of our daily living as we prepare for the temple? Here are several ideas that may be helpful:

Ponder the word. Study the word of God as given in the scriptures and through the voice of the living prophets. Herein are the attributes of godliness identified, clarified, and put forward for emulation (see Jacob 3:2; Alma 32:28; D&C 138:1–11).

Choose the best patterns. Organize and structure your life after the best models and examples: the Lord's prophets and servants, faithful family members, and righteous neighbors and colleagues. Especially seek to follow in the footsteps of the Savior (see Matt. 16:24).

Be clean. Cleanliness is next to godliness as reflected in purity of thought (see Prov. 23:7) as well as in actions (see James 1:22; Mosiah 5:15).

Be obedient. Godliness entails righteousness (see D&C 27:14; 98:30). Faith is the foundation of righteousness (see Rom. 3:22; 9:30–32); hence this principle is most important as we seek after godliness (see 2 Pet. 1:3–12; Moro. 10:32–33; D&C 4:6).

Be a leader in all walks of life. Godliness entails being a good example. Through our example we can lift and bless others (see 1 Tim. 4:12; Alma 17:11; 3 Ne. 12:16).

Be prepared. Recognize that those who lead a godly life may well suffer persecution (see 2 Tim. 3:12). Understand the blessings and the challenges.

Remember. Create a way to remember the things that are required for the acquisition of the attributes of godliness: surround yourself with reminders (pictures, charts, posters, notes, wall and table ornaments—anything that will bring the principles of godliness to mind throughout the day). Guard against forgetting due to the ease of the way (see Hel. 12:1–2). Remember the goodness and mercy of the Lord in all things (see Mosiah 4:11).

This kind of focus on godliness will ensure that we move forward "with an eye single to the glory of God" (D&C 4:5; see also Morm. 8:15; D&C 27:2; 55:1; 59:1; 82:19) as we prepare for the temple.

Principles of Godliness

As we prepare to enter the house of the Lord, where godliness is manifested with radiant clarity and covenant authority, we should keep in mind such principles as the following:

The process of acquiring godliness extends into the eternities. We can act now with godly obedience and charity so that we can obtain a full measure of godliness in the hereafter, to be redeemed "in the due time of the Lord" (D&C 76:38). We do not leave this earth perfect in ourselves, but rather "perfect in Christ" (Moro. 10:32, see also Moro. 10:33). Similarly, we do not enter the temple perfect in ourselves but rather with a perfect commitment to become as the Savior and to ultimately enter His rest and glory. The key lies in enduring to the end, as the Savior counseled: "Behold, I am the law, and the light. Look unto me, and endure to the end, and ye shall live; for unto him that endureth to the end will I give eternal life" (3 Ne. 15:9). The temple offers to us a sanctified rehearsal of this process—a microcosm of the macrocosm of returning to our heavenly home. The Prophet Joseph Smith declared:

> God has in reserve a time, or period appointed in His own bosom, when He will bring all His subjects, who have obeyed His voice and kept His commandments, into His celestial rest. This rest is of such perfection and glory, that man has need of a preparation before he can, according to the laws of that kingdom, enter it and enjoy its blessings. This being the fact, God has given certain laws to the human family, which, if observed, are sufficient to prepare them to inherit this rest. (*HC,* 2:12)

We can acquire godliness through faith and diligence. Godliness comes as a result of unshakable commitment and undeviating righteousness. President Lorenzo Snow emphasized the following:

> Purity, virtue, fidelity, and godliness must be sought ambitiously, or the crown cannot be won. Those principles must be incorporated with[in] ourselves—woven into our

constitutions—becoming a part of us, making us a center, a fountain of truth, of equity, justice, and mercy, of all that is good and great; that from us may proceed the light, the life, the power, and the law to direct, to govern, and assist to save a wandering world—acting as the sons of God, for and in behalf of our Father in heaven. These qualifications can be had only as they are sought and obtained; so that in the morning of the Resurrection we will possess those acquisitions only which we secured in this world! Godliness cannot be conferred, but must be acquired—a fact of which the religious world seems strangely and lamentably unconscious. (*TLS,* 79)

The individual, having infinite potential, can become as great as he or she wants to become. Going to the temple is always a reminder of our divine heritage and limitless potential. The temple is the gateway to perfection and godliness, the confirmation of our destiny to become like our Father in Heaven and His Only Begotten Son. We turn again to Lorenzo Snow for guidance on this subject. Before he joined the Church, the young Lorenzo was promised the following by Patriarch Joseph Smith Sr.:

> "You will be great, and as great as you want to be, as great as God Himself, and you will not wish to be greater." I could not understand this, but years after in Nauvoo while talking upon a principle of the gospel, the Spirit of God rested powerfully upon me and showed me more clearly than I can now see your faces a certain principle and its glory, and it came to me summarized in this brief sentence: "As man is now, God once was; as God is now man may be." The Spirit of God was on me in a marvelous manner all that day, and I stored that great truth away in my mind. (*TLS,* 2)

President Snow later commented as follows on this grand insight:

> "As man now is, God once was; As God now is, man may be." That fulfilled Father Smith's declaration. Nothing was

ever revealed more distinctly than that was to me. Of course, now that it is so well known it may not appear such a wonderful manifestation; but when I received it, the knowledge was marvelous to me. This principle, in substance, is found also in the scriptures. The Lord said to John, as recorded in the third chapter of his Revelation: "To him that overcometh will I grant to sit with me in my throne, even as I also overcame, and am set down with my Father in his throne." (*TLS*, 2)

Godliness is a form of power. In the scriptures we read: "Yea, verily I say unto you, I gave unto you a commandment that you should build a house, in the which house I design to endow those whom I have chosen with power from on high" (D&C 95:8). To take upon ourselves a measure of the quality of godliness within the temples of God—through our faithfulness and obedience—is to bring power to bear in our lives, the productive and protective power that comes from the gospel of Jesus Christ and from the blessings of the Spirit. President Ezra Taft Benson taught:

> Yes, there is a power associated with the ordinances of heaven—even the power of godliness—which can and will thwart the forces of evil if we will be worthy of those sacred blessings. This community will be protected, our families will be protected, our children will be safeguarded as we live the gospel, visit the temple, and live close to the Lord. This temple will be a light to all in this area—a symbol of all we hold dear. It will be an inspiration not only to Latter-day Saints, but to many others as well. God bless us as Saints to live worthy of the covenants and ordinances made in this sacred place. May it be a constant reminder that life is eternal and that covenants made by us in mortality can be everlasting. (*TETB*, 256)

The Mysteries of Godliness

How does one become like God? To the world, unschooled in the ways of the Lord and untutored by the Holy Spirit, this is an unfathomable mystery. But to those who frequent the halls of the holy temples of God and avail themselves of the blessings and endowments of truth bestowed there upon the faithful through the keys of the priesthood, the process becomes less and less of a mystery and more and more of a lucid and understandable revelation of glory and hope. The temple is a school for the practice of godliness, a sacred tutorial in the process of repelling all enticements of Satan and yielding "to the enticings of the Holy Spirit" (Mosiah 3:19), that we might eventually be worthy to enter the presence of Deity and once more be at home in heaven.

David E. Sorensen, formerly of the Presidency of the Seventy, taught:

> Temples stand as a constant physical reminder of the grace and the goodness of the Father. This helps communities of Saints strengthen themselves. President George Q. Cannon said: "Every foundation stone that is laid for a temple, and every temple completed . . . lessens the power of Satan on the earth, and increases the power of God and Godliness."
>
> Temples have always symbolized being in the presence of the Lord. "Let them make me a sanctuary; that I may dwell among them," said the Lord. "And there I will meet with thee, and I will commune with thee" (Ex. 25:8, 22). There is a closeness to God that comes through consistent worship in the house of the Lord. We can come to know Him and feel welcome, "at home," in His house. (*Ensign*, Nov. 1998, 64)

Through the temple we learn the great mystery of how to become as our Father in Heaven and His Only Begotten Son are. We learn how to prepare to take upon ourselves the divine nature by covenant, through the exercise of faith and hope. Indeed, the temple is a process by which we rehearse the magnificent event of coming back into the presence of our Father in Heaven.

Modern-day revelation has given us this extraordinary insight into the workings of the priesthood: "And this greater priesthood administereth the gospel and holdeth the key of the mysteries of the kingdom, even the key of the knowledge of God. Therefore, in the ordinances thereof, the power of godliness is manifest. And without the ordinances thereof, and the authority of the priesthood, the power of godliness is not manifest unto men in the flesh; For without this no man can see the face of God, even the Father, and live" (D&C 84:19–22).

Through the sacred ordinances of the temple we are endowed with the blessings of light and truth by means of which the power of godliness can become accessible to faithful and devoted sons and daughters of God. The Melchizedek Priesthood holds the keys of the mysteries of the kingdom—the sealing powers that transcend earthly boundaries so that temple ordinances are recognized in the courts on high. Such things are understood only through the Spirit—and only on the basis of our obedience to the laws and commandments of God. President Joseph Fielding Smith explained: "The Lord promised the saints that he would reveal to them the mysteries of his kingdom on certain conditions, as we read in the Doctrine and Covenants, section 76:1–10. *These truths cannot be understood except by obedience to the law of the gospel on which the reception of this knowledge is based.* It was for the same reason the Lord told Nicodemus, 'Except a man be born again, he cannot see the kingdom of God'" (*DS*, 1:297; emphasis in original).

In our preparations for attending the temple, we should look forward with joy to the opportunity to receive and understand these "mysteries" of the gospel. These are not things to be anticipated with a sense of apprehension or foreboding. They are blessings of enlightenment, comfort, and peace. We should move forward toward this day with a consistent and dedicated desire to serve the Lord in all holiness and conviction. President Lorenzo Snow gave this counsel:

> *Develop the character traits of godliness.* Be upright, just, and merciful, exercising a spirit of nobility and godliness in all your intentions and resolutions—in all your acts and dealings. Cultivate a spirit of charity, be ready to do for others more than you would expect from them if circumstances were reversed. Be ambitious to be great, not in the estimation of the worldly minded, but in the eyes of God, and to be

great in this sense: "Love the Lord your God with all your might, mind and strength, and your neighbor as yourself." You must love mankind because they are your brethren, the offspring of God. Pray diligently for this spirit of philanthropy, this expansion of thought and feeling, and for power and ability to labor earnestly in the interest of Messiah's kingdom. (*TLS,* 10; emphasis in original)

TIME TO MEDITATE AND PONDER

1. President Harold B. Lee stated: "A mystery may be defined as a truth which cannot be known except by revelation" (*THBL,* 574–75). By what process does revelation come to the members of the Church?

2. What is meant by the expression "with an eye single to the glory of God" (D&C 4:5)? How does this relate to the process of acquiring godliness?

3. How can we demonstrate a higher level of godliness in our everyday lives?

4. How does the famous saying of President Lorenzo Snow—"As man now is, God once was; As God now is, man may be" (*TLS,* 2)—help you in your quest for becoming more like our Heavenly Father and His Son?

5. The Savior said, "Look unto me, and endure to the end, and ye shall live" (3 Ne. 15:9). How does this relate to the process of going to the temple—the house of godliness?

CHAPTER 11
A HOUSE OF CHARITY

Guiding Principle: Charity is the essence of the divine; it is the heritage of the sons and daughters of God, the framework in which we view our brothers and sisters as fellowcitizens with the Saints.

> *There is a love from God that should be exercised toward those of our faith, who walk uprightly, which is peculiar to itself, but it is without prejudice; it also gives scope to the mind, which enables us to conduct ourselves with greater liberality towards all that are not of our faith, than what they exercise towards one another. These principles approximate nearer to the mind of God, because it is like God, or Godlike.*
> —JOSEPH SMITH, *HISTORY OF THE CHURCH,* 3:304.

The temple is a house of charity, for charity is a key part of the divine nature. We participate in the temple ordinances to help not only ourselves, but also our family, our extended family, and our departed family. Our motivation is essentially charitable in its roots and foundation. The sealing powers of the priesthood sanctify our charity by binding the generations together. Family history work is a work of charity deriving from the loving-kindness of God in preparing a way for all of His children to receive the blessings of the temple.

Charity is the ultimate attribute of godliness. It constitutes the essence of obtaining the divine nature of Christ through faith, virtue, knowledge, temperance, patience, brotherly kindness, and godliness—ever with humility and diligence (see D&C 4:6). This pure love of Christ is total, complete, enduring, and characteristic of a divine being. When we are possessed of this love, our desires are like unto those of our Savior—to bless and serve mankind.

"Charity never faileth" (1 Cor. 13:8; see also Moro. 7:46). Christ did not fail His Father, nor did He fail us. His pure love motivated His great sacrifice—the eternal, infinite, vicarious Atonement. When we possess that kind of love, we govern our lives according to the principles of the Atonement. When we possess that kind of love—the pure love of Christ, the love for all people, the desire to bless and serve—we then possess the eternal quality of charity, and we never fail. In the strength of the Lord we can do all things, just as Ammon demonstrated (see Alma 26:12). In the strength of charity, through the Atonement of Christ, we begin to acquire this unconditional, godly love, this divine nature of Christ: "And charity suffereth long, and is kind, and envieth not, and is not puffed up, seeketh not her own, is not easily provoked, thinketh no evil, and rejoiceth not in iniquity but rejoiceth in the truth, beareth all things, believeth all things, hopeth all things, endureth all things" (Moro. 7:45).

How can we increase the presence of charity in our lives as we prepare for the temple? Here are some simple but effective ideas to help all of us:

Start with yourself. Ask Heavenly Father in sincere prayer for a blessing of charity, then make a personal commitment and a plan for improvement (see D&C 4:6). Accept the motto: "Do as Jesus would do." Count your blessings—the desire to do good will increase and the desire to serve others will be strengthened. To become *full* of charity requires a change of heart toward ourselves, others, and God. Follow the promptings of the Spirit so that the avenues of charity will be opened unto you.

Make your home the schoolhouse of charity. Teach charity. Set an example by cultivating the qualities of charity toward loved ones. Recognize and honor even small acts of charity on the part of others.

Do it for the right reasons. Charity never judges. Act from love alone. By this we can know that our motivation is pure—if we are ready and willing to forego recognition and credit for the good deed.

Have a plan for charitable giving. As much as possible, share resources, time, talents, knowledge, goods, and money with those who need help. Budget to give away a certain amount of all these for charitable purposes. Remember to pay a full tithe. Often the greatest act of charity is to give of yourself, your counsel, your solace, your support, your encouragement, and your companionship.

In these and similar ways we can enhance the quality of charity in our thoughts and deeds and thus be better prepared for the house of the Lord, which He has given to us out of a pure motivation of charity—His love.

The Path to the Temple Is the Path of Charity

The spiritual price we pay for the transcendent blessings of the temple is charity. What a small cost! What a modest investment for the blessings of eternity! This promise is found in the scriptures: "Every one that thirsteth, come ye to the waters, and he that hath no money; come ye, buy, and eat; yea, come, buy wine and milk without money and without price" (Isa. 55:1).

The fruit of the gospel of Jesus Christ comes to us freely from the Lord. In return, He asks us to take upon ourselves abundantly the divine nature by giving freely of our time and substance as we exercise charity in the kingdom of God and toward all His children. Often this may come at considerable sacrifice—but never without the blessings and attending grace of the Lord. President Ezra Taft Benson has provided us with a moving illustration of the kind of charity that is contemplated for those who frequent the house of the Lord:

> When I think of charity, I again think of my father and that day he was called on his mission. I suppose some in the world might say that his acceptance of that call was proof he did not really love his family. To leave seven children and an expectant wife at home alone for two years, how could that be true love?
>
> But my father knew a greater vision of love. He knew that "all things shall work together for good to them that love God" (Rom. 8:28). He knew that the best thing he could do for his family was to obey God.
>
> While we missed him greatly during those years, and while his absence brought many challenges to our family, his acceptance proved to be a gift of charity. Father went on his mission, leaving Mother at home with seven children. (The eighth was born four months after he arrived in the field.) But there came into that home a spirit of missionary work that never left it. It was not without some sacrifice. Father had to sell our old dry farm in order to finance his mission. He had to move a married couple into part of our home to take care of the row crops, and he left his sons and wife the responsibility for the hay land, the pasture land, and a small herd of dairy cows.
>
> Father's letters were indeed a blessing to our family. To us children, they seemed to come from halfway around the world, but they were only from Springfield, Massachusetts; and Chicago, Illinois; and Cedar Rapids and Marshalltown, Iowa. Yes, there came into our home, as a result of Father's mission, a spirit of missionary work that never left it.
>
> Later the family grew to eleven children—seven sons and four daughters. All seven sons filled missions, some of them two or three missions. Later, two daughters and their husbands filled full-time missions. The two other sisters, both widows—one the mother of eight and the other the

mother of ten—served as missionary companions in Birmingham, England.

It is a legacy that still continues to bless the Benson family even into the third and fourth generations. Was not this truly a gift of love? (*Ensign*, Nov. 1986, 45)

In many ways, charity is the integrating essence of the divine nature of Christ. The first principles and ordinances of the gospel—faith, repentance, baptism, and receiving the gift of the Holy Ghost—are the foundation elements of our preparations to enter the temple. As we are nourished by the word of God and learn how to endure in our covenant loyalty and obedience, we remain worthy to enter the house of the Lord. Elder William Grant Bangerter of the First Quorum of the Seventy declared in this context:

> The gospel is *faith in the Lord, Jesus Christ.* This implies a willingness to accept His doctrine and take upon us His name, being obedient to His commandments. *The gospel is repentance* and a cleansing from all iniquity. *It is baptism* whereby we have made the covenant and promise. It is the right to have the *companionship of the Holy Ghost,* which, when we have a correct frame of mind, will teach us as we go through the temple. *The gospel is the scriptures.* The answer to almost any appropriate question about the temple will be found in the scriptures for those who seek it. *The gospel is prayer, humility, teachableness, charity.* It is *commitment* and it is *covenant* and *ordinances.* It is also *blessings.* (*Ensign*, May 1982, 71; emphasis in original)

There are those pervasive challenges thrown in our pathway from time to time that might tend to weaken our resolve or dilute our commitment to prepare for the temple. In such cases we need to remember that "charity never faileth" (1 Cor. 13:8; see also Moro. 7:46). One woman whose husband is not a member of the Church wrote: "Though my husband and I do not share the same faith, we still work together in teaching our children to live by righteous principles. . . . All marriages require continuing effort. However, when everyone in the home is willing to exercise charity, we can make our earthly family a wonderful one even before achieving that goal of a temple sealing. We can make it a family prepared to accept eternally binding covenants" (*Ensign,* Apr. 2000, 34).

We can all rejoice over the blessings that await us in the temple. We can gratefully depart from the environment of malaise and unholiness so often characteristic of modern society and enter worthily into a realm of peace, tranquility, and holy inspiration where we learn how to enrich our lives spiritually and become engaged in the magnificent program for extending universal blessings to all of God's children through the sealing ordinances of the temple. In this regard, President James E. Faust has counseled:

> We unavoidably stand in so many unholy places and are subjected to so much that is vulgar, profane, and destructive of the Spirit of the Lord that I encourage our Saints all over the world, wherever possible, to strive to stand more often in holy places. Our most holy places are our sacred temples. Within them is a feeling of sacred comfort. We should seek to be worthy to take our families to the temple to be sealed together for eternity. We should also search for the records of our kindred dead so that they too can be sealed to us in one of the temples. We must strive for holiness by being "an example of the believers, in word, in conversation, in charity, in spirit, in faith, in purity." In this way we can maintain and strengthen our own individual relationship with our God. (*Ensign,* May 2005, 62)

Time to Meditate and Ponder

1. In what ways is it true to say that temple work is founded on the principle of charity?

2. "Charity never faileth" is the celebrated statement from the scriptures. One might also say that our labors to prepare for the temple will never fail if established on charity—the pure love of Christ. Why is this the case?

3. How can we demonstrate our charity toward those who have passed beyond the veil before they could receive the blessings of the gospel and the temple?

4. How can we demonstrate our charity toward family members who have not yet accepted the opportunity to be active in temple work?

CHAPTER 12
A HOUSE OF HUMILITY

Guiding Principle: For the humble the Lord reserves choice blessings of guidance and inspiration in the holy temples of God.

> *People ask me frequently what is my favorite verse of scripture. I have many and this is one of them, "Be thou humble; and the Lord thy God shall lead thee by the hand, and give thee answer to thy prayers" (D&C 112:10). What a promise to those who walk without arrogance, to those who walk without conceit, to those who walk without egotism, to those who walk humbly. "Be thou humble; and the Lord thy God shall lead thee by the hand, and give thee answer to thy prayers." What a solid and wonderful promise that is.*
> —GORDON B. HINCKLEY, *TEACHINGS OF GORDON B. HINCKLEY*, 265.

Humility is a cardinal virtue of growth that illuminates our pathway toward the temple. Humility is an essential part of the divine nature. When we acknowledge and understand our relationship to and dependence upon God, we begin to become humble. In the state of humility—being submissive, easily entreated, and teachable (see Alma 7:23)—we receive the fruits or the blessings of humility, including peace, inspiration, hope, and the guidance of the Lord. We understand the nothingness of man in comparison to the majesty of God. We will have a broken heart and a contrite spirit. Humility causes us to relate to God in gratitude and love and thus become more like the Savior, who taught: "Whosoever therefore shall humble himself as this little child, the same is greatest in the kingdom of heaven" (Matt. 18:4). Said Brigham Young: "We have to humble ourselves and become like little children in our feelings—to become humble and childlike in spirit, in order to receive the first illuminations of the spirit of the Gospel, then we have the privilege of growing, of increasing in knowledge, in wisdom, and in understanding" (*Discourses,* 228).

How can we cultivate a more humble and teachable disposition and thus become more like the Savior, whose home the temple is? Here are a few ideas regarding the various aspects of humility to consider:

Humility is the beginning of spirituality. Remember to pray for humility (see Hel. 3:35). Understand that all are equal in the sight of God (see Alma 1:26). Cultivate a broken heart (see Ps. 34:18), listen to spiritual input (see Alma 7:23; 13:28), acknowledge our dependence upon God (see Mosiah 4:5), and accept with gratitude the grace of God as an eternal blessing to His children (see Ether 12:27).

Humility is a quality of strength. Humility signals a partnership with Jesus Christ, in whose name all things are possible (see Matt. 19:26). Choose therefore to make humility part of your nature (see 1 Pet. 5:5). Seek to be humbled by the word of God and His goodness rather than being compelled to be humble (see Alma 32:16; 48:20). Seek to be humble, for in humility we can learn to depend upon the strength of the Lord, who renders unto us the courage and fortitude to stand firm on principle. President Ezra Taft Benson taught, "Humility does not mean timidity. A person can be humble, powerful, and courageous. The Prophet Joseph is a good example. Humility is an acknowledged recognition of our dependence on a higher power. In this work, we will never be successful unless we have that spirit of humility" (*TETB*, 369–70).

Humility belongs in the family. Grow together. Humility in a family setting means listening to every voice, having family councils to make plans and decisions that bless the lives of everyone, and suppressing any manifestation of anger, sarcasm, or abuse of any kind. Become humble like a child, and life will suddenly be filled with the wonder of endless learning and growth.

Humility belongs in the workplace. Value everyone alike. Humility means a willingness to listen without judgment until there is clarity of thought and direction.

Humility belongs in society. Humility makes society flow. Humility is a cousin to courtesy and a sibling of forgiveness. It is that oil that renders interpersonal relationships smooth and wholesome. Humility is the foundation for respect. Treat all with kindness, love, and respect. Never put down another to elevate yourself.

When we invest a spirit of humility in all our relationships—at home, in the workplace, and in society—we are truly making ourselves more temple worthy, for we are consistently making the example of our Savior a governing factor in our lives. Humility brings peace and rest into our environment. Coleen K. Menlove, former Primary general president, observed: "As we replace fear with faith and then demonstrate our humility, we are blessed with a feeling of peace" (*Ensign,* Sept. 2004, 24).

HUMILITY AT EVERY STATION IN LIFE

Moses, in all of his power and influence, was by nature most humble. "Now the man Moses was very meek, above all the men which were upon the face of the earth" (Num. 12:3). Such meekness was no deterrent to his filling the commission to ascend the natural temple of the Lord (Mount Sinai) and commune in person with Jehovah. In fact, it was Moses' submissiveness and humility that helped qualify him for his prophetic office and calling. Isaiah likewise demonstrated great humility when he was called as a prophet of God (see Isa. 6:1–8), as did Jeremiah (see Jer. 1:6–8). The prophets of God, by nature, are humble and self-effacing, willing to submit to the will of the Lord in everything, just as the Savior submitted to the will of the Father. Said President Lorenzo Snow:

> The Lord chooses humble men. The Lord has not chosen the great and learned of the world to perform His work on the earth. It is not those who have been trained and educated in the colleges and seminaries of learning, but humble men devoted to His cause whom He has chosen to take charge of the affairs of His Church, men who are willing to be led and guided by the Holy Spirit, and who will of necessity give the glory unto Him knowing that of themselves they can do nothing. (*TLS*, 77)

Humility is a hallmark of discipleship and priesthood leadership within the fold of Christ. Willingness to be led by the Spirit of the Lord is a quality that distinguishes the Saints of God—from the most meek and lowly person in the fold to the ranks of the chosen prophets, seers, and revelators appointed to be God's messengers of the covenant. A most instructive illustration of this fact came to light on the occasion of the unexpected death of President Harold B. Lee on December 26, 1973. Since President N. Eldon Tanner, First Counselor in the First Presidency, was out of town at the time, Second Counselor Marion G. Romney was directing the affairs of the Church during the illness of Harold B. Lee and was at the hospital with Spencer W. Kimball, President of the Quorum of the Twelve. President Tanner explains what then happened:

> Immediately upon the death of President Lee, President Romney turned to President Kimball and said, "You are in charge." Remember, the Prophet Joseph Smith had said that without the President there was no First Presidency over the Twelve.
>
> Not one minute passed between the time President Lee died and the Twelve took over as the presiding authority of the Church.

Following President Lee's funeral, President Kimball called a meeting of all of the Apostles for Sunday, December 30, at 3 PM in the Salt Lake Temple Council Room. President Romney and I had taken our respective places of seniority in the council, so there were fourteen of us present.

Following a song, and prayer by President Romney, President Kimball, in deep humility, expressed his feelings to us. He said that he had spent Friday in the temple talking to the Lord, and had shed many tears as he prayed for guidance in assuming his new responsibilities and in choosing his counselors.

Dressed in the robes of the holy priesthood, we held a prayer circle; President Kimball asked me to conduct it and Elder Thomas S. Monson to offer the prayer. Following this, President Kimball explained the purpose of the meeting and called on each member of the quorum in order of seniority, starting with Elder Ezra Taft Benson, to express his feelings as to whether the First Presidency should be organized that day or whether we should carry on as the Quorum of the Twelve. Each said, "We should organize now," and many complimentary things were spoken about President Kimball and his work with the Twelve. (*Ensign*, Nov. 1979, 42)

The extraordinary display of humility by President Spencer W. Kimball and his pattern of meekly importuning the Lord in the temple for guidance and direction is a noble example for us all to follow—especially as we, too, prepare to enter the temple and seek the Lord's blessings there.

The temple is a house of humility. Going there is a privilege, one that yields marvelous blessings for the humble, the meek, and the teachable. We go to the temple in humility—just as if we were entering the presence of God. We do not go in fear, but with broken hearts and contrite spirits. As we prepare to enter the temple, we are reminded of King Benjamin's counsel that we are as nothing in comparison with the majesty of God (see Mosiah 4:5, 11)—but we are also reminded that we are everything in God's plan, for we are destined to be heirs of all that He has (see D&C 84:33–38). As God Himself explained to Moses, "For behold, this is my work and my glory—to bring to pass the immortality and eternal life of man" (Moses 1:39).

Inspired Counsel of the Prophets

In our preparations to seek the Lord humbly in His holy temple, let us remember the words of wisdom spoken by His anointed servants. Here are a few examples to follow:

Principle: The simple truths of the gospel, planted in the hearts of the Saints, yield a mighty harvest of joy, peace, and comfort.
President Brigham Young:
> I delight extremely in plain simplicity. . . . The hearts of the meek and humble are full of joy and comfort continually. (*Discourses,* 228)

Principle: Humility is the counterbalance to pride, the framework for importuning the Lord in reverence to forgive us for our weaknesses, that we might receive His blessings and guidance.
President Harold B. Lee:
> Humility is a rare quality. Before you can ask Him for a temporal blessing you've got to be like the brother of Jared. In all humility you've got to plead your weakness and ask for His pity and His forgiveness in order that you can receive the blessing. Someone has aptly said that humility is a rare virtue. When men become humble they soon become proud they're humble. I think there's a lot of that. Humility is one of the rarest qualities in all the world. (*THBL,* 618)

Principle: King Benjamin taught a great lesson in humility. Said he: "I would that ye should remember, and always retain in remembrance, the greatness of God, and your own nothingness, and his goodness and long-suffering towards you, unworthy creatures, and humble yourselves even in the depths of humility, calling on the name of the Lord daily, and standing steadfastly in the faith of that which is to come, which was spoken by the mouth of the angel" (Mosiah 4:11).

President Spencer W. Kimball:
> How does one get humble? To me, one must constantly be reminded of his dependence. On whom dependent? On the Lord. How remind one's self? By real, constant, worshipful, grateful prayer. (*TSWK,* 233)

Principle: Humility is a virtue of light and charity; pride is characteristic of darkness and self-conceit. Humility draws us nearer to God; pride builds up a wall that separates us from Him.

President Howard W. Hunter:
> Humility is an attribute of godliness possessed by true Saints. It is easy to understand why a proud man fails. He is content to rely upon himself only. This is evident in those who seek social position in fields of business, government, education, sports, or other endeavors. Our genuine concern should be for the success of others. The proud man shuts himself off from God, and when he does he no longer lives in the light. The Apostle Peter made this comment: "Be clothed with humility: for God resisteth the proud, and giveth grace to the humble. Humble yourselves therefore under the mighty hand of God, that he may exalt you in due time." (1 Pet. 5:5–6.) (*THWH,* 266)

TIME TO MEDITATE AND PONDER

1. One of President Gordon B. Hinckley's favorite passages of scripture is this: "Be thou humble; and the Lord thy God shall lead thee by the hand, and give thee answer to thy prayers" (D&C 112:10). How does this scripture relate to our becoming prepared to enter the temple?

2. What did the Savior mean when He declared, "Whosoever therefore shall humble himself as this little child, the same is greatest in the kingdom of heaven" (Matt. 18:4)?

3. In what ways does humility represent strength?

4. How does humility make us more receptive to truth?

5. Why does the Lord choose the humble and meek to accomplish His work?

6. On the eve of his calling as President of the Church, where did President Spencer W. Kimball go to seek guidance? How can we follow his example?

7. Why do you think President Harold B. Lee maintained that "humility is one of the rarest qualities in all the world" (*THBL*, 618).

8. According to President Spencer W. Kimball, what is the most important key to becoming humble before the Lord?

9. Why is it that pride inevitably results in failure?

CHAPTER 13
A HOUSE OF DILIGENCE

Guiding Principle: The temple is a beacon of light from which are dispensed the powers and truths to sustain our diligent commitment to endure to the end in righteousness. The more often we frequent the sacred halls of the house of the Lord, the more attuned we become to His nature and His designs for our eternal salvation and exaltation.

> *We consider that God has created man with a mind capable of instruction, and a faculty which may be enlarged in proportion to the heed and diligence given to the light communicated from heaven to the intellect; and that the nearer man approaches perfection, the clearer are his views, and the greater his enjoyments, till he has overcome the evils of his life and lost every desire for sin; and like the ancients, arrives at that point of faith where he is wrapped in the power and glory of his Maker, and is caught up to dwell with Him. But we consider that this is a station to which no man ever arrived in a moment: he must have been instructed in the government and laws of that kingdom by proper degrees, until his mind is capable in some measure of comprehending the propriety, justice, equality, and consistency of the same.*
> —JOSEPH SMITH, *HISTORY OF THE CHURCH,* 2:8.

The attributes of success in the quest to become more like the Savior are really crowned with diligence, meaning devotion and perseverance. Diligence is an attribute we aspire to gain as we seek to take upon ourselves the divine nature. Diligence is the glow of commitment that moves us forward as we prepare ourselves in every needful way to enter the temple—whether for the first time or frequently thereafter. Diligence is the power of momentum as we strive to attain our spiritual goals. When one is dedicated, steadfast, and loyal to the cause, success is a welcome outcome. Devotion and perseverance—the two complementary aspects of diligence—compensate for so many inadequacies. We should all seek to maintain diligence in following the counsel of Nephi: "Wherefore, ye must press forward with a steadfastness in Christ, having a perfect brightness of hope, and a love of God and of all men. Wherefore, if ye shall press forward, feasting upon the word of Christ, and endure to the end, behold, thus saith the Father: Ye shall have eternal life" (2 Ne. 31:20).

Those whose hearts and minds are imbued with a living testimony of the gospel thrive on diligence and inspire diligence in those they serve. As President Thomas S. Monson declared: "To the . . . question, 'What prompts such devotion on the part of every worker?' the answer can be stated simply: an individual testimony of the gospel of the Lord Jesus Christ, even a heartfelt desire to love the Lord with all one's heart, mind, and soul, and one's neighbor as oneself" (*Be Your Best Self* [Salt Lake City: Deseret Book, 1979], 181).

Diligence in our activities to prepare for the temple can be enhanced through some of following strategies:

Build persistence into your goals from the beginning. Commit to following eternal principles. Set goals about which you have passion strong enough to sustain you through the rough times (see Alma 21:23; 27:27). Prepare thoroughly; preparation precedes power and ensures that you will not fear (see D&C 38:30).

Follow a plan of resilience. Have a vision, but divide it into a sequence of little victories that you can measure on a daily and weekly basis. Break your plan down into the critically important things you need to do each day to move forward. Take reversals in stride by having alternate routes in mind to attain your goal. Keep your commitment to your purposes with all your heart, mind, and strength. Never give up. Use a systematic timetable for your temple preparation: study the scriptures every day, pray to be ready, spend time on the temple grounds, talk with your loved ones and trusted colleagues and friends, counsel with your Church leaders, and invoke the Spirit to help you stay on track. Never, never give up.

Have an active team in place. Develop and pursue your goals cooperatively with your loved ones and associates. Working as a team to reach meaningful objectives—such as going to the temple—will augment and magnify devotion and persistence. Follow the example of heroes of diligence, past and present: the prophets, the pioneers, your forebears who plied the trails of sacrifice and devotion. Pray for the wisdom, willpower, and strength to succeed at all your worthy goals.

Keep the rewards in mind. Take time each day to remember your covenants and commitments, rise to your highest potential, serve the best interests of your loved ones and friends, make your home and community a better place, and build a reputation of persistence and industry. The rewards of being diligent in the faith will be gratitude, togetherness, satisfaction, peace, harmony, and happiness. The testimony of industry and loyalty that we record in the pages of our own book of life will contribute lasting value to the dynamic chronicle of how the kingdom of God expands and grows in this, the last dispensation of the gospel.

President Gordon B. Hinckley has given us this inspiring portrait of how our diligence plays an important role in furthering the Lord's design to bless all of humanity:

> We serve as teachers in quorums and auxiliary organizations; we serve as missionaries at home and abroad; we serve as researchers in family history and as temple workers—hopefully each with diligence in our little corner—and from all of this there emerges a remarkable and wonderful pattern, a phenomenon grand in its comprehensiveness, as

broad as the earth and encompassing all of the generations of men.

If each of us does not do well that which is his or hers to do, then there is a flaw in the entire pattern. The whole tapestry is injured. But if each of us does well his or her part, then there is strength and beauty.

I need not remind you that this cause in which we are engaged is not an ordinary cause. It is the cause of Christ. It is the kingdom of God our Eternal Father. It is the building of Zion on the earth, the fulfillment of prophecy given of old and of a vision revealed in this dispensation. (*Ensign*, Nov. 1989, 51)

Monuments of Diligence

When in February 1846 the Saints were forced to evacuate their beloved Nauvoo—the City of Joseph—and move onward yet again in their quest for peace and security, they left their magnificent temple behind. Parley P. Pratt reminisced about that occasion: "Our houses, our farms, this Temple and all we leave will be a monument to those who may visit the place of our industry, diligence and virtue. . . . There is no sacrifice required at the hands of the people of God but shall be rewarded to them an hundred fold, in time or eternity" (*Ensign*, July 2005, 40).

Following the exodus, Brigham Young stated in a general epistle to the Church dated December 23, 1847, at Winter Quarters, the following regarding the Saints' diligence:

> Thousands have since been wandering to and fro, destitute, afflicted, and distressed for the common necessaries of life, or, unable to endure, have sickened and died by hundreds, while the Temple of the Lord is left solitary in the midst of our enemies, an enduring monument of the diligence and integrity of the Saints. . . . Come, then, ye Saints of Latter-day, and all ye great and small, wise and foolish, rich and poor, noble and ignoble, exalted and persecuted, rulers and ruled of the earth, who love virtue and hate vice, and help us to do this work, which the Lord hath required at

our hands; and inasmuch as the glory of the latter house shall exceed that of the former, your reward shall be an hundred fold, and your rest shall be glorious. Our universal motto is, *"Peace with God and good will to all men."* (quoted in *Ensign,* July 1971, 37; emphasis in original)

"Peace with God and good will to all men" is indeed an appropriate motto for all gospel service and especially for temple service. Temples are monuments of diligence and peace. The edifices of the kingdom of God, including the sacred temples, do not feature the symbol of the cross so pervasive throughout Christendom. The cross reminds us of the consummate sacrifice of the Lord on our behalf—something that we would do well to ponder at all times and especially as we partake of the sacrament. But the icon of the cross is transcended by the witness of the Resurrection and by the confirmation of the Spirit that the Savior overcame death and became the Author of eternal life: "I am the light of the world: he that followeth me shall not walk in darkness, but shall have the light of life" (John 8:12). If the cross, then, is not the symbol of our faith, what is? Faithful temple-goers themselves are the primary monuments of diligence and fortitude. President Gordon B. Hinckley emphasized this point some years ago, on the occasion of the open house for the newly renovated temple in Mesa, Arizona, when a Protestant minister inquired of him why our Church buildings do not display the cross as a monument of our Christian faith. President Hinckley responded thus:

> I do not wish to give offense to any of my Christian colleagues who use the cross on the steeples of their cathedrals and at the altars of their chapels, who wear it on their vestments, and imprint it on their books and other literature. But for us, the cross is the symbol of the dying Christ, while our message is a declaration of the Living Christ.
>
> He then asked: "If you do not use the cross, what is the symbol of your religion?"
>
> I replied that the lives of our people must become the most meaningful expression of our faith and, in fact, therefore, the symbol of our worship. (*Ensign,* Apr. 2005, 3)

Truly our preparation for entering the temple of God is a preparation for exemplary diligence. It is an exercise in allowing our inner light to be manifested to the world. The Savior said in the Sermon on the Mount: "Ye are the light of the world. A city that is set on an hill cannot be hid. Neither do men light a candle, and put it under a bushel, but on a candlestick; and it giveth light unto all that are in the house. Let your light so shine before men, that they may see your good works, and glorify your Father which is in heaven" (Matt. 5:14–16).

The light of the gospel is universal. All are invited to receive it and allow it to resonate within their lives. "Blessed are the poor in spirit," declared the Lord during His ministry, "for theirs is the kingdom of heaven" (Matt. 5:3). Faithful and diligent sons and daughters of God in all walks of life bring forth the light of the gospel in their lives as they increase in spirituality, productivity, and service. Elder Richard G. Scott of the Quorum of the Twelve described this process in the following story of inspiration:

> I know that the plan of happiness can lift and bless those who live it anywhere.
>
> On Christmas Eve 37 years ago, in the light of a full moon, I climbed a small hill in the isolated village of Quiriza, Bolivia. Four young elders and I had spent the day crossing over a mountain pass on a treacherous road. Then we struggled up a riverbed to see if the teachings of the Savior would help a destitute people. What we saw that day was discouraging—undernourished children, adults subsisting on meager crops, some with eyes glazed from seeking refuge with alcohol and drugs. I looked at the tiny, barren village below: a cluster of adobe thatched-roof houses beaten by the harsh environment. The only evidence of life was barking dogs searching for food. There was no electricity, telephone, running water, roads, proper sanitation, nor doctors there. It seemed so hopeless. Yet a solemn prayer confirmed that we should be there. We found a humble people who embraced the restored gospel with determination to live it. They did that under harsh

conditions where severe poverty, alcohol, drugs, witchcraft, and immorality were in plentiful supply.

Under the guidance of exceptional missionaries, the people learned to work hard to cultivate the fields. They produced a harvest of nutritious vegetables and raised rabbits for better protein. But the best lessons came from beloved missionaries who taught them of a God who loved them, of a Savior who gave His life that they might succeed. Their physical appearance began to change. The light of truth radiated from their happy faces. As devoted, loving emissaries of the Lord, missionaries patiently taught truth to a willing people. Wives and husbands learned how to live in harmony, teach truth to their children, pray, and sense guidance of the Spirit. . . .

As you continue to center your mind and heart in [the Lord], He will help you have a rich and full life no matter what happens in the world around you. (*Ensign,* May 2004, 100)

Our youth, especially, are grateful for the opportunity to render diligent service in the temples of the Lord as they perform baptisms for the dead. This is particularly true when they also complete their own family history work and bring with them to the temple the names of their forebears so that they can perform the vicarious service in behalf of their own ancestors. This kind of service brings immeasurable joy, as Don L. Searle, managing editor of the *Ensign,* illustrated in the following story:

> When young members of the Carlsbad Ward, Roswell New Mexico Stake, began preparing for their annual excursion to the Dallas Texas Temple, they knew their experience would be different from that of previous years: this time they were committed to provide names of their own ancestors for temple ordinances.
>
> Paul Hanna, ward Young Men president, says these temple experiences and the preparations for them brought home to the young people "that they have family that have gone on before them." Now those ancestors "are not just names. They're real people. They lived."

> Brother Hanna had noted the diligence of these youth in preparing for the temple excursion, had seen many of them show great spiritual sensitivity as they searched out their ancestors. But now, seeing them in the temple, he was reminded that "it won't be too many years until they're the leaders of the Church. It gave me confidence in the leadership we'll have in the future." (*Ensign,* Feb. 1997, 54)

Truly, diligence is the mortar that binds together the segments of our ongoing campaigns and efforts to help build the kingdom of God in faith and obedience to the principles of the gospel. Preparing with diligence to enter the house of the Lord will pay enormous dividends in the form of divine blessings for now and for the eternities.

Additional Inspired Counsel from the Prophets

Let us give heed to the advice and counsel of the Lord's anointed regarding the need for diligence as we move forward toward the temple. Here are a few examples:

The Prophet Joseph Smith:
In conclusion we would say, brethren and sisters, be faithful, be diligent, contend earnestly for the faith once delivered to the Saints; let every man, woman and child realize the importance of the work, and act as if success depended on his individual exertion alone; let all feel an interest in it. (*HC,* 4:214)

President Brigham Young:
They who secure eternal life are doers of the word as well as hearers. (*Discourses,* 290)

President Lorenzo Snow:
We should be diligent in God's service. Having received the light of the everlasting gospel, and partaken of the good things of the kingdom, and being of the seed of Israel and heirs to great and glorious promises, we should labor with fidelity and diligence to accomplish what God has designed to do through us. We should be men and women of faith

and power as well as good works; and when we discover ourselves careless or indifferent in the least, it should be sufficient for us to know it in order to mend our ways and return to the path of duty. (*TLS,* 48; emphasis in original)

President Joseph F. Smith:
In Christ's Church we cannot be neutral or inert. We must either progress or retrograde. It is necessary for the Latter-day Saints to keep pushing on in order that they may keep their faith alive and their spirits quickened to the performance of their duties. Let us remember that we are engaged in God's work—and when I say God's work, I mean that we are engaged in the work which the Almighty has instituted in the earth for our salvation individually. Every man should be laboring for his own good and as far as possible for the good of others. There is no such thing in the science of life as a man laboring exclusively for himself. We are not intended to be alone in time nor in eternity. Each individual is a unit in the household of faith, and each unit must feel his or her proportion of the responsibility that devolves upon the whole. Each individual must be diligent in performing his duty. (*Gospel Doctrine,* 115)

In all of these sayings we are counseled to step forward with courage and diligence to perform the Lord's work, just as He commanded us: "Verily I say, men should be anxiously engaged in a good cause, and do many things of their own free will, and bring to pass much righteousness" (D&C 58:27). To follow this divine counsel in all diligence is to act in accordance with the Lord's specific instruction to "enlarge the place of thy tent, and let them stretch forth the curtains of thine habitations: spare not, lengthen thy cords, and strengthen thy stakes" (Isa. 54:2). To lengthen the cords of the kingdom and to strengthen her stakes and stretch out her curtains is accomplished more fully as each individual in the fold lengthens his or her steps forward in all diligence. Perhaps the most celebrated formulation of this principle originated with President Spencer W. Kimball, who counseled: "Let us 'lengthen our stride.' So much depends upon our willingness to make up our minds, collectively and individually, that present levels of performance are not acceptable, either to ourselves or to the Lord" (*TSWK,* 174).

The temple is a house of diligence—the diligence of all who have labored to place the temples in service, the diligence of the faithful temple workers who provide selfless service to keep the temples running smoothly according to divine authority and protocol, and the diligence of all who prepare themselves humbly and devotedly to enter these sacred halls of learning with a willingness to make enduring covenants. The Lord declared, "Let the work of my temple . . . be continued on and not cease; and let your diligence, and your perseverance, and patience, and your works be redoubled, and you shall in nowise lose your reward" (D&C 127:4).

To dedicate ourselves in diligence to the work of the temples is, in many respects, analogous to the process by which finished temples are dedicated to the Lord. Here are the inspiring words from the dedication of the Kirtland Temple:

> That thy glory may rest down upon thy people, and upon this thy house, which we now dedicate to thee, that it may be sanctified and consecrated to be holy, and that thy holy presence may be continually in this house; And that all people who shall enter upon the threshold of the Lord's house may feel thy power, and feel constrained to acknowledge that thou hast sanctified it, and that it is thy house, a place of thy holiness. (D&C 109:12–13)

By extension of this process, let us pray to the Lord that His glory may rest upon our own diligent preparations to enter His house and that we may be capacitated thereby to feel His power within the temple and be able to rejoice and acknowledge that the temple is, indeed, a place of holiness.

Time to Meditate and Ponder

1. The Prophet Joseph Smith promised that our faculty for learning would be enlarged "in proportion to the heed and diligence given to

the light communicated from heaven" (*HC,* 2:8). How does this provide encouragement for our preparations to enter the temple?

2. Nephi taught us: "Wherefore, ye must press forward with a steadfastness in Christ, having a perfect brightness of hope, and a love of God and of all men. Wherefore, if ye shall press forward, feasting upon the word of Christ, and endure to the end, behold, thus saith the Father: Ye shall have eternal life" (2 Ne. 31:20). How does this relate specifically to our preparations for entering the temple?

3. Many others are willing to assist us in our diligent preparations for the temple. How can we recognize their desire to help and enlist their support as we move forward?

4. How are the temples of God enduring monuments to diligence?

5. Even more than the temples, those who attend the temple are fitting monuments to diligence and faith. President Gordon B. Hinckley has declared: "The lives of our people must become the most meaningful expression of our faith and, in fact, therefore, the symbol of our worship" (*Ensign,* Apr. 2005, 3). How can you personally be a fulfillment of that very prophetic observation?

6. Lorenzo Snow taught, "The most important work that Latter-day Saints can do on this earth is that of opening the door for the salvation of their kindred dead" (*TLS,* 96). How does this statement help us magnify our diligence in preparing for temple work?

7. President Spencer W. Kimball is celebrated for his motto: "Lengthen your stride" (*TSWK,* 174). How can we "lengthen our stride" with respect to our own program of preparing to enter the house of the Lord?

PART TWO
ENTERING THE TEMPLE

Guiding Principle: The temple is a place of spiritual transformation. Those who attend the temple in devotion and faithfulness find so often that burdens are rendered lighter, cares are changed into opportunities for prevailing in the strength of the Lord, and anxiety is transformed into peace and hope through the power of the gospel to enliven within us the promise of the Lord for a life everlasting with our eternal family.

> *Blessings of Temple Service: Take advantage of the blessings of the house of the Lord. What a privilege. Every man or woman who goes to the temple comes out of that building a better man or woman than he or she was when entering into it. That's something that's remarkable that happens with all of us. Is life filled with cares for you? Do you have problems and concerns and worries? Do you want for peace in your heart and an opportunity to commune with the Lord and meditate upon His way? Go to the house of the Lord and there feel of His spirit and commune with Him and you will know a peace that you will find nowhere else. Take advantage of it. What a great and wonderful blessing it is.*
> —GORDON B. HINCKLEY, "EXCERPTS FROM RECENT ADDRESSES OF PRESIDENT GORDON B. HINCKLEY," *ENSIGN*, APR. 1996, 72.

CHAPTER 14
OBTAINING A TEMPLE RECOMMEND

Guiding Principle: The authentic temple recommend is written upon the heart of the individual, just as Jeremiah prophesied concerning the latter-day Restoration: "But this shall be the covenant that I will make with the house of Israel; After those days, saith the Lord, I will put my law in their inward parts, and write it in their hearts; and will be their God, and they shall be my people" (Jer. 31:33). Because we are the people of the Lord, we bear our temple recommends in our hearts and in our countenances—for therein is the confirmation of our personal worthiness to enter the house of the Lord, having done our utmost to take upon ourselves the divine nature in all its aspects.

> *What a unique and remarkable thing is a temple recommend. It is only a piece of paper with a name and signatures, but in reality it is a certificate that says the bearer is "honest, true, chaste, benevolent, virtuous" and that he or she believes in doing good to all, that "if there is anything virtuous, lovely, or of good report or praiseworthy," he or she seeks after such. (A of F 1:13.)*
> —GORDON B. HINCKLEY, "KEEPING THE TEMPLE HOLY," *ENSIGN*, MAY 1990, 52.

Jacob, brother of Nephi, provided priceless counsel to the Saints of his day concerning their ultimate return to the presence of the Savior: "O then, my beloved brethren, come unto the Lord, the Holy One. Remember that his paths are righteous. Behold, the way for man is narrow, but it lieth in a straight course before him, and the keeper of the gate is the Holy One of Israel; and he employeth no servant there; and there is none other way save it be by the gate; for he cannot be deceived, for the Lord God is his name. And whoso knocketh, to him will he open" (2 Ne. 9:41–42).

When we return to the gates of our heavenly home, we will be met there by the Savior in person, for "he employeth no servant there." In the temples of the Lord, on this side of the veil, He does indeed employ trusted and valiant servants to greet us at the gates and welcome us into these sacred precincts of holiness. Those servants are priesthood officials who are called to represent the Lord in His house and assigned to confirm our worthiness to enter. They do so by examining the temple recommend that we have received from our local leaders—and by discerning from our demeanor and aura of spirituality that we are honorably presenting ourselves as worthy to come into the temple.

The temple recommend is a precious document. It confirms our compliance with the standards and ideals of the gospel of Jesus Christ. It bears the endorsement signatures of our bishop and stake president as judges in Israel. It bears our own personal signature as a witness before God that we have truthfully answered the searching questions of worthiness, that we are authentic disciples of Jesus Christ with the desire and commitment to become more like the Savior, and that we now seek further light and knowledge in His holy house. The recommend functions much like a passport that gives us authorized access to new frontiers. It is a comfort and a joy to the bearer who holds this certificate in trust as evidence of goodwill and humble devotion to the Lord. President Gordon B. Hinckley confirmed this point in regard to temple service:

> Let us work toward qualifying every member of this Church to hold a temple recommend. That is the passport

to the house of the Lord. That is the passport to the place where we glimpse a little of heaven. That is the passport to the place where we lose ourselves in the service of others. That is the passport to the place where we always come away better men and women than we were when we entered. (*TGBH*, 631)

President Hinkley also stated:

> I would hope that every Latter-day Saint who is old enough would have a temple recommend. It says something. It is a priceless, priceless thing to have a temple recommend. It says that we are faithful, that we are doing what we ought to be doing, that we are living the gospel, that we are sustaining our authorities, that we are observing the Word of Wisdom, that we are paying our tithing, that we are treating our families properly, that we are treating our neighbors properly, that we are the kind of people we ought to be. Perhaps you cannot get to the temple very often. But even if you cannot get to the temple, I would like to suggest that you go to your bishops and get a temple recommend and carry it with you and regard it as a precious and true thing. It is a credit card, if you please, with the Lord. (*TGBH*, 631–32)

QUESTIONS CONCERNING THE TEMPLE RECOMMEND

Who are the judges in Israel that certify recommends?

Those who have the responsibility to confirm our worthiness to enter the temple are the bishops and stake presidents in Zion. Prior to 1891, the President of the Church was the one to sign temple recommends. After that, the responsibility was given to bishops and stake presidents. These leaders are our brothers in the gospel who have a commitment to serve the Lord and maintain the order, vitality, and glory of the kingdom of God. Thank heaven that we have honorable leaders among us whose only motivation is to do good and tend the vineyard of the Lord with an eye single to His glory. Theirs is a "labour of love," as Paul described it (Heb. 6:10). Their service inspires gratitude in the hearts of the faithful, much as Paul extolled the exemplary devotion of his colleagues: "We give thanks to God always for you all, making mention of you in our prayers; Remembering without ceasing your work of faith, and labour of love, and patience of hope in our Lord Jesus Christ, in the sight of God and our Father; Knowing, brethren beloved, your election of God" (1 Thes. 1:2–4; see also Philip. 1:3–5; 2 Thes. 1:3).

As we look forward in our preparations to enter the temple, we can depend on the wisdom and honor of the judges in Israel (see D&C 58:17; 107:72, 76) who give us the opportunity to express ourselves in regard to specific questions of worthiness. They are the stewards of righteousness and the curators of obedience in the context of the eternities.

It is a sacred obligation of a Zion people to ensure that the temple is kept sacred and holy. Those who attend the temple worthily do so with the conviction that they have done all in their power to comply with the standards of temple service. Those who stand as stewards at the gates of the temple are watchful and diligent in sanctioning entry to the Lord's house. In all that we do, we reach out to others in the spirit of love and encouragement, supporting them in their preparations to go the temple—the symbol of the infinite and eternal upon the landscape of mortality. "Everything that occurs in the temple is eternal in its consequences," observed President Gordon B. Hinckley. "I submit that every man who holds the Melchizedek Priesthood has an obligation to see that the house of the Lord is kept sacred and free of any defilement. This obligation rests primarily and inescapably upon the shoulders of bishops and stake presidents. They become the judges of worthiness concerning those eligible to enter the temple. Additionally, each of us has an obligation—first, as to his own personal worthiness, and secondly, as to the worthiness of those whom he may encourage or assist in going to the house of the Lord (*Ensign,* May 1990, 50).

The temple recommend is, in a way, a covenant to keep our covenants. It is a document to which we affix our signature of compliance with specific standards established by the Lord as a means to ensure that we receive choice blessings of the eternities. Our priesthood leaders also sign this document as an expression of their faith in our commitment to align our lives with the example of the Savior. President N. Eldon Tanner explained the essence of priesthood responsibility concerning the recommend procedure:

> You bishops and stake presidents might approach an interview for a temple recommend something like this:
>
> "You have come to me for a recommend to enter the temple. I have the responsibility of representing the Lord in interviewing you. At the conclusion of the interview there is provision for me to sign your recommend; but mine is not the only important signature on your recommend. Before the recommend is valid, you must sign it yourself." . . .
>
> And so it is. The Lord gives the privilege to members of the Church to respond to those questions in such interviews. Then if there is something amiss, the member can get his life in order so that he may qualify for the priesthood advancement, for a mission, or for a temple recommend. (*Ensign,* Nov. 1978, 42)

How long must one wait following baptism before seeking a temple recommend?

The period of time following baptism is at least one year—in order to allow sufficient opportunity for individuals to complete a thorough preparation, gain a solid foundation in gospel principles, and achieve a clear understanding of the purposes of the temple and the sacred nature of the covenant obligations that one accepts in going there. President Harold B. Lee explained this point as follows:

> We have a number of those who want to go to the temple soon after they have been baptized. It has been a long-standing rule now outlined in the [*General Handbook of Instructions*] which says it should be *at least* a year. We put that *at least* one year. The reason why we say at least a year is to hope that the bishops and stake presidents will interview carefully enough to make sure that they have

been in the Church long enough to have their feet on the ground and that they know the basic doctrines of the Church before we expect them to understand the higher ordinances, the temple ordinances. The questions then for those going to the temple should not be only for worthiness but also for readiness to receive the ordinances of the temple. (*THBL*, 584)

What is the proper age and maturity for youth doing baptisms for the dead?

The opportunity for young people to participate in baptisms for the dead is a singularly significant initiation into the sacred ordinances of the temple. Youth who regularly serve in this way establish a strong foundation of appreciation and understanding for the eternal implications of temple work. Those who seek to be recommended for this purpose need to demonstrate worthiness of character, show that they have a testimony of the gospel of Jesus Christ, and exhibit a high degree of maturity in spiritual matters. President Joseph Fielding Smith made the following observations concerning the worthiness of young people who seek to go to the temple:

> Children should not go to the temple until they are old enough to understand the purpose of their going. They should be taught the principles of the gospel, and to have faith in God, and in the mission of Jesus Christ, and should gain a testimony of the truth *before* they receive the blessings of the temple.
>
> I believe that a young man or a young woman should seek after these blessings in the temple, and just as soon as they are old enough to understand the meaning of temple ordinances, they should have them. Moreover, *they should not go to the temple until they do have a testimony of the truth and a knowledge of the gospel,* no matter how old they may be. It is not intended that these sacred covenants should be given to those who do not have faith and who have not proved themselves worthy by obedience to the gospel. (*DS,* 254; emphasis in original)

On March 11, 2003, the First Presidency distributed a letter in which the following counsel was included: "Millions of our ancestors have lived upon the earth without receiving the benefit of temple ordinances. We particularly encourage newer members and youth of the Church who are 12 years of age and older to live worthy to assist in this great work by serving as proxies for baptisms and confirmations" (*Liahona,* Mar. 2004, 47).

What is the nature of the temple recommend interview?

The temple recommend interview is not to be seen as an examination that one must pass. Rather, it is a milestone in our quest for becoming more like the Savior. It is an opportunity to go forward with the assurance that we are doing all in our power to align ourselves with the saving truths of the gospel. It is a conversation with our trusted leaders in which we are candid and truthful about our progress in becoming worthy of the Lord's choicest blessings. It is an audience of confidentiality with those who rejoice with us in the good that we have accomplished and encourage us to do better continually. Elder Richard G. Scott provided the following general overview concerning the recommend interview process:

> If you are now ready to receive the ordinances of the temple, prepare carefully for that crowning event. Before entering the temple, you will be interviewed by your bishop and stake president for your temple recommend. Be honest and candid with them. That interview is not a test to be passed but an important step to confirm that you have the maturity and spirituality to receive the supernal ordinances and make and keep the edifying covenants offered in the house of the Lord. Personal worthiness is an essential requirement to enjoy the blessings of the temple. Anyone foolish enough to enter the temple unworthily will receive condemnation. (*Ensign,* May 1999, 5)

The interview reviews several vital issues relating to worthiness, including honesty and moral cleanliness. It gives us the opportunity to confirm our commitment to live a life of purity and valor—that we are willing to separate ourselves from embracing the ways of the world and distinguish ourselves, as Peter declared, as part of God's kingdom: "But ye are a chosen generation, a royal priesthood, an holy nation, a peculiar people; that ye should shew forth the praises of him who hath called you out of darkness into his marvellous light" (1 Pet. 2:9). The issues concerning temple worthiness are of vital importance in the grand scheme of our eternal happiness. "Why are these issues so crucial?" inquired Elder Russell M. Nelson. He gave this response:

> Because they are spiritual separators. They help to determine if we truly live as children of the covenant, able to resist temptation from servants of sin. These interviews help to discern if we are willing to live in accord with the will of the true and living God or if our hearts are still set upon riches and . . . vain things of the world.
>
> Such requirements are not difficult to understand. Because the temple is the house of the Lord, standards for admission are set by Him. One enters as His guest. To hold a temple recommend is a priceless privilege and a tangible sign of obedience to God and His prophets. (*Ensign,* May 2001, 32)

Temple worthiness embraces many interrelated factors, including, among other things, our faith and testimony, our sustaining of the Lord's chosen servants, our moral cleanliness, our relationships of harmony with family members, our honesty, our activity and service in the Church, and our compliance with the law of tithing and the Word of Wisdom. In an article entitled "Your Temple Recommend," published in the *New Era* (Apr. 1995, 6–9), President Howard W. Hunter summarized these key issues covered in the temple recommend interview as follows:

> You must believe in God the Eternal Father, in his Son Jesus Christ, and in the Holy Ghost
>
> You must sustain the General Authorities and local authorities of the Church.
>
> You must be morally clean to enter into the holy temple.

> You must ensure that there is nothing in your relationship with family members that is out of harmony with the teachings of the Church.
>
> To enter the temple you must be honest in all of your dealings with others.
>
> To qualify for a temple recommend, you should strive to do your duty in the Church, attending your sacrament, priesthood, and other meetings.
>
> To enter the temple you must be a full-tithe payer and live the Word of Wisdom.

Going to the temple is a sacred privilege reserved for the faithful and obedient in the fold of Christ. Those who go there are focused on the things of eternity. They seek within those walls the blessings of a merciful God who endows His children with the powers and rights of perpetuating the family beyond the grave and guides them to make all preparations to return one day to His presence. President Hunter emphasizes in the same article: "The temples we dedicate are dedicated to our Heavenly Father. These temples are his houses, built in his name for his glory and for his purposes. Our hearts and hands must be clean and pure and our thoughts must be focused on things of an eternal nature when we go to the temple. We hope you will feel that entering the temple is a privilege given to worthy Church members and not a right that automatically comes with Church membership" (*New Era,* Apr. 1995, 6).

What is the obligation regarding the temple garment?

The temple garment is a symbol of worthiness to be in the house of the Lord. Within the temple, all have similar attire. White is the bonding color. This practice is a unifying manifestation that all of God's children are alike before Him and that all can be blessed in equal measure with the opportunity to come into His presence one day, having lived a life of purity and worthiness, having endured to the end. Elder John A. Widtsoe explained this point as follows:

> In the temples all are dressed alike in white. White is the symbol of purity. No unclean person has the right to enter

God's house. Besides, the uniform dress symbolizes that before God our Father in heaven, all men are equal. The beggar and the banker, the learned and the unlearned, the prince and the pauper sit side by side in the temple and are of equal importance if they live righteously before the Lord God, the Father of their spirits. It is spiritual fitness and understanding that one receives in the temple. All such have an equal place before the Lord. (*Ensign,* Jan. 1972, 56)

Those who participate in temple ordinances are clothed in the garments of the holy priesthood. The garment serves as a shield and protection for the Saints, and a reminder of sacred covenants they have entered into. Following the reception of the temple endowment, the garment is to be worn at all times. (See *Ensign,* Aug. 1997, 19–23.)

How frequently does one renew a temple recommend?

Under current practice, a recommend is valid for a period of two years.

How does one dress when entering the temple?

We present ourselves before the Lord in His holy house attired in our Sunday best. The temple is a place of dignity and neatness. In the temple we change into the white clothing designated for temple service, with all sisters dressed alike, and all brethren dressed alike—all mingling as equals before the Lord, all reflecting a spirit of camaraderie as "fellowcitizens with the saints, and of the household of God" (Eph. 2:19). Elder Russell M. Nelson has provided this counsel concerning attire to wear when going to the temple:

> One prepares physically for the temple by dressing properly. It is not a place for casual attire. "We should dress in such a way that we might comfortably attend a sacrament meeting or a gathering that is proper and dignified."
>
> "Within the temple, all are dressed in spotless white to remind us that God is to have a pure people." Nationality, language, or position in the Church are of secondary

significance. In that democracy of dress, all sit side by side and are considered equal in the eyes of our Maker.

Brides and grooms enter the temple to be married for time and all eternity. There brides wear white dresses—long sleeved, modest in design and fabric, and free of elaborate ornamentation. Grooms also dress in white. And brethren who come to witness weddings do not wear tuxedos. (*Ensign*, May 2001, 32)

The temple provides us with the opportunity to set aside, for a time, the casualness of the world. We come forward with the deportment of reverence in how we dress and speak. We come with good cheer—for that is a commandment of the Lord (see D&C 61:36; 68:6)—but also with the desire to follow the Lord's counsel to "let the solemnities of eternity rest upon your minds" (D&C 43:34). Elder L. Aldin Porter confirmed this instruction as follows: "The world's standards tend to be very casual in dress and speech. But we must not be casual as we take upon ourselves the teachings, ordinances, and covenants of the temple. I hope young adults will come to the temple dressed in their Sunday best, displaying an attitude of reverence in dress, actions, and speech. We can learn what the Lord has for us only if we attend the temple in a sacred and respectful way" (*New Era*, Oct. 2004, 8).

An Example of Faith: The Precious Recommend

Faith and courage are precursors to obtaining a temple recommend. Anne C. Pingree, second counselor in the Relief Society general presidency, tells this moving story about faithful Saints in West Africa who endured all hardships to obtain temple recommends:

> I will never forget a sauna-hot day in the lush rain forest of southeastern Nigeria. My husband and I had traveled to one of the most remote locations in our mission so he could conduct temple recommend interviews with members in the Ikot Eyo district. Some in this growing district had been Church members less than two years. All

the members lived 3,000 miles away from the nearest temple in Johannesburg, South Africa. None had received their temple endowment.

These members knew the appointed day each month we would come to their district, but even we didn't know the exact hour we would arrive; nor could we call, for telephones were rare in that part of West Africa. So these committed African Saints gathered early in the morning to wait all day if necessary for their temple recommend interviews. When we arrived, I noticed among those waiting in the searing heat were two Relief Society sisters dressed in bold-patterned wrappers, white blouses, and the traditional African head-ties.

Many hours later, after all the interviews were completed, as my husband and I drove back along that sandy jungle trail, we were stunned when we saw these two sisters still walking. We realized they had trekked from their village—a distance of 18 miles round trip—just to obtain a temple recommend they knew they would never have the privilege of using. (*Ensign,* Nov. 2003, 13)

In that same spirit, may we all seek to obtain and maintain a temple recommend with full devotion and commitment to the cause of eternal happiness. When we meet the Savior at the gates of the Holy City on that glorious day, we shall not, in all likelihood, present a document certifying our worthiness—rather, we will *be* that document. Our hearts will reflect the light of the gospel. Our minds will be sanctified. Our eyes will emit the radiance of purity. Our voice will be the voice of gladness and gratitude. Our demeanor will be one of humility and complete submission to the will of the Lord. Our spirit will be rendered holy through the grace of the Atonement and by our having endured to the end in obedience. Let us work in all diligence and faith toward that moment.

Time to Meditate and Ponder

1. Jacob declared that "the keeper of the gate is the Holy One of Israel; and he employeth no servant there" (2 Ne. 9:41). How is

presenting a temple recommend at the front desk of the temple analogous to knocking on the door and seeking to come in unto the Lord, the "keeper of the gate"?

2. President Gordon B. Hinckley has referred to a temple recommend as a "passport to the house of the Lord" (*TGBH*, 631). How is a recommend similar to a passport?

3. How are the bishops and stake presidents of the Church "judges in Israel" concerning temple worthiness?

4. Why is it essential for new converts to wait at least one year before seeking a temple recommend?

5. The Savior characterized the Saints as "children of the covenant" (3 Ne. 20:26). How does temple activity fulfill this characterization? How can we confirm that we are truly "children of the covenant"?

6. What is appropriate dress for entering the temple?

7. Why is it desirable to have a temple recommend even if we do not have ready access to a temple?

CHAPTER 15
UNDERSTANDING THE SYMBOLISM OF THE TEMPLE

Guiding Principle: The temple confirms the presence and operation of the infinite within our finite mortal environment. It is the symbol of the divine origins of mankind in the premortal realms and the emblem of the glorious and eternal destiny of the Lord's faithful—by virtue of the grace of the Father and Son and the atoning sacrifice of the Messiah. Truly the temple is a witness of the verity of God's plan of eternal salvation and exaltation for all mankind.

> *Each temple built by The Church of Jesus Christ of Latter-day Saints stands as an expression of the testimony of this people that God our Eternal Father lives, that He has a plan for the blessing of His sons and daughters of all generations, that His Beloved Son, Jesus the Christ, who was born in Bethlehem of Judea and crucified on the cross of Golgotha, is the Savior and Redeemer of the world, whose atoning sacrifice makes possible the fulfillment of that plan in the eternal life of each who accepts and lives the gospel. Every temple, be it large or small, old or new, is an expression of our testimony that life beyond the grave is as real and certain as is mortality. There would be no need for temples if the human spirit and soul were not eternal. Every ordinance performed in these sacred houses is everlasting in its consequences.*
> —GORDON B. HINCKLEY, "THIS PEACEFUL HOUSE OF GOD," *ENSIGN*, MAY 1993, 72.

The temple rises in magnificence. It points toward the heavens. It emits light from its beautiful windows. It lifts the spirit upward with a force of buoyancy and edification. In fact, the word *edify* derives linguistically from a Latin word meaning to build a building (or edifice)—in this case a temple of God. The very shape and structure of the temple is a manifestation of the doctrines and truths that govern and define its operation and function—for the temple is concerned with lifting us upward into the presence of God through light and truth. The lofty image of the Angel Moroni on the topmost pinnacle of the temple, trumpet raised to sound the good news of the gospel, is a reminder of the vision of John the Revelator: "And I saw another angel fly in the midst of heaven, having the everlasting gospel to preach unto them that dwell on the earth, and to every nation, and kindred, and tongue, and people, Saying with a loud voice, Fear God, and give glory to him; for the hour of his judgment is come: and worship him that made heaven, and earth, and the sea, and the fountains of waters" (Rev. 14:6–7).

Those who are preparing to enter the temple of God are well advised to spend some time—where that is possible—on the grounds of the temple. There they will feel the spirit of these grand houses of holiness long before they enter through the doorway and into the inner chambers of peace and glory. Temple grounds are also sacred places that are dedicated to the Lord. Such grounds invite visitors to come there to meditate and consider things of eternity. Temple grounds are frequently sites where landscape architects have provided a rich tapestry of verdure and floral grandeur to delight the eye and gladden the heart.

The temple buildings themselves reflect a high commitment to quality and structural excellence. We want to present before the Lord houses that represent the very highest imperatives of craftsmanship and artistry, for they represent His home on earth. Said President Gordon B. Hinckley: "We have been criticized for the cost of these structures, a cost which results from the exceptional quality of the workmanship and the materials that go into them. Those who criticize do not understand that these houses are dedicated as the abode of

Deity and, as Brigham Young stated, are to stand through the Millennium" (*Ensign,* May 1993, 72).

Truly the temples are constructed according to the highest standards of architectural excellence so that they will be fitting venues for accommodating priesthood ordinances of the highest standards of eternal truth—those relating to celestial exaltation.

Both without and within, the temple serves as a symbol of the majesty of the gospel of Jesus Christ and its exalting principles. Scholar Victor L. Ludlow explains some of the details of this structural symbolism:

> The purpose of temples—uniting people and preparing them for eternity—is expressed in the location and design of the buildings themselves. Whenever possible, temples are built in a central location, representing the center of the earth, or on elevated ground, representing the meeting of earth with heaven. . . .
>
> The external structure and foundation of most temples is rectangular, and the interior design and upper levels usually include a circular or a progressive pattern focused on the celestial room as one comes from the temple courtyard or grounds into the temple itself. . . . The rectangular shape establishes a firm footing and recalls the gathering from the four corners of the earth; the circular design gathers us together and reminds us that all the elect are joined into one eternal family, like a circle that has no beginning and no end. . . .
>
> Each building is usually mounted by one or more spires ascending into heaven, for the temple is where Saints receive revelation from God, and only through the ordinances of the temple do they gain passage to him in the celestial realm. (Victor L. Ludlow, *Principles and Practices of the Restored Gospel* [Salt Lake City: Deseret Book, 1992], 363)

The temples of God reflect a seamless blend of symbolism and functionality. The structure of the temple is designed to be highly conducive to efficiency and reverence in carrying out the sacred business of the institution. Initially, the visitor notes that the purpose and character of the temple are memorialized through the external inscriptions "House of the Lord" and "Holiness to the Lord." One passes through the doorway of the temple into the foyer and comes up to the recommend desk, where gracious and pleasant officials dressed in white suits examine temple recommends and confirm worthiness to enter the temple. Already the symbolic overtones of our preparation to enter the presence of God are impressed upon the soul.

Within the temple are beautifully decorated gathering rooms and hallways leading to the various sections of activity: dressing rooms to prepare for temple participation, a baptismal chamber for carrying out baptismal ordinances for the dead, a chapel for meditating and bringing together groups of people for orderly movement into the endowment sessions, rooms for the initiatory ordinances of washing and anointing, endowment rooms for instruction and participation in sacred covenants, and the celestial room as the pinnacle of the endowment experience—symbolically reflective of coming into the presence of God and partaking of His rest and glory. In addition, the temple has smaller sealing rooms for performing the sealing ordinances of the temple, including eternal marriage. Some temples contain larger auditoriums where priesthood gatherings can take place in the form of solemn assemblies for special instruction and worship.

The temple can readily kindle within us distant memories of our premortal life in the heavenly realms of the Creator. There is a sense of familiarity within the walls of the temple, for the cleanliness and holiness of those rooms can easily evoke within us a quiet recollection of the grandeur of heaven, where we "received [our] first lessons in the world of spirits and were prepared to come forth in the due time of the Lord to labor in his vineyard for the salvation of the souls of men" (D&C 138:56). Vaughn J. Featherstone, a former member of the First Quorum of the Seventy, reminisced about the structural power of the temple to impress upon the soul the divine purposes of the plan of exaltation:

> "Holiness to the Lord" is a divine phrase that touches me deeply each time I read it on one of our temples. It is more

than a statement; it is a vision of eternal adoration and love for the Master. I know in my heart that I had a recollection of that phrase from my premortal life. As I go to the temple, the veil always seems thin. The first time I saw the solemn assembly room in the Salt Lake Temple, I felt that I had been there before. This was also true of the celestial room, the sealing rooms, and the rooms on the fourth floor where the Brethren meet. This does not contradict the doctrine of the Church, for in Moses 3:5 we read: "And every plant of the field before it was in the earth, and every herb of the field before it grew. For I, the Lord God, created all things, of which I have spoken, spiritually, before they were naturally upon the face of the earth." (Vaughn J. Featherstone, *More Purity Give Me* [Salt Lake City: Deseret Book, 1991], 127)

The temple is an integrated manifestation of symbolic truth. Often the smallest details participate in the glorious unfolding of divine principles before our eyes. Elder Boyd K. Packer of the Quorum of the Twelve points out that the symbolism of the temple is even reflected by the intricate carvings on the doorknobs in the Salt Lake Temple: "As you move from room to room and set your hand to turn the knob you find that pioneer craftsmen have carefully fashioned the design of the latch and lock. The tribute 'Holiness to the Lord' is engraved in circular fashion on each knob. When you enter this or any dedicated temple you are in the house of the Lord" (Boyd K. Packer, *The Holy Temple* [Salt Lake City: Bookcraft, 1980], 4).

Teaching Truth through Symbolism

The Lord is the Master Teacher. His house provides instruction for the eternities. During His mortal ministry, the Lord made abundant use of parables and analogies to confirm gospel principles and effect the transfer of truth to His disciples in miraculous and memorable ways. Likewise, symbolism and analogy abound in the presentations of the temple, where the chronicle of man's journey of life is unfolded in a panoramic view. This unfolding vision of the eternal work of

God in behalf of His children is imparted to the mind and heart through symbolic instruction that invites us to ponder reverently upon the truths being conveyed. Elder L. Aldin Porter, former president of the Salt Lake Temple, explained on one occasion what people can expect when they come to the temple to receive their own endowments:

> They come to make covenants, and they come to be taught. A temple recommend gives them entrance to the temple and the right to receive the ordinances and covenants, but it does not give them an education in the temple, the Lord's university. This education is going to take effort.
>
> Young adults shouldn't be surprised if some aspects of the temple seem a little confusing at first. In the scriptures, the Lord often teaches with parables and symbolism. He does so in the temple as well. Understanding the symbolism will require some pondering and prayer. If young adults will look, in faith, beyond the symbols, they will find lessons of eternal substance.
>
> What we learn and feel in the temple is largely determined by how reverent we are. Reverence is more than silence. Reverence is, among other things, a respect for sacred gifts. (*New Era,* Oct. 2004, 8)

The fabric of the gospel message, with its associated ordinances, is a blend of symbolism and instruction. The Lord, in His mercy, uses the everyday things of mortal reality to teach us the principles of salvation and exaltation. Baptism is reflective of birth and of a cleansing process (see Moses 6:59–60); the sacrament is reflective of taking nourishment—namely, the "bread of life" (John 6:35, 48) and the "living waters" (John 4:10; see also D&C 63:23); dressing becomes symbolic of taking upon ourselves the "armor of God" (see Eph. 6:10–18; D&C 27:15–18) and of donning the sacred garments of the temple; going through doorways and passing through veils becomes reflective of entering into the presence of God (see Matt. 7:7). Sacred symbolism supports the transfer of truth from the bosom of the Savior (see D&C 35:20) into the hearts and minds of the faithful and devout through the operation of the Spirit—"even the Comforter which was sent forth to teach the truth" (D&C 50:14).

When we go to the temple, we will be favored with a magnificent banquet of wisdom and truth imparted through divine symbolism and sustained by a vision of hope and joy. We can pray for the Spirit to open our minds to a greater understanding of this marvelous endowment of truth from the Lord. Repeated visits to the temple will bring an unfolding of added appreciation for the insights and revelations imparted there concerning the purpose of life, our relationship with God, and our ultimate destiny of immortality and eternal life.

Time to Meditate and Ponder

1. What symbolic qualities of the temple structure and appearance make the greatest impression upon your soul?

2. What is the significance of the Angel Moroni statue on the topmost spire of the temple?

3. Why does the Lord often teach us through parables and symbolism?

4. In what ways can we plan to understand the deep and impressive symbolism used in the temple?

CHAPTER 16
PARTICIPATING IN TEMPLE ORDINANCES

Guiding Principle: The Lord has established the prerequisites for entering into His presence. He has organized the system of laws and ordinances that pertain to the celestial realm where He lives. He has designed the temple experience to endow us with the covenant armor of knowledge and the preparatory shield of truth to secure our passage home again. Without these authorized ordinances and this designated preparation, "the power of godliness is not manifested to man in the flesh" (D&C 84:21).

> *The question is frequently asked "Can we not be saved without going through with all these ordinances, &c.?" I would answer, No, not the fullness of salvation. Jesus said, "There are many mansions in my Father's house, and I will go and prepare a place for you." House here named should have been translated kingdom; and any person who is exalted to the highest mansion has to abide a celestial law, and the whole law too.*
>
> *But there has been a great difficulty in getting anything into the heads of this generation. . . . Even the Saints are slow to understand. . . . How many will be able to abide a celestial law, and go through and receive their exaltation, I am unable to say, as many are called, but few are chosen.*
> —JOSEPH SMITH, *HISTORY OF THE CHURCH*, 6:184; EMPHASIS IN ORIGINAL.

The temple is a house of sacred ordinances—ordinances that are absolutely essential for our salvation and exaltation as we complete the journey back home to the presence of the Father and the Son. In October 1841, the Lord revealed through the Prophet Joseph Smith the following concerning the temple in Nauvoo: "And verily I say unto you, let this house be built unto my name, that I may reveal mine ordinances therein unto my people; For I deign to reveal unto my church things which have been kept hid from before the foundation of the world, things that pertain to the dispensation of the fulness of times" (D&C 124:40–41).

In chapter 10 concerning the subject of godliness, we took note of the significant passage of scripture concerning the higher ordinances of the priesthood: "Therefore, in the ordinances thereof, the power of godliness is manifest. And without the ordinances thereof, and the authority of the priesthood, the power of godliness is not manifest unto men in the flesh; For without this no man can see the face of God, even the Father, and live" (D&C 84:21–22).

The place ordained of the Lord for the performance of these ordinances is the holy temple. Paul, looking forward to the period of the Restoration, prophesied: "That in the dispensation of the fulness of times he might gather together in one all things in Christ, both which are in heaven, and which are on earth; even in him" (Eph. 1:10). The truths of all dispensations coalesce in the temple experience. The power to turn the hearts of the children to their fathers and the hearts of the fathers to their children has been restored through the ministration of Elijah. The great sealing ordinances that bind families for all eternity are operative once again. We are grateful to be part of this mighty movement instituted of God for the blessing of mankind. President Joseph Fielding Smith, confirming the restoration of the fullness of the priesthood with all its holy powers, has stated:

> But now we have the fulness of the *power* of the priesthood. The Lord has restored the keys and authorities of all the dispensations and has made it possible, *by the power of Elijah,* to make every act performed by authority of force when men are dead or out of the world. Let us remember

that all contracts, bonds, oaths, or performances, which are not entered into by the authority of this sealing power, are of no efficacy or virtue after men are dead. The house of the Lord is a house of order and everything in it is obedient to divine law. (*DS,* 3:134; emphasis in original)

The suite of temple ordinances that belong to this eternal doctrine include:

Baptism for the dead.
The endowment, including the initiatory ordinances of washing and anointing.
The sealing ordinance, including temple marriage for time and all eternity.

Each of these ordinances will be considered in the pages to follow.

BAPTISM FOR THE DEAD

Jesus taught the inquiring Nicodemus, "Verily, verily, I say unto thee, Except a man be born of water and of the Spirit, he cannot enter into the kingdom of God" (John 3:5). Rebirth through faith, repentance, and the administration of priesthood ordinances is essential for salvation. The countless millions of God's children who did not have the opportunity to hear the gospel while on earth will have that opportunity in the spirit realm. The Apostle Peter confirmed this good news as follows: "For Christ also hath once suffered for sins, the just for the unjust, that he might bring us to God, being put to death in the flesh, but quickened by the Spirit: By which also he went and preached unto the spirits in prison; Which sometime were disobedient, when once the longsuffering of God waited in the days of Noah, while the ark was a preparing, wherein few, that is, eight souls were saved by water" (1 Pet. 3:18–20). And furthermore, "For for this cause was the gospel preached also to them that are dead, that they might be judged according to men in the flesh, but live according to God in the spirit" (1 Pet. 4:6).

When President Joseph F. Smith was pondering these very passages of scripture on October 3, 1918, the glorious vision of the

Savior's work in behalf of those in the spirit world was unfolded to his view. He was privileged to behold the righteous departed Saints, organized as emissaries of the Lord, teaching their spirit colleagues the plan of salvation so that they, too, might elect to come unto Christ and be saved: "The dead who repent will be redeemed, through obedience to the ordinances of the house of God, And after they have paid the penalty of their transgressions, and are washed clean, shall receive a reward according to their works, for they are heirs of salvation" (D&C 138:58–59).

The vision that President Smith saw that day, now memorialized as section 138 of the Doctrine and Covenants, confirmed the revelations given earlier to the Prophet Joseph Smith concerning this extraordinary subject:

> Now the great and grand secret of the whole matter, and the *summum bonum* of the whole subject that is lying before us, consists in obtaining the powers of the Holy Priesthood. For him to whom these keys are given there is no difficulty in obtaining a knowledge of facts in relation to the salvation of the children of men, both as well for the dead as for the living. Herein is glory and honor, and immortality and eternal life—The ordinance of baptism by water, to be immersed therein in order to answer to the likeness of the dead, that one principle might accord with the other; to be immersed in the water and come forth out of the water is in the likeness of the resurrection of the dead in coming forth out of their graves; hence, this ordinance was instituted to form a relationship with the ordinance of baptism for the dead, being in likeness of the dead. . . .
>
> This, therefore, is the sealing and binding power, and, in one sense of the word, the keys of the kingdom, which consist in the key of knowledge. And now, my dearly beloved brethren and sisters, let me assure you that these are principles in relation to the dead and the living that cannot be lightly passed over, as pertaining to our salvation. For their salvation is necessary and essential to our salvation, as Paul says concerning the fathers—that they

without us cannot be made perfect—neither can we without our dead be made perfect. (D&C 128:11–12, 14–15)

Through the sacrifice and toil of the Saints in the early days of the Restoration, a baptismal font in the Nauvoo Temple was prepared (even before the remainder of the building was completed) and dedicated by Brigham Young on November 8, 1841, with the Prophet Joseph Smith in attendance. The first baptismal event for the dead in this dispensation had been performed on August 15, 1840, in the Mississippi River, with others following over the next few weeks (see Church Educational System, *Church History in the Fulness of Times* [Salt Lake City: The Church of Jesus Christ of Latter-day Saints, 2000], 251). On January 19, 1841, the Lord commanded that a temple be built for this purpose: "For this ordinance belongeth to my house, and cannot be acceptable to me, only in the days of your poverty, wherein ye are not able to build a house unto me" (D&C 124:30). On October 3, 1841, the Prophet announced that the Lord had commanded that no further baptisms for the dead be performed until they could be attended to in the temple (see *HC,* 4:426). Finally, on November 8, 1841, the temporary baptismal font was ready for dedication.

Thus the Saints were joyfully able to present themselves before the Lord in obedience to His commandment: "And if my people will hearken unto my voice, and unto the voice of my servants whom I have appointed to lead my people, behold, verily I say unto you, they shall not be moved out of their place" (D&C 124:45).

Similarly, when we do all in our power to prepare for and participate in temple ordinances for ourselves and for our kindred dead, we shall not be moved out of our place but enjoy the blessings of the Spirit to attend our every contribution toward the building up of the kingdom of God.

In all temples of the Lord, the ordinance of baptism for the dead is performed under the authorization and direction of the holy priesthood. Each temple contains a beautiful font—resting on the backs of twelve oxen, symbolic of the twelve tribes of Israel—constructed for the sacred purpose of performing proxy baptisms in behalf of the departed. The Savior declared to Peter, "And I will give unto thee the keys of the kingdom of heaven: and whatsoever thou shalt bind on earth shall be bound in heaven: and whatsoever thou shalt loose on earth shall be loosed in heaven" (Matt. 16:19). That promise was fulfilled soon thereafter on the Mount of Transfiguration, where, in the presence of the Savior, Moses and Elias (Elijah) appeared to Peter, James, and John—and the voice of the Father was heard bearing witness of the Son. Priesthood keys, including the sealing powers, were bestowed upon the three Apostles as a presidency (see Matt. 17:1–8). The same keys and sealing powers, restored through the visit of Elijah to the Kirtland Temple on April 3, 1836, are active in our day so that the departed spirits will also have the opportunity to come unto Christ, having exercised faith unto repentance, and having the requisite physical ordinances performed by worthy representatives—"saviours" on "mount Zion" (Obad. 1:21)—as agents of the Lord, acting vicariously for the salvation of the dead.

The Endowment

Endowment means "gift"—in this case, the bestowal of a priceless treasure of knowledge and covenant ordinances designed to empower individuals to return to the presence of God in order to enjoy the infinite blessings of exaltation in the celestial kingdom. May 4, 1842, was a special day in the history of the Church and the history of temple work in this dispensation. On that day the Prophet Joseph Smith undertook the process of inaugurating the ceremony of the endowment among a select group of associates in his red brick store in Nauvoo. Here are his words concerning that important occasion:

> *Wednesday, 4.*—I spent the day in the upper part of the store, that is in my private office (so called because in that room I keep my sacred writings, translate ancient records, and receive revelations) and in my general business office, or lodge room . . . in council with General James Adams, of Springfield, Patriarch Hyrum Smith, Bishops Newel K. Whitney and George Miller, and President Brigham Young and Elders Heber C. Kimball and Willard Richards, instructing them in the principles and order of the Priesthood,

attending to washings, anointings, endowments and the communication of keys pertaining to the Aaronic Priesthood, and so on to the highest order of the Melchisedek Priesthood, setting forth the order pertaining to the Ancient of Days, and all those plans and principles by which any one is enabled to secure the fullness of those blessings which have been prepared for the Church of the First Born, and come up and abide in the presence of the Eloheim in the eternal worlds. In this council was instituted the ancient order of things for the first time in these last days. And the communications I made to this council were of things spiritual, and to be received only by the spiritual minded: and there was nothing made known to these men but what will be made known to all the Saints of the last days, so soon as they are prepared to receive, and a proper place is prepared to communicate them, even to the weakest of the Saints; therefore let the Saints be diligent in building the Temple, and all houses which they have been, or shall hereafter be, commanded of God to build; and wait their time with patience in all meekness, faith, perseverance unto the end, knowing assuredly that all these things referred to in this council are always governed by the principle of revelation. (*HC,* 5:1–2)

Elder James E. Talmage has expressed this doctrine in somewhat more detail:

> The Temple Endowment, as administered in modern temples, comprises instruction relating to the significance and sequence of past dispensations, and the importance of the present as the greatest and grandest era in human history. This course of instruction includes a recital of the most prominent events of the creative period, the condition of our first parents in the Garden of Eden, their disobedience and consequent expulsion from that blissful abode, their condition in the lone and dreary world when doomed to live by labor and sweat, the plan of redemption by which the great transgression may be atoned, the period of

the great apostasy, the restoration of the Gospel with all its ancient powers and privileges, the absolute and indispensable condition of personal purity and devotion to the right in present life, and a strict compliance with Gospel requirements. . . .

The ordinances of the endowment embody certain obligations on the part of the individual, such as covenant and promise to observe the law of strict virtue and chastity, to be charitable, benevolent, tolerant and pure; to devote both talent and material means to the spread of truth and the uplifting of the race; to maintain devotion to the cause of truth; and to seek in every way to contribute to the great preparation that the earth may be made ready to receive her King,—the Lord Jesus Christ. With the taking of each covenant and the assuming of each obligation a promised blessing is pronounced, contingent upon the faithful observance of the conditions.

No jot, iota, or tittle of the temple rites is otherwise than uplifting and sanctifying. In every detail the endowment ceremony contributes to covenants of morality of life, consecration of person to high ideals, devotion to truth, patriotism to nation, and allegiance to God. (*The House of the Lord* [Deseret Book, 1968], 83–84)

The endowment instructs and then extends the opportunity to enter into sacred covenants with the Lord on the basis of those principles of truth; it teaches and then extends specific promises in return for honoring those covenants throughout life. The endowment is a canopy of grace unto the living and the dead; it is a glorious heavenly arrangement with Deity that will secure everlasting joy for the faithful "heirs of God, and joint-heirs with Christ" (Romans 8:17). President Howard W. Hunter has provided the following concise summary of the endowment:

> The endowment is another ordinance performed in our temples. It consists of two parts: first, a series of instructions, and second, promises or covenants that the person receiving

the endowment makes—promises to live righteously and comply with the requirements of the gospel of Jesus Christ. The endowment is an ordinance for the great blessing of the Saints—both living and dead. Thus it is also an ordinance performed by the living in behalf of deceased individuals; it is performed for those for whom baptismal work has already been performed. (*Ensign,* Feb. 1995, 2)

The first part of the endowment consists of initiatory ordinances comprised of sacred washings and anointings—symbolic cleansing rites—performed in special rooms of the temple, "that we may be clean before the Lord" (*Ensign,* Mar. 2002, 17). The scriptures give an account of these ordinances of washings and anointings as follows:

And again, verily I say unto you, how shall your washings be acceptable unto me, except ye perform them in a house which you have built to my name? For, for this cause I commanded Moses that he should build a tabernacle, that they should bear it with them in the wilderness, and to build a house in the land of promise, that those ordinances might be revealed which had been hid from before the world was. Therefore, verily I say unto you, that your anointings, and your washings, and your baptisms for the dead, and your solemn assemblies, and your memorials for your sacrifices by the sons of Levi, and for your oracles in your most holy places wherein you receive conversations, and your statutes and judgments, for the beginning of the revelations and foundation of Zion, and for the glory, honor, and endowment of all her municipals, are ordained by the ordinance of my holy house, which my people are always commanded to build unto my holy name. (D&C 124:37–39)

The temple endowment is a sacred ordinance given with one objective in mind: to ensure the happiness and joy of those who benefit from its covenant blessings—both now and in the hereafter. In confirmation of this verity, President Harold B. Lee declared: "The temple endowment is a guide to happiness. Somehow we must get across the fact to all our people, young and old, that in our holy temples the temple endowment is the sure guide to happiness here and eternal life in the world to come" (*THBL*, 584).

The Sealing Ordinance

In addition to baptisms for the dead and the endowment, the temple is the sole venue for the performance of sacred sealings (both for the living and for the dead), whereby families are bound together for eternity—husbands and wives to each other in eternal marriage and children to their parents. No more glorious doctrine is to be found in the gospel of Jesus Christ. The heaven-ordained perpetuity of the family in the eternities is a magnificent concept that gives hope and courage to those who live worthy of the sealing blessings given in the temples of God. And what is the ultimate destiny of those who rise in dignity and godliness to obtain all the truths and all the ordinances of the temple in obedience to the laws of heaven? They are on course to receive their exaltation and eternal life in the kingdom of the Almighty, to know Him and His Son, and to continue in their progress until they are gods, even the children of God from everlasting to everlasting, with the supernal blessing of having their lives continue forever. President Joseph Fielding Smith reviews the monumental scriptural revelation on this subject (section 132 of the Doctrine and Covenants) and offers commentary under the title "Celestial Marriage Makes Gods in Eternity":

> But if we are married for time and for all eternity and it is sealed upon our heads by those who have the authority so to seal, and *if we then keep our covenants and are faithful to the end,* we shall come forth in the Resurrection from the dead and receive the following promised blessings:
> "*Then shall they be gods,* because they have no end; therefore shall they be from everlasting to everlasting, because they continue; then shall they be *above all,* because all things are subject unto them. Then shall they be gods, because they have *all power,* and the angels are subject unto them."

Who are the angels? Those who would not abide the law.

"Verily, verily, I say unto you, except ye abide my law ye cannot attain to this glory."

Abide what law? The law of the new and everlasting covenant, which is all the covenants.

"For strait is the gate, and narrow the way that leadeth unto *the exaltation and continuation of the lives,* and few there be that find it, because ye receive me not in the world neither do ye know me.

"But if ye receive me in the world, then shall ye know me, and shall receive your *exaltation*; that where I am ye shall be also."

What a wonderful promise! And it is open to us; it is a free gift; it doesn't cost us anything: *only righteousness, faith, obedience;* and surely we can pay that price. It means, of course, giving up the things of the world; but is that a sacrifice? Does anybody consider that giving up the things that pertain to this world is a sacrifice? Some people would look upon it that way, but it isn't. You cannot sacrifice anything for the gospel of Jesus Christ. It would be just as consistent if a man gave me a dollar and I gave him ten cents, and then I would go out and say that was a great sacrifice I made.

So if you want to enter into exaltation and become as God, that is a son of God or a daughter of God, and receive a *fulness* of the kingdom, then you have got to abide in his law—not merely the law of marriage but all that pertains to the new and everlasting covenant—and then you have the "continuation of the lives" forever, for the Lord says:

"This is *eternal lives*—to know the only wise and true God, and Jesus Christ, whom he hath sent. I am he. Receive ye, therefore, my law." (*DS,* 2:62–63; emphasis in original)

The efficacy of these sacred sealing ordinances is assured through the operation of the keys of the priesthood vested in the President of the Church—and in the Quorum of the Twelve in the event of a succession in the presidency. Without the keys and the ordinances of the priesthood, the work of the temples would cease. Earthly keys are pervasive and can be reproduced at will; but heavenly keys—the keys to organize and operate the temples of God—are precious and unique, granted only under strict governance of the laws of the priesthood as directed by the Lord.

President Joseph Fielding Smith used an interesting illustration concerning keys:

> I picked up a key on the street one day, and took it home, and it opened every door in my house. You cannot find a priesthood key on the street, for that key is never lost that will open the door that enters into our Father's mansions. You have got to go where the key is given. And each can obtain the key, if you will; but after receiving it, you may *lose* it, by having it taken away from you again, unless you abide by the agreement which you entered into when you went to the house of the Lord. (*DS*, 2:40–41; emphasis in original)

The pathway leading through the garden of faith, repentance, baptism, and receiving the gift of the Holy Ghost continues on until it reaches the doorway marked "Holiness to the Lord"—the doorway of the temple. In the temple—and only there—are made available to the obedient and worthy the keys of admittance to the abode of God and His Eternal Son, Jesus Christ. In this same passage from President Joseph Fielding Smith just quoted, he goes on to provide the following summary of the eternal implications and blessings of the temple ordinances:

> The Lord has given unto us privileges, and blessings, and the opportunity of entering into covenants, of accepting ordinances that pertain to our salvation beyond what is preached in the world; beyond the principles of faith in the Lord Jesus Christ, repentance from sin, and baptism for the remission of sins, and the laying on of hands for the gift of the Holy Ghost; and these principles and covenants are received nowhere else but in the temple of God.

> *If you would become a son or a daughter of God and an heir of the kingdom, then you must go to the house of the Lord and receive blessings which there can be obtained and which cannot be obtained elsewhere; and you must keep those commandments and those covenants to the end....*
>
> ***The ordinances of the temple, the endowment and sealings, pertain to exaltation in the celestial kingdom, where the sons and daughters are.*** *The sons and daughters are not outside in some other kingdom. The sons and daughters go into the house, belong to the household, have access to the home. "In my Father's house are many mansions." Sons and daughters have access to the home where he dwells, and you cannot receive that access until you go to the temple. Why? Because you must receive certain key words as well as make covenants by which you are able to enter. If you try to get into the house, and the door is locked, how are you going to enter, if you haven't your key? You get your key in the temple, which will admit you.* (DS, 2:40; emphasis in original)

Naturally, these ordinances must proceed on the basis of careful planning and management. Those who are to be sealed with the blessings of marriage for time and eternity in the temple will need to ensure that they are also complying with all applicable laws of the area and country where they live concerning required licenses, physical tests, waiting time, consent forms, those authorized under the law to perform marriages, and so on. It is also wise to schedule with the temple of choice well in advance regarding the timing of endowments and the temple marriage. In the case of a temple marriage, invited guests must be endowed and have current temple recommends. Such wedding companies should typically be rather small, since sealing rooms are modest in size. If a couple desires a special sealer authorized to seal in the temple of choice, this request should be made well in advance. The temple authorities can provide helpful counsel in regard to dress, grooming, time of arrival, policies for taking pictures on the temple grounds, and so forth.

Sacred, not Secret

What transpires in the holy temples of the Lord is sacred. Ordinances and instructions are not to be discussed outside the temple—except in very general terms, after the pattern used by Church leaders in the kinds of quotations we have included in the present volume. The word of God contained in the scriptures and the pronouncements given as counsel by His holy prophets in public meetings are matters that we are free to discuss in our own Church gatherings and family home evenings. But the particulars of the message of God imparted in the holy temples are to remain within those walls. They are holy and sacred matters—not to be received and articulated except within the house of the Lord. President Harold B. Lee has provided helpful counsel in this regard:

> There is a caution that I want to make about these ordinances in the temple. There is a difference between the revelations that the Lord has given to us—what we might call "open" revelations that might be discussed in the world, and private or "safeguarded" revelations. The teachings which are contained in the four standard Church works which are taught as a part of the temple endowment anyone is free to talk about—section 76, section 88, section 110, other things that pertain to priesthood—all of that which is in open revelations may be taught. But there are certain things that are reserved solely for teaching inside of the temple walls, not to be discussed outside. . . . Moses was commanded to have a sacred place in the tabernacle, and one of the first buildings they built in the Holy Land was a temple, that the ordinances might be kept from the outside world (see D&C 124:38).
>
> We must remember this. Sometimes we hear stories of those—I am sure well intentioned and perhaps not intended to be vicious—but, in order to try and impress somebody, people speak of things in public meetings that ought never to be discussed outside of the temple walls. We are talking about intimate things that we have been told repeatedly and we have covenanted that they are not to be spoken of outside the temple. (*THBL*, 576)

Keeping sacred and private the spiritual truths and experiences received in, and confined to, the precincts of the holy temple is a matter of solemn obligation. President Gordon B. Hinckley said, "I remind you of the absolute obligation to not discuss outside the temple that which occurs within the temple. Sacred matters deserve sacred consideration. We are under obligation, binding and serious, to not use temple language or speak of temple matters outside" (*Ensign,* May 1990, 52).

TIME TO MEDITATE AND PONDER

1. The scriptures tell us that the "power of godliness" is "manifest" in the ordinances of the higher priesthood, namely, in the sacred temple ordinances (see D&C 84:21–22). These ordinances are designed to prepare us for which ultimate and transcending event?

2. In what ways do the ordinances of the temple—baptisms for the dead, the endowment, the sealing ordinances—strengthen our hope and give us comfort for the future?

3. How are the temple and its ordinances a compelling witness for the mercy and loving-kindness of God and His Only Begotten Son?

4. What scriptural evidence do we have that a comprehensive system of missionary work was inaugurated by the Savior in the spirit world and is being carried out concurrent with missionary work on the earth?

5. Elder James E. Talmage described the nature of the covenant promises we make in the temple during the endowment as follows: "To observe the law of strict virtue and chastity, to be charitable, benevolent, tolerant and pure; to devote both talent and material means to the spread of truth and the uplifting of the race; to maintain devotion to the cause of truth; and to seek in every way to contribute to the great preparation that the earth may be made ready to receive her King,—the Lord Jesus Christ" (*The House of the*

Lord, 83–84). How are these themes, in effect, a continuation and consummation of the preparations that people go through to become worthy to enter the temple?

6. President Harold B. Lee declared, "The temple endowment is a guide to happiness" (*THBL,* 584). How can you infuse into your temple preparation an attitude and a commitment to be happy in the sense stated by Lehi that "men are, that they might have joy" (2 Ne. 2:25)? How is the temple a testimony of happiness for you?

7. The scripture on eternal marriage states: "This is eternal lives—to know the only wise and true God, and Jesus Christ, whom he hath sent. I am he. Receive ye, therefore, my law" (D&C 132:24). Why do you feel the word is stated in the plural—lives?

8. What happens in the temple is sacred, not secret. How can we explain the difference to those not of our faith?

CHAPTER 17
TEMPLE COVENANTS

Guiding Principle: With the Restoration of the gospel and kingdom of God in the latter days, the Lord instituted a new and everlasting covenant with all who would take upon themselves His name to become renewed and sanctified as heirs of His glory in the celestial realm. This new and everlasting covenant embraces all of our solemn promises of obedience and love enacted by ordinance—whether by baptism, ordination, endowment, sealing, or another means pertaining to the operation of the holy priesthood—that we might be lifted up, edified, and exalted as worthy and royal recipients of the eternal blessings of God. The temple is the ultimate venue for solemnizing our new and everlasting covenant with Deity.

> *What is the new and everlasting covenant? . . .* The new and everlasting covenant is the sum total of all gospel covenants and obligations. . . . *Now there is a clear-cut definition in detail of the new and everlasting covenant. It is everything—the fulness of the gospel. So marriage properly performed, baptism, ordination to the priesthood, everything else*—every contract, every obligation, every performance that pertains to the gospel of Jesus Christ, which is sealed by the Holy Spirit of promise *according to his law here given,* is a part of the new and everlasting covenant.
> —JOSEPH FIELDING SMITH, *DOCTRINES OF SALVATION,* 1:156, 158; EMPHASIS IN ORIGINAL.

Temple work is based on covenants of the most sacred order. Our Heavenly Father works through covenants. He relates to His children through covenants of mercy, love, and grace. The word *covenant* derives from the Latin term *convenire,* meaning "coming together." The sense of the word *covenant* as used in gospel terminology is "agreement"—a harmonizing bond between the parties involved, with a promise based on the fulfillment of the agreement.

Consistently there is an "if/then" pattern given in the expression of a covenant. A simple example—though one that is profound in its implications—is the sacrament prayer that we hear each week in the process of renewing our covenants. We are reminded that *if* we are willing to take upon ourselves the name of the Son and keep His commandments, *then* we will have His Spirit to be with us. That is the essence of the agreement that we have with our Father in Heaven: to be faithful and obedient, with the promise of having the guidance and direction of the Holy Ghost in our lives.

The process of taking upon ourselves the divine nature of the Father and the Son—as Peter counseled (see 2 Pet. 1:3–8)—is also accomplished under the aegis of a covenant arrangement. Look at the promise extended by the Lord through His spokesperson, Peter: *if* we bring into our thoughts and actions the qualities of faith, virtue, knowledge, temperance, patience, brotherly kindness, godliness, charity, humility, and diligence, *then* we have these blessings to look forward to: "For if these things be in you, and abound, they make you that ye shall neither be barren nor unfruitful in the knowledge of our Lord Jesus Christ. . . . Wherefore the rather, brethren, give diligence to make your calling and election sure: for if ye do these things, ye shall never fall: For so an entrance shall be ministered unto you abundantly into the everlasting kingdom of our Lord and Saviour Jesus Christ" (2 Pet. 1:8, 10–11).

Thus, by taking on the divine nature in preparation for visiting the temple, we harvest three grand blessings: fruitfulness in the knowledge of Jesus Christ, the assurance that we will never fall, and an entrance into the kingdom of our Lord—not insignificant promises by any measure!

Similarly, section 121 of the Doctrine and Covenants, which the Prophet Joseph Smith sent to the Saints in the form of an epistle written from Liberty Jail in March 1839, contains a striking "if/then" structure. If we will serve in our callings by persuasion, long-suffering, gentleness, meekness, love unfeigned, kindness, pure knowledge, charity, and virtue, "then shall thy confidence wax strong in the presence of God; and the doctrine of the priesthood shall distil upon thy soul as the dews from heaven. The Holy Ghost shall be thy constant companion, and thy scepter an unchanging scepter of righteousness and truth; and thy dominion shall be an everlasting dominion, and without compulsory means it shall flow unto thee forever and ever" (D&C 121:45–46).

By way of contrast, those who operate with pride and unrighteous dominion, striving to hide their sins, will inevitably suffer the withdrawal of the Spirit and experience an end to the power and authority of their priesthood (see D&C 121:37–38). We see that the penalty for noncompliance with the terms of the covenant is made clear, as is so often the case in the scriptural expression of covenant agreements.

It is well, then, as we prepare to participate in the sacred ordinances of the temple, to understand the binding nature of the covenants made in the house of the Lord. These covenants originated before the foundation of the world, when it was decided that the mortal experience would serve as a probationary exercise of agency: "And we will prove them herewith, to see if they will do all things whatsoever the Lord their God shall command them; And they who keep their first estate shall be added upon; and they who keep not their first estate shall not have glory in the same kingdom with those who keep their first estate; and they who keep their second estate shall have glory added upon their heads for ever and ever" (Abr. 3:25–26; see also Jude 1:6).

Throughout the history of the earth, the Lord has extended to His people the opportunity to enter into covenants with Him that they might "keep their second estate" with devotion and courage as they progress along the pathway toward salvation and eternal life. From the summit of Sinai, the Lord recounted to Moses the miracle of deliverance from Egypt and commanded him to say to the people: "Now therefore, if ye will obey my voice indeed, and keep my covenant, then ye shall be a peculiar treasure unto me above all people: for all the earth is mine: And ye shall be unto me a kingdom of priests, and an holy nation" (Ex. 19:5–6).

Becoming a holy nation—a covenant people—was the promise attached to the agreement of the Lord with Abraham and his posterity, long before the time of Moses:

> And I will make of thee a great nation, and I will bless thee above measure, and make thy name great among all nations, and thou shalt be a blessing unto thy seed after thee, that in their hands they shall bear this ministry and Priesthood unto all nations; And I will bless them through thy name; for as many as receive this Gospel shall be called after thy name, and shall be accounted thy seed, and shall rise up and bless thee, as their father; And I will bless them that bless thee, and curse them that curse thee; and in thee (that is, in thy Priesthood) and in thy seed (that is, thy Priesthood), for I give unto thee a promise that this right shall continue in thee, and in thy seed after thee (that is to say, the literal seed, or the seed of the body) shall all the families of the earth be blessed, even with the blessings of the Gospel, which are the blessings of salvation, even of life eternal. (Abr. 2:9–11; see also Gen. 12:3; 17:2)

The Prophet Joseph Smith observed, "If there is anything calculated to interest the mind of the Saints, to awaken in them the finest sensibilities, and arouse them to enterprise and exertion, surely it is the great and precious promises made by our Heavenly Father to the children of Abraham" (*HC,* 4:128). These same promises extend to us in the latter days. Under the terms of the Abrahamic covenant, we are to be spiritual emissaries to the world, bringing the blessings of the gospel and the priesthood to all nations, kindreds, tongues, and peoples. The promises to the faithful and obedient are vast and all-encompassing: that we will have the gospel and the priesthood to guide our lives, holy places to which we can gather, a posterity of grand scope (both here and in the eternities), and the hope and assurance of immortality and exaltation in the presence of the Father and the Son—all of this if we will but be faithful! By what power is this to be accomplished? By the power of the priesthood, given to us under the terms and conditions of the oath and covenant of the priesthood as revealed in modern-day revelation:

> For whoso is faithful unto the obtaining these two priesthoods of which I have spoken, and the magnifying their calling, are sanctified by the Spirit unto the renewing of their bodies. They become the sons of Moses and of Aaron and the seed of Abraham, and the church and kingdom, and the elect of God. And also all they who receive this priesthood receive me, saith the Lord; For he that receiveth my servants receiveth me; And he that receiveth me receiveth my Father; And he that receiveth my Father receiveth my Father's kingdom; therefore all that my Father hath shall be given unto him. And this is according to the oath and covenant which belongeth to the priesthood. Therefore, all those who receive the priesthood, receive this oath and covenant of my Father, which he cannot break, neither can it be moved. But whoso breaketh this covenant after he hath received it, and altogether turneth therefrom, shall not have forgiveness of sins in this world nor in the world to come. (D&C 84:33–41)

Under the terms of this covenant, if we are faithful in magnifying and fulfilling our priesthood covenants, *then* we will be sanctified by the Spirit, experience a renewal of our bodies, become sons of the Abrahamic lineage and the elect of God, and receive "all that my Father hath"—a breathtaking vista of blessings. By contrast, those who fully abdicate their heritage and potential will not have forgiveness "in this world nor in the world to come."

This stark juxtaposition of opposites—transcendent, eternal blessings for the obedient versus eternal condemnation for those who "altogether" turn away from their covenants—is a derivative function of our moral agency, granted to us by our Heavenly Father. The same urgency applies to the covenants that we are favored to receive in the temples of the Lord. As we prepare to enter into these divine covenants, we should understand what is at stake: the opportunity to receive the highest possible blessings that can come to us from God—even all that He has—based on our undeviating commitment to honor our covenant vows or, alternately, the judgment of God in the event we abandon these sacred vows and utterly turn therefrom. Through the blessings of the Spirit, and through prayer, fasting, and devoted study, we can lay a foundation of valor that will secure our ability to receive the light and truth dispensed in the temple and use it faithfully to endure to the end.

Wisdom of Latter-day Prophets Concerning Covenants

As we prepare to enter the temple—whether for the first time or upon repeated visits—we can keep in mind the counsel and guidance of the Lord's prophets. Here are a few examples:

1. We enter the presence of the Lord only through the power and promises of sacred covenants. President John Taylor spoke about the need to abide by the principles of a celestial glory if we hope to enter the presence of the Father and Son in the hereafter:

> If men do not live according to the laws of a celestial kingdom, they are not going into a celestial glory; they cannot pass by the angels and the Gods, who are set to guard the way of life. Straight is the gate, and narrow is the way that leads to life, and few there be that find it.
>
> Is God merciful? Yes. Will he treat his children well? Yes. He will do the very best he can for all. But there are certain eternal laws by which the Gods in the eternal worlds are governed and which they cannot violate, and do not want to violate. These eternal principles must be kept, and one principle is that no unclean thing can enter into the kingdom of God. What, then, will be the result? Why, the people . . . who do not keep the celestial law . . . will have to go into a lesser kingdom, into a terrestrial, or perhaps a telestial, as the case may be. Is that according to

the law of God? Yes, for if they are not prepared for the celestial kingdom, they must go to such a one as they are prepared to endure.... [W]e are here in a school to learn, and it is for the elders of Israel who are desirous to do the will of God, and keep his commandments, to put themselves in the way of doing so, to seek to the Lord for his guidance and direction, to repent of their follies, their nonsense, and wickedness of every kind, and to come out for God and his kingdom, and to seek to build up the Zion of God and the kingdom of God upon the earth, and if we do this, God will bless us and exalt us in time and throughout the eternities that are to come. (*Gospel Kingdom,* 19)

2. We are to follow the Word in order to obtain exaltation. President Joseph F. Smith emphasized the need to abide by principles of eternal truth as revealed to us by the Savior: "The kingdom of God must be erected upon the principles which Christ has revealed, upon the foundation of eternal truth; Jesus himself being the chief cornerstone. Those holy and sublime principles must be observed and honored in our lives, in order that we may obtain an exaltation with the sanctified in the kingdom of God" (*Gospel Doctrine,* 91)

3. Only those in the celestial kingdom will be in the presence of the Father and the Son. God has prepared many "mansions" in the life hereafter—many realms where His children may dwell through the eternities, in accordance with the degree of obedience and valor they exhibit in the present probationary state. The highest and most lofty of these realms is the celestial kingdom, the home of the Father and the Son. Temple work is designed to ensure our admittance into this glorious kingdom, to live in the presence of our God forever. President George Albert Smith confirmed that we are to honor our covenants at a celestial level of obedience:

> And may I say that there are comparatively few people in all the world who understand that there will be a Resurrection. The Lord has again revealed this in our day. He has impressed it upon us and has given us to understand that

when the time comes for that Resurrection, if we are worthy, that we will be quickened celestial bodies, and from then on, we will dwell in the celestial kingdom, the highest of all kingdoms. But he has taught us also that there are other places where we may go. If we don't want to go to the celestial kingdom, by being less careful and particular about keeping the commandments of God, we may go into the terrestrial kingdom, and if we are still more careless, we may find our way into the telestial kingdom, which is the least of the kingdoms of glory. (*TGAS,* 36)

4. The temple is the only place where covenants of exaltation are given. Receiving and honoring our temple covenants is the only means whereby we can receive the blessings of the celestial kingdom. Participating in the blessings of this order of the holy priesthood—instituted from the foundations of the world as the only avenue whereby we, as descendants of Adam and Eve, together with our families, could receive a celestial inheritance in the presence of God—brings comfort, hope, joy, and the assurance of exaltation and everlasting life. President Ezra Taft Benson explained this aspect of the new and everlasting covenant as follows:

> How did Adam bring his descendants into the presence of the Lord?
>
> The answer: Adam and his descendants entered into the priesthood order of God. Today we would say they went to the house of the Lord and received their blessings. The order of priesthood spoken of in the scriptures is sometimes referred to as the patriarchal order because it came down from father to son. But this order is otherwise described in modern revelation as an order of family government wherein a man and woman enter into a covenant with God—just as did Adam and Eve—to be sealed for eternity, to have posterity, and to do the will and work of God throughout their mortality.
>
> If a couple are true to their covenants, they are entitled to the blessing of the highest degree of the celestial

kingdom. These covenants today can only be entered into by going to the house of the Lord.

Adam followed this order and brought his posterity into the presence of God. He is the great example to follow.... When our children obey the Lord and go to the temple to receive their blessings and enter into the marriage covenant, they enter into the same order of the priesthood that God instituted in the beginning with father Adam.

This order of priesthood can only be entered into when we comply with all the commandments of God and seek the blessings of the fathers as did Abraham by going to our Father's house. They are received in no other place on this earth! Our Father's house is a house of order. We go to His house to enter into that order of priesthood which will entitle us to all that the Father hath, if we are faithful. For as the Lord has revealed in modern times, Abraham's seed are "lawful heirs" to the priesthood (see D&C 86:8–11). (*Ensign,* Aug. 1985, 9–10)

5. All covenants, including temple covenants, are conditioned upon our faithfulness. The Prophet Joseph Smith taught: "There is a law, irrevocably decreed in heaven before the foundations of this world, upon which all blessings are predicated—And when we obtain any blessing from God, it is by obedience to that law upon which it is predicated" (D&C 130:20–21).

This doctrine applies with special solemnity to our temple covenants, given the ultimate and eternal consequence involved. The promised blessings inherent in these sacred covenants are conditioned upon our obedience in honoring and keeping our part of the agreement with the Lord. President Spencer W. Kimball reminded us of these binding obligations:

> Our very presence in this world is the result of a covenant we have made and a promise of and the result of faithfulness. Our baptism is a covenant in which the Lord promises us celestial life if we live celestial laws. To fail to do so we are cheating both him and us, but more especially ourselves.

> This is true also of other ordinances. We receive the higher priesthood with an oath and a covenant with the Father, which covenant "He cannot break neither can it be moved," but we may break it and fail, and in so doing we break a vow and are dishonest with ourselves and him. Our free agency permits our doing what we wish to do, but it does not immunize us from the results of our failures.
>
> The endowment in the holy temple is another contract of covenants which we solemnly make with our Heavenly Father. For faithfulness we are again promised unimaginable blessings. We may cheat, but the deprivations and sorrows and remorses will come to us who cheat. (*TSWK,* 504)

By honoring our temple covenants with exactitude, acting in gratitude and love for the Father and the Son, extending our arm in charitable service to our fellowmen, and enduring to the end, we have the assurance of a celestial abode in the eternities. The Savior promised us: "I give unto you these sayings that you may understand and know how to worship, and know what you worship, that you may come unto the Father in my name, and in due time receive of his fulness. For if you keep my commandments you shall receive of his fulness, and be glorified in me as I am in the Father; therefore, I say unto you, you shall receive grace for grace" (D&C 93:19–20).

Those who honor their covenants have the promise that they will receive the blessings of grace from the Lord. It is this measure of mercy that enhances our ability to remain steadfast and obedient—despite the adversities and temptations we face. The Lord, in His infinite wisdom and mercy, has prepared a way for us to partake of His grace in sufficient measure to ensure a celestial inheritance. What is that way? It is the gospel plan of light and truth, ordinances and covenants, culminating in the magnificent temple rites and services. When we come into the temple, we come unto Christ in the ultimate sense proclaimed by Moroni at the end of the Book of Mormon: "Yea, come unto Christ, and be perfected in him, and deny yourselves of all ungodliness; and if ye shall deny yourselves of all ungodliness, and love God with all your might, mind and strength, then is his grace sufficient for you, that by his grace ye may be perfect in Christ; and if by the grace of God ye are perfect in Christ, ye can in nowise deny the power of God" (Moro. 10:32).

At the heart of these sacred covenants of perfection is the Atonement of the Savior. It is in and through the redeeming power of the Atonement that the grace of the Lord is extended to all, "this being the intent of this last sacrifice, to bring about the bowels of mercy, which overpowereth justice, and bringeth about means unto men that they may have faith unto repentance" (Alma 34:15). Therefore, we are empowered through obedience and covenant valor to honor our sacred promises, being strengthened through the blessings and grace of the Lord, being blessed by the Holy Spirit with the assurance of our ultimate triumph over sin and death as "joint-heirs with Christ" (Rom. 8:17) in the eternal glory of the eternities.

Elder David E. Sorensen of the Presidency of the Seventy observed the close connection between the Atonement and our ability to participate in temple work worthily:

> One reason for the power of covenants may be due to the capability they have for effecting changes in our lives, especially sacred covenants. This capacity comes in part because when we make a covenant with God, we are making a promise to our Heavenly Father who knows us best, who knows exactly what we feel and think and intend in our heart of hearts—and this provides unique motivation to keep our promises. Additionally, sacred covenants are even more powerful than regular covenants or promises because by entering a covenant that is sealed by the Holy Spirit of Promise (the Holy Ghost), we gain special access to the grace of God to help us keep the promises we have made.
>
> The purpose of temple work is to make more effective the Atonement of Jesus Christ, and since covenants can be such an effective tool for change, covenants feature prominently in the temple and particularly are a key component of the endowment. Consider how the covenants of baptism, the sacrament, and the laying on of hands are all centered upon the Savior and His atoning sacrifice and

how they lead us to change our lives. In a similar way, the covenants we make when we receive the endowment can propel us to even greater changes and greater Christlike behavior. Put another way, we might ask, How do we gain access to the fulness of the Atonement, this additional dispensation of grace? Only by covenants, which are entered into only through ordinances, which can be performed only through priesthood keys. The Prophet Joseph Smith taught, "Being born again, comes by the Spirit of God through ordinances."

These truths help us understand the spiritual power of temple work and how that power can come into a person's life by covenant. Then, keeping the covenant brings the promised blessing in time and in eternity. (*Liahona,* Aug. 2002, 30)

Time to Meditate and Ponder

1. According to President Joseph Fielding Smith, which covenants are included in the "new and everlasting covenant?"

2. What is the "if/then" character of sacred covenants? Think of this in connection with one or more of the following:

> the sacrament
> the counsel of the Apostle Peter concerning taking on the divine nature
> the operation of the priesthood as explained in Doctrine and Covenants 121
> plans for the probationary experience of mortality as established in the premortal realm
> the covenant promises of the Lord to ancient Israel at Sinai
> the Abrahamic covenant
> the oath and covenant of the priesthood (see D&C 84:33–42)
> temple covenants

3. How can we ensure our faithfulness and honor in keeping our sacred covenants?

4. What blessings come to us and to our loved ones as a result of honoring temple covenants?

5. The temple is the only place where the covenants of exaltation are given. Why is this so?

6. The Lord promised, "For if you keep my commandments you shall receive of his [the Father's] fulness" (D&C 93:20). What does it mean to receive of His "fulness"? How does this promise influence our striving to be prepared to enter the temple?

PART THREE
TEMPLE SERVICE FOR A LIFETIME

Guiding Principle: The momentum of temple service increases as we invest ourselves in full accord with the doctrines and covenants of this holy work. The Savior taught, "For whosoever will save his life shall lose it: and whosoever will lose his life for my sake shall find it" (Matt. 16:25). When we "lose" our life in devoted and consistent temple service, we "find" it again through the transformational process of becoming "a new creature" (2 Cor. 5:17) through the power of the new and everlasting covenant leading to exaltation and eternal life in the celestial kingdom.

> *Let the work of my temple, and all the works which I have appointed unto you, be continued on and not cease; and let your diligence, and your perseverance, and patience, and your works be redoubled, and you shall in nowise lose your reward, saith the Lord of Hosts (D&C 127:4).*
>
> *Brethren, shall we not go on in so great a cause? Go forward and not backward. Courage, brethren; and on, on to the victory! Let your hearts rejoice, and be exceedingly glad. Let the earth break forth into singing. Let the dead speak forth anthems of eternal praise to the King Immanuel, who hath ordained, before the world was, that which would enable us to redeem them out of their prison; for the prisoners shall go free (D&C 128:22).*

CHAPTER 18
THE ETERNAL FAMILY—
THE JOY OF FAMILY
HISTORY WORK

Guiding Principle: Temple work embraces the whole of the history of mankind, from the premortal period, to the journey throughout mortality, to the dawning of the millennial reign, and onward to the consummating Judgment prior to the ultimate disposition of souls among the eternal realms. No one is forgotten. All are important. All are part of God's family. Our perfectibility is contingent upon the mission of gathering together in one the grand matrix of family history of our forebears preceding us, that the faithful and devout among them may accept our vicarious service on their behalf and join with us, by virtue of the Atonement and the associated sealing powers of the temple, as heirs of glory in the celestial realm.

> *The greatest responsibility in this world that God has laid upon us is to seek after our dead. The apostle says, "They without us cannot be made perfect"; for it is necessary that the sealing power should be in our hands to seal our children and our dead for the fulness of the dispensation of times—a dispensation to meet the promises made by Jesus Christ before the foundation of the world for the salvation of man.*
> —JOSEPH SMITH, *HISTORY OF THE CHURCH,* 6:313.

When we go to the temple of the Lord to avail ourselves of the personal blessings that await us there—the sacred endowment, the sealing blessings—we experience a twofold miracle. The first part is that we have embarked on a momentous journey of joy toward the ultimate promised destination—the abode of Deity where we can receive "crowns of eternal lives in the eternal worlds" (D&C 132:55). The second part is that we are moved upon by the Spirit of Elijah to take up our role as saviors on Mount Zion (see Obad. 1:21) in behalf of our ancestors who have passed beyond the veil. The universal Atonement—together with the keys of the sealing powers, which recognize no boundaries between this mortal realm and the expanse of eternity—plants firmly in our hearts, through the Spirit of the Lord, the hope of salvation and exaltation for all our loved ones as well as for ourselves. "And hope maketh not ashamed; because the love of God is shed abroad in our hearts by the Holy Ghost which is given unto us" (Rom. 5:5). This kind of love, sustained by the Spirit of Elijah, turns the hearts of the fathers to the children and the hearts of the children to their fathers—giving rise to a sacred commission of vicarious charity centered in temple service.

When we do all in our power to ensure that the spiritual needs of our own family are taken care of—whereby all can be sanctified and bound together through the sealing powers of priesthood ordinances obtained in the temple—then our mind is turned to our greater family, the family of our own lineage, whose members depend upon us to perform proxy acts of service on their behalf, to the end "that they might be judged according to men in the flesh, but live according to God in the spirit" (1 Pet. 4:6). Recall how Enos, having prayed mightily for forgiveness until the Lord benevolently granted his petition on the basis of faith, next turned his mind and heart toward his fellow beings, with overpowering anxiety for their well-being and salvation (see Enos 1). So it is with temple work. We put our own spiritual life in order, then we help our own family to do the same, then we work tirelessly for the salvation and blessing of our predecessors in the family line by gathering together an accurate record of their lives and arranging for the essential ordinance work to be done in the temple. President Howard W. Hunter described this sacred commission as follows:

> In the ordinances of the temple, the foundations of the eternal family are sealed in place. Our first great purpose in this work is to save ourselves and our own families. The Lord has not given me the responsibility to save your family, but he has given me the responsibility of saving my own family. My own family will be the unit through which I may obtain exaltation and continuation of the seeds.
>
> Joseph Smith the Prophet said: "If you have power to seal on earth and in heaven, then we should be wise. The first thing you do, go and seal on earth your sons and daughters unto yourself, and yourself unto your fathers in eternal glory." (*HC,* 6:253.) This is the real work of what we call priesthood genealogy. It is the work of saving and exalting all of Father's children if they will hearken unto his commandments and obey his laws and ordinances.
>
> Our purpose is to see that every man lives worthy of receiving, in the house of the Lord, those great and marvelous blessings which will associate him in an eternal family unit. We long to see the day when every Melchizedek Priesthood bearer will love his wife, and the family which he expects or may now have, enough to stand together in sacred places and be sealed together as an eternal family. When this has been performed in our own behalf, we should then labor unceasingly to provide these same blessings for those who gave us the opportunity to be born into mortality and died without the privilege of hearing these sacred truths. (*THWH,* 244)

The pathway that lies ahead of us, after we have made our vows with the Lord in the holy temple through sacred covenants, is to gather together the genealogical history of our forebears and find joy and fulfillment by performing the requisite temple ordinances in their behalf. Again, from President Hunter: "What a glorious thing it is for us to have the privilege of going to the temple for our own blessings.

Then after going to the temple for our own blessings, what a glorious privilege to do the work for those who have gone on before us. This aspect of temple work is an unselfish work. Yet whenever we do temple work for other people, there is a blessing that comes back to us. Thus, it should be no surprise to us that the Lord does desire that his people be a temple-motivated people" (*Ensign,* Feb. 1995, 5).

IN THE SPIRIT OF ELIJAH

What is it that opens hearts and minds to the sacred privilege of doing temple work in behalf of others? Is it not the Spirit of the Lord acting upon us to the end that the commission and power of Elijah might be fulfilled as a blessing unto all mankind? The Prophet Joseph Smith declared: "The spirit, power, and calling of Elijah is, that ye have power to hold the key of the revelation, ordinances, oracles, powers and endowments of the fulness of the Melchizedek Priesthood and of the kingdom of God on the earth; and to receive, obtain, and perform all the ordinances belonging to the kingdom of God, even unto the turning of the hearts of the fathers unto the children, and the hearts of the children unto the fathers, even those who are in heaven" (*HC,* 6:251).

The appearance of Elijah the Prophet in the Kirtland Temple on April 3, 1836, to restore the keys of the sealing power, inaugurated an era of unprecedented interest in family history throughout the world. When we respond to our callings in the Spirit of Elijah, there is an excitement that comes into our lives, a feeling of dynamic enthusiasm to be engaged in the work of salvation in behalf of others. We can take full and productive advantage of this disposition of eagerness and passion for doing good by systematically applying the following guidelines:

>   Cultivate and magnify the desire to do family history and temple work.
>   Take advantage of up-to-date technology.
>   Follow recommended procedures.
>   Savor the blessings of temple work.
>   Follow the Spirit in all things.

CULTIVATE AND MAGNIFY THE DESIRE TO DO FAMILY HISTORY AND TEMPLE WORK

The hosts of our departed relatives in the spirit world—and we are all brothers and sisters in the gospel—wait upon us yearningly to take action on their behalf. Sometimes, it seems, their wait is prolonged unduly as we muster the courage and energy to be about the Lord's business as "saviours" on "mount Zion" (Obad. 1:21). In the encouragement and admonition of the prophets we can find means to increase our motivation to action. Said the Prophet Joseph Smith:

> What is this office and work of Elijah? It is one of the greatest and most important subjects that God has revealed. He should send Elijah to seal the children to the fathers, and the fathers to the children.
>
> Now was this merely confined to the living, to settle difficulties with families on earth? By no means. It was a far greater work. Elijah! what would you do if you were here? Would you confine your work to the living alone? No; I would refer you to the Scriptures, where the subject is manifest: that is, without us, they could not be made perfect, nor we without them; the fathers without the children, nor the children without the fathers.
>
> I wish you to understand this subject, for it is important; and if you will receive it, this is the spirit of Elijah, that we redeem our dead, and connect ourselves with our fathers which are in heaven, and seal up our dead to come forth in the first resurrection; and here we want the power of Elijah to seal those who dwell on earth to those who dwell in heaven. This is the power of Elijah and the keys of the kingdom of Jehovah. (*HC,* 6:251–52)

Our commission to do the holy work of the temples reaches back, like the Atonement of Christ, into the premortal realm, having been established from the foundation of the earth. It was ever ordained that we should be associates of the Redeemer—emulators of His example and understudies of His consummate mission of sacrifice—by performing, as He did, vicarious service in behalf of those who could not accomplish it for themselves. President Howard W. Hunter assured us that "we who live in this day are those whom God appointed before birth to be his priesthood representatives on the earth in this dispensation. We are the House of Israel. In our hands lie the sacred powers of bringing to pass the ennobling work of being saviors on Mount Zion in the latter days" (*THWH*, 231).

What we invest in our family history labors is essentially an abundant measure of our love, which radiates back in time toward the love that our ancestors had for us as their descendants, the coming generation. These two streams of love find their confluence in the temples of God, where bonds are formed, families united, destinies sealed, and the pathway to eternal glory secured. President Ezra Taft Benson emphasized that love is truly at the heart of our desire to do family history work and perform the sealing ordinances in behalf of our kindred spirits:

> We are largely a product of our progenitors, their strength sustains us, their weaknesses, if any, warn us of traits and tendencies to curb and avoid. Their love and devotion bring to fulfillment the Savior's great law of love with combined loved ones and families joyfully together in time and throughout eternity. We owe them much more than we can ever repay. A noble heritage has always been regarded as one of life's greatest treasures. (*TETB*, 161)

Such teachings reinforce our commitment to follow through with devotion as we attend to the sacred task of participating in a holy partnership with the Lord to assist in securing the salvation and exaltation of our family members. The work and glory of the Lord is to "bring to pass the immortality and eternal life of man" (Moses 1:39). Our work and glory, as the Lord revealed to Hyrum Smith, is to "keep my commandments, yea, with all your might, mind and strength" (D&C 11:20). No commandment exceeds in importance the commandment concerning temple work; no worship transcends in significance the worship we perform in the temple as we come to understand more deeply the nature of the Father and Son and our eternal relationship with Them; no joy can exceed the joy we feel in performing willing service within those sacred walls on behalf of our loved ones now and from yesteryear. President Howard W. Hunter has clearly confirmed in our day that "as we attend the temple and perform work for the dead, we acquire a deep sense of alliance with God and a better understanding of his plan for the salvation of the human race. We learn to love our neighbors as ourselves. Truly there is no work equal to that done in the temple" (*THWH*, 236).

Take Advantage of Up-to-Date Technology

Through advances in modern technology and information science, family history work has taken on promising new dimensions. We begin and further the quest, of course, by consulting personal records and documentation, reading private family histories, and interacting with informative relatives. But there is, in addition, a dazzling world of computerized research capability awaiting the avid genealogist. For example, FamilySearch.org, a Web-based research system available without cost, is a powerful tool that enables people to search millions of records instantly as they construct pedigrees of their ancestors. Sponsored by The Church of Jesus Christ of Latter-day Saints, FamilySearch.org is described on its home page as the "largest collection of free family history, family tree and genealogy records in the world."

The Church is continually deploying new advances in computerized and Internet-based programs and resources to assist in the vital process of organizing names for the sacred work being performed in the temples of the Lord. Consult your nearest family history center (identified on FamilySearch.org) for the latest information and guidance.

Follow Recommended Procedures

The design of accomplishing family history work is logical and orderly. We start with our own immediate family to ensure that the sealing blessings of the temple have been made available within the most important circle of our existence. Then we proceed to expand the quest to our forebears with the objective to ensure that the temple work is performed on their behalf, linking the generations together that all might be sanctified and preserved intact as an assembly unto the Most High. President Joseph Fielding Smith outlined a wise and productive approach to follow in fulfilling the commission to be avidly engaged in family history work:

> Now the duty of a man in his own family is to see that he and his wife are sealed at the altar. If married out in the world before they joined the Church, or if they have been in the Church and have been unable to go to the temple, it is that man's duty to go to the temple, have his wife sealed to him and have their children sealed, so that the family group, that unit to which he belongs, is made intact so that it will continue throughout all eternity. That is the first duty that a man owes to himself, to his wife, and to his children. He receives this blessing by virtue of the priesthood.
>
> Then it is his duty to seek his record as far back as he can go and do the same thing for each unit. He should begin with his father and mother and their children, and his grandfather and his children, great-grandfather and his children, and have the work done in like manner, linking each generation with the one that goes before. That is the responsibility resting upon every man who is at the head of a household in this Church.
>
> Now the Lord has not placed upon any man in this Church the responsibility of doing the temple work for his neighbor. If you want to help your neighbor, there is no objection. If he needs help and you can help him, he will appreciate it. But your responsibility is to do your own work for your *own* line, going from son to father, going clear back as far as you are able to carry this record. When you do that, then you place yourself in line, through the fulness of the priesthood, eventually to receive the fulness of the glory of God. (*DS,* 2:207; emphasis in original)

We are laying a great foundation in family history work. We are reaching back with the arm of charity to effect an enduring link with our ancestors. As we do our duty in our capacity as saviors on Mount Zion, we are gaining the favor of our Heavenly Father and His Son. But at the same time, our vision is to also be focused on the future. We are to train our children and grandchildren in this great enterprise of salvation. After all, we occupy more roles than just our current ones of father or mother, son, or daughter—we will also become ancestors for future generations.

Being faithful in maintaining our own personal journal and compiling the stories of our immediate ancestors is one key approach to being a great ancestor. In this regard, President Ezra Taft Benson has declared, "Our responsibility to keep a journal and to write our own personal histories and those of our ancestors, particularly those who belong to the first four generations of our pedigree, has not changed" (*TETB*, 162).

Savor the Blessings of Temple Work

The abundant rewards and joys of doing temple work for ourselves and our ancestors provide an effective catalyst for our ongoing involvement. There is no more compelling theme, no more motivating power, than to open the door of access to treasured celestial blessings for our families and our progenitors in the spirit of the Savior's atoning mission. President Thomas S. Monson has observed:

> An appreciation for the temple endowment and the sealing ordinances will bring the members of our families closer together and there will be quickened within each family member a desire to make available these same blessings to our loved ones who have gone beyond. We will come to say with George Elliott, "I desire no future that would break the ties of the past, for heaven would not be heaven without family and friends."
>
> This vicarious work performed in our temples must be carried forth in the same spirit of selfless devotion and sacrifice that characterized the life of the Master. When we remember him, it becomes easier for us to do our individual parts in this vital work. Each time we gaze upon one of

these holy houses, may we be reminded of the eternal opportunities which are found inside, not only for ourselves, but for our dead. Let us be mindful that decisions pertaining to the temple are eternal decisions with eternal consequences. (*Pathways to Perfection* [Salt Lake City: Deseret Book, 1973], 206–207)

Follow the Spirit in All Things

This is the work of the Lord. He is the "author of eternal salvation" (Heb. 5:9) and the "finisher of our faith" (Heb. 12:2; see also Moro. 6:4). He guides the work of the temple through the manifestation of His Spirit. As we pray and fast for guidance and direction, He will respond, often well ahead of our pleading: "And it shall come to pass, that before they call, I will answer; and while they are yet speaking, I will hear" (Isa. 65:24).

The work of salvation for the dead is attended by miracles—miracles without number—as the Saints search and find, explore and discover, reach out and are filled with knowledge that is crucial to vicarious temple work. The veil is thin, and the forces of good on the other side are marshaled to help in ways often unseen and undetected. Through our faith and diligence, answers will be forthcoming, doors will be opened, and the Spirit of the Lord will illuminate the pathway forward to the completion of the work that lies before us. Said President Harold B. Lee:

> *There is divine help in genealogical research.* [In our genealogical research] the Lord is not going to open any doors until we get as far as we can on our own. We have to go toward that blank wall and then we have to have enough faith to ask the Lord to help to make an opening so that we can take the next step. And there can be information given to you from sources that reveal the fact that heaven and earth are not far away.
>
> Many of you have lived to a time in life where you have had loved ones who have gone on. You have had certainty of the nearness, sometimes, of those who have

drawn very near to you. And sometimes they have brought to you information that you could not have otherwise had.

The Lord will help open doors as we do genealogy. I have a conviction born of a little experience to which I bear testimony that there are forces beyond this life that are working with us. . . . I have the simple faith that when you do everything you can, researching to the last of your opportunity, the Lord will help you to open doors to go further with your genealogies, and heaven will cooperate, I am sure. (*THBL,* 584; emphasis in original)

We are not alone in this work. The Spirit of Elijah is active across the world. Hearts are being softened; minds are being drawn toward an understanding of the need to link together the families that constitute the flow of our generations on earth; service is being rendered in the temples of God—with increasing scope and fervor in the latter days—for the purpose of bringing the sealing blessings of heaven to our departed loved ones. This power is active on both sides of the veil, for those who have gone beyond and wait upon the day of their deliverance from the spirit realm through the redemptive power of the Lord extend their influence for good in support of our selfless service. President Spencer W. Kimball has confirmed that we receive help from beyond the veil:

Research is aided from the spirit world. I am sure that the veil is thin. My grandfather, being one of a family, searched all his life to get together his genealogical records; and when he died, in 1868, he had been unsuccessful in establishing his line back more than the second generation beyond him. I am sure that most of my family members feel the same as I do—that there was a thin veil between him and the earth, after he had gone to the other side, and that which he was unable to do as a mortal he perhaps was able to do after he had gone into eternity. After he passed away, the spirit of research took hold of men—his family in the West and two distant relatives, not members of the Church, in the East. For seven years these two men—

> Morrison and Sharples—unknown to each other, and unknown to the members of the family in the West, were gathering genealogy. After seven years, they happened to meet and then for three years they worked together. The family feels definitely that the spirit of Elijah was at work on the other side and that our grandfather had been able to inspire men on this side to search out these records; and as a result, two large volumes are in our possession with about seventeen thousand names. (*TSWK,* 542)

Let us therefore pray for strength to accomplish our duties in connection with the magnificent enterprise of salvation for the dead that is centered in the temples of God. With the help of the Lord, we will generate the desire equal to the task, find the resources to accomplish the research, follow the recommended procedures successfully, and savor the blessings—all by following the guidance of the Spirit in every aspect of the work. Our journey will not be unlike that of ancient Israel: "And the Lord went before them by day in a pillar of a cloud, to lead them the way; and by night in a pillar of fire, to give them light; to go by day and night" (Ex. 13:21). As we labor day and night on behalf of our deceased brothers and sisters, the Lord will attend our footsteps and grant us a reward of eternal glory: "And the sons of Moses and of Aaron shall be filled with the glory of the Lord, upon Mount Zion in the Lord's house, whose sons are ye; and also many whom I have called and sent forth to build up my church" (D&C 84:32).

Time to Meditate and Ponder

1. According to the Prophet Joseph Smith, what is the "greatest responsibility in this world that God has laid upon us" (*HC,* 6:313)?

2. President Howard W. Hunter taught that "we are foreordained to be saviors on Mount Zion" (*THWH,* 231). That being the case, in the premortal realm we must have associated with the very people for whom we are currently doing vicarious temple work. How does that help to increase and empower our motivation to do the work?

3. What role do gratitude and love play in the performance of our temple obligations?

4. What modern technology systems are available to assist us in family history work?

5. What are the blessings of doing family history and temple work?

6. The prophets assure us that we are not alone in this work. How can we secure the help of unseen forces in completing our assignment to do family history and temple work?

CHAPTER 19
ENDURING TO THE END WITH THE TEMPLE IN VIEW

Guiding Principle: The temple is an emblem of the gospel's power to effect a mighty change in our lives, drawing us forward toward a destination of exaltation. To be drawn unto the Lord, and to be transformed through His power of deliverance, is to complete our covenant work in the Church and kingdom of God, culminating in the sacred rites of the temple, and then to endure to the end with courage, loyalty, and honor.

> *In another usage familiar and unique to Latter-day Saints, the words saved and salvation are also used to denote exaltation or eternal life (see Abr. 2:11). This is sometimes referred to as the "fulness of salvation" (Bruce R. McConkie,* The Mortal Messiah, *4 vols. [1979–81], 1:242). This salvation requires more than repentance and baptism by appropriate priesthood authority. It also requires the making of sacred covenants, including eternal marriage, in the temples of God, and faithfulness to those covenants by enduring to the end. If we use the word salvation to mean "exaltation," it is premature for any of us to say that we have been "saved" in mortality. That glorious status can only follow the final judgment of Him who is the Great Judge of the living and the dead.*
> —DALLIN H. OAKS, "HAVE YOU BEEN SAVED?" *ENSIGN*, MAY 1998, 55.

The daily life of one who frequents the house of the Lord is to be consistent with a pattern of enduring to the end in righteousness and obedience. The counsel of the Lord to newly baptized members is that they should cultivate and manifest "a godly walk and conversation . . . that there may be works and faith agreeable to the holy scriptures—walking in holiness before the Lord" (D&C 20:69). This same counsel serves us well as a governing principle for the remainder of our lives.

If we look to the temple, we will find truth, life, and joy in abundance. If we keep our eye focused on the temple, we will not stumble by the wayside and yield to the enticings of evil influences. "And faith, hope, charity and love, with an eye single to the glory of God, qualify him for the work" (D&C 4:5). What work are we qualifying for? The work of salvation and exaltation as saviors on Mount Zion, the work of extending the blessings of temple covenants to the living and the dead in preparation for the Second Coming.

This book has presented a sequence of ideas and recommendations for preparing to enter the temple throughout our lives. We need to prepare *every* time we enter the house of the Lord. The process of cleansing and sanctification is an ongoing and lifelong undertaking that can be conducted only "in the strength of the Lord" (Alma 20:4). "Behold, I am the law, and the light. Look unto me, and endure to the end, and ye shall live; for unto him that endureth to the end will I give eternal life" (3 Ne. 15:9).

Enduring to the end is a function of staying on the straight and narrow road that ascends the hill of the Lord where His temple radiates the spirit of the eternities. In this light, President Gordon B. Hinckley presented the following portrait of those who are enduring to the end by steadfastly following a vision of temple work:

> When I leave the office about 6 o'clock in the evening and drive from the parking ramp up on to Main Street and up to North Temple I see scores of people walking in the direction of this building, their little suitcases in hand. I say to myself, "These are the very pick and flower of the Church." These are they who understand the whole, broad mission of this work. They know that the Church is more

than a social organization. They know that it involves more than meeting together to receive instruction. They know that it means more than recreation and sociability. They know that it is concerned with matters of eternity. They know that it deals with all of the children of God and their eternal well-being. (*TGBH,* 623)

As a review of the material that we have been discussing in this book, we offer a brief outline of ten steps to follow—from the perspective of the temple and temple work—in order to endure to the end.

Ten Steps for Enduring to the End

1. Be grateful for the temple and its blessings. The temple has a wonderful way of generating within us enduring feelings of gratitude. How blessed we are to live in a time when temples abound throughout the world and to have the privilege of entering these sanctuaries of peace, comfort, and hope as often as circumstances will allow. While conducting a research project on the scriptural patterns of guidance and wisdom concerning gratitude, the authors of this volume found some one thousand references to gratitude and associated qualities (thanks, praise, rejoicing, "glory in," "delight in," and similar terms) in the four standard works. Those references indicate that the causes for and sources of gratitude in our lives center on five key categories of blessings: God, the gospel, goodness of people, the gathering, and gifts. From the standpoint of the temple, we can fortify our capacity to endure to the end by strengthening our gratitude for these blessings.

Gratitude for God. Be grateful for His infinite greatness, love, mercy, long-suffering, justice, grace, glory, and kindness in having restored to the earth the temple with all of its ordinances and sealing powers.

Gratitude for the gospel. Be grateful for the Atonement of the Savior accomplished through His miraculous and vicarious act of redemption—which forms the centerpiece of all temple ceremonies and ordinances.

Gratitude for the goodness of people. Be grateful for the selfless service and sacrifice of the prophets of God who devote their lives to the building up of the kingdom of God—including the building and operation of temples; for our loved ones who constitute our eternal families; and for the dedicated Saints who give so liberally of their time and talents to keep the temples open day and night.

Gratitude for the gathering. Be grateful for the Restoration of the gospel that extends the blessings of the kingdom of God to all kindreds, tongues, and peoples under the aegis of the Abrahamic covenant and gathers in the faithful to stand in "holy places"—especially the temples of God—in order to enjoy the blessings of salvation and exaltation.

Gratitude for gifts. Be grateful for the bounteous heavenly endowment of truth and light, peace and comfort, strength and faith, and for every gift of the Spirit—all of which are reflected in, and augmented by, the work performed in the temple.

Temple worship is the epitome of selfless service. Those who frequent the halls of God's house are motivated by the desire for increased devotion, expanded joy, and magnified holiness before the Lord—for themselves and for their kindred dead. President Gordon B. Hinckley has declared the following concerning temple work and its profound influence for good in our lives:

> Those who come to the temples to do work for the dead generally know very little of those in whose service they labor. They expect no thanks for that service. They come out of a sense of love and duty. There is an absence of selfishness, except as they desire to refine and enhance their own spirituality in the process. If there were more temple work done in the Church, there would be less of selfishness, less of contention, less of demeaning others. The whole Church would increasingly be lifted to greater heights of spirituality, love for one another, and obedience to the commandments of God. (*TGBH*, 622)

By remembering the temple as the font of gratitude in our lives, we can indeed be "lifted to greater heights of spirituality, love for one another, and obedience" as we strive to endure to the end.

2. Maintain a current temple recommend. We have already taken note that our recommend, in many ways, is a passport to the eternities. It is a source of abundant comfort and joy—to know that we have achieved the level of worthiness required for entry into the house of the Lord. The recommend is a tangible certificate of endurance to the end, for it reminds us of the ongoing obligation to honor our covenants with valor and obedience.

3. Return often to the temple. The Church booklet entitled *Preparing to Enter the Holy Temple* reminds us of the importance of returning to the house of the Lord as frequently as possible:

> The temple ceremony will not be fully understood at first experience. It will be only partly understood. Return again and again and again. Return to learn. Things that have troubled you or things that have been puzzling or things that have been mysterious will become known to you. . . .
>
> When you have the opportunity to attend an endowment session in the temple or to witness a sealing, ponder the deeper meaning of what you see demonstrated before you. And in the days following your visit keep these things on your mind; quietly and prayerfully review them and you will find that your knowledge will increase.
>
> One of the great values of the temple experience is that it presents the broad, sweeping panorama of God's purposes relating to this earth. Once we have been through the temple (and we can return and refresh our memories) the events of life fit into the scheme of things. We can see in perspective where we are, and we can quickly see when we are off course. (*Preparing to Enter the Holy Temple,* 10)

We all desire communion with our Heavenly Father and His Only Begotten Son. We all yearn for Their guidance and blessing in our lives. The temple is a choice venue for receiving that guidance and inspiration. President Ezra Taft Benson asked the important question: "Do we return to the temple often to receive the personal blessings that come from regular temple worship?" He then reminds us that "prayers are answered, revelation occurs, and instruction by the Spirit takes place in the holy temples of the Lord" (*TETB,* 179).

Because of the transcendent spiritual blessings that continual service in the temple brings, it stands to reason that we are to remain ever vigilant in order to counteract those negative influences that will tend to dissuade us from going. Elder Boyd K. Packer warns, "Temple work brings so much resistance because it is the source of so much spiritual power to the Latter-day Saints" (*Ensign,* Feb. 1995, 36). The temple beckons to us as a magnificent opportunity for demonstrating our sense of priorities, for displacing the superficial and unimportant things in our lives with those activities that accord more fully with the realization of eternal blessings. Moreover, the temple is an influence that galvanizes our desire to help others come to the temple, enlisting us to encourage, support, and reinforce their efforts to serve the Lord in His holy house. On March 11, 2003, the First Presidency issued a letter to Church leaders in which they stated, in part, the following:

> We are grateful for the increased availability of temples worldwide and invite adult members to have a current temple recommend and visit the temple more often. Where time and circumstances permit, members are encouraged to replace some leisure activities with temple service. . . .
> We request that local priesthood leaders encourage temple-worthy members to consider ways in which more frequent daytime temple attendance could occur. Home and visiting teachers may wish to arrange transportation for those who need it, particularly during the daytime.
> All of the ordinances which take place in the house of the Lord become expressions of our belief in that fundamental and basic doctrine of the immortality of the human soul. As we redouble our efforts and our faithfulness in going to the temple, the Lord will bless us. (*Ensign,* Mar. 2004, 45)

The temple is a source of light and inspiration—just the elements of life that need constant renewal and replenishment as we seek to take upon ourselves the divine nature and to bring blessings to our departed family progenitors. In this same spirit, Elder David B. Haight counseled: "Come to the temples worthily and regularly. Not only do you bless those who are deceased, but you may freely partake of the promised personal revelation that may bless your life with power, knowledge, light, beauty, and truth from on high, which will guide you and your posterity to eternal life" (*Ensign,* May 1992, 16). Returning to the house of the Lord regularly and serving the Lord faithfully in those sacred premises through vicarious ordinance work is manifest evidence that we are enduring to the end.

4. Include the temple in your prayers. Do we remember to include in our prayers the sacred work of the temples and those countless thousands of temple workers who invest their time and efforts to accomplish their commission as "saviours" on "mount Zion" (Obad. 1:21)? Do we pray to our Father in Heaven that He will continue to prosper the work of gathering family history information worldwide in support of temple work? Do we pray for strength and guidance for ourselves as we strive to support the Lord in this magnificent effort? On the occasion of the dedication of the temple that bore his name, Solomon declared: "Now, my God, let, I beseech thee, thine eyes be open, and let thine ears be attent unto the prayer that is made in this place. Now therefore arise, O Lord God, into thy resting place, thou, and the ark of thy strength: let thy priests, O Lord God, be clothed with salvation, and let thy saints rejoice in goodness" (2 Chr. 6:40–41).

In our times, the Prophet Joseph Smith set a pattern for temple-related supplication through his inspired dedicatory prayer for the Kirtland Temple on March 27, 1836—now included in the Doctrine and Covenants as section 109. It is instructive to read and reread this passage of scripture and savor repeatedly the uplifting sentiments and instructive counsel contained in it. Later, in an epistle to the Church dated September 6, 1842, concerning baptism for the dead, the Prophet Joseph brought forth an anthem of exultant praise and encouragement for the Saints:

> Brethren, shall we not go on in so great a cause? Go forward and not backward. Courage, brethren; and on, on

to the victory! Let your hearts rejoice, and be exceedingly glad. Let the earth break forth into singing. Let the dead speak forth anthems of eternal praise to the King Immanuel, who hath ordained, before the world was, that which would enable us to redeem them out of their prison; for the prisoners shall go free. Let the mountains shout for joy, and all ye valleys cry aloud; and all ye seas and dry lands tell the wonders of your Eternal King! And ye rivers, and brooks, and rills, flow down with gladness. Let the woods and all the trees of the field praise the Lord; and ye solid rocks weep for joy! And let the sun, moon, and the morning stars sing together, and let all the sons of God shout for joy! And let the eternal creations declare his name forever and ever! And again I say, how glorious is the voice we hear from heaven, proclaiming in our ears, glory, and salvation, and honor, and immortality, and eternal life; kingdoms, principalities, and powers! (D&C 128:22–23)

Through earnest prayer and humble supplication we can invoke the blessings of our Father in Heaven to help us place the temple at the center of our quest to endure to the end. Moreover, we can use the temple experience as the opportunity to invoke the blessings of our Heavenly Father upon our family members and associates who need special guidance and succor. The practice of entering the names of loved ones upon a slip of paper for inclusion upon the prayer rolls of the temple is a choice opportunity, on occasion, to importune the Lord in His holy house for His loving care and blessing.

5. Feast on the word of God, filling your own "temple" with the Spirit. We are the temple of God (see 1 Cor. 3:16–17; 6:19). When we fill our temple with light and truth, we will dispel the darkness of evil that lurks menacingly around us, and we will thus become more holy disciples of the Lord: "That which is of God is light; and he that receiveth light, and continueth in God, receiveth more light; and that light groweth brighter and brighter until the perfect day" (D&C 50:24). Nephi taught: "Wherefore, I said unto you, feast upon the words of Christ; for behold, the words of Christ will tell you all things what ye should do" (2 Ne. 32:3).

The process of enduring to the end is rendered more secure and energized when we continually feast upon the words of life. Let us study the scriptures to learn more about the Atonement, about the fundamental principles of the gospel, and about temple work. Let us read from the Book of Mormon daily—remembering to include frequently those passages that were given at the temple in Zarahemla by King Benjamin (see Mosiah 3–5) and by the Savior at the temple in Bountiful (see 3 Ne. 11–28). Let us place ourselves in a position of worthiness to be receptive to the word of the Lord: "And the scriptures shall be given, even as they are in mine own bosom, to the salvation of mine own elect" (D&C 35:20).

6. Continue to take on the divine nature. We have seen that preparing to enter the temple of the Lord is an exercise in systematically taking upon ourselves the divine nature, including such qualities as faith, virtue, knowledge, temperance, patience, brotherly kindness, godliness, charity, humility, and diligence (see 2 Pet. 1:3–8; D&C 4). Enduring to the end, particularly in regard to temple work, comprises the cultivation and augmentation of all of these qualities:

Faith in the eternal power of the Almighty to bring to pass the immortality and eternal life of man.

Virtue as the bloom of worthiness for admittance into the temple.

Knowledge of exalting truth as bestowed in the temple.

Temperance and moderation befitting a disciple of Christ.

Patience to learn line upon line and to gather family history data for use in the temples.

Brotherly kindness to complete vicarious work as saviors on Mount Zion.

Godliness to become more like the Father and the Son as we learn in the temple how to enter Their presence.

Charity to practice the pure love of Christ in all that we do—within or without the temple walls.

Humility to be submissive always to the will of the Father and the Son in doing temple work.

Diligence to carry on the mission of the temple by honoring our covenants to the end.

A systematic plan to improve in these qualities as we visit the temple will enable us to harvest a marvelous and bounteous array of spiritual blessings not accessible in any other way.

7. Make your home like unto a temple of God. Like the temple, a righteous home is a holy place where the family can live in gratitude and reverence before our Father in Heaven. We can make our homes a place where the Spirit can dwell, a place where our prayers can be answered, a place where family relationships are harmonious and uplifting, a place where the Lord would feel welcome if we were favored to have Him come to bless us there.

On one occasion, Elder L. Aldin Porter was asked the question: "How will the temple ordinances and covenants bless a marriage?" He responded: "The Lord has said: 'When we obtain any blessing from God, it is by obedience to that law upon which it is predicated' (D&C 130:21). Laws of eternal happiness are given in the temple, where we covenant to obey those laws. Keeping those covenants will help us establish a happy and productive home in this life and a continuation of that happiness into eternity" (*New Era,* Oct. 2004, 8).

The temple provides the key for family happiness, now and in the hereafter. Those who visit the house of the Lord regularly tend to bring that same spirit of love, reverence, and hope into their home, thus helping to transform it into a holy place unto the Lord. A major part of enduring to the end is organizing and maintaining a home in which the spirit of temple work flourishes and touches the lives of all who enter.

8. Teach your family and others about the temple. There are simple and effective ways in which we can teach about the temple to our families and others in our circle of influence. We can express to them our joy in the blessings that flow from temple service. We can demonstrate in our demeanor and language the quality of discipleship fostered and cultivated through temple activity. We can radiate the light of the temple in our personalities so that our children will have the desire to follow in our footsteps as "children of the covenant" (3 Ne. 20:26). In this context, Elder David B. Haight has counseled:

> When you return from the temple, share with your children and loved ones at home your feelings about what you experienced. Speak not of the sacred ordinances, but of the love and power manifest by them.
>
> Let your children see you behave—toward them and your eternal companion—in kindlier, more loving ways. Your consistently positive expressions about what you experience in the temple will create in your children a desire to receive those same blessings and provide them with strong motivation to resist the temptations which could disqualify them from temple blessings. (*Ensign,* May 1992, 16)

The Lord will inspire us to teach our families the eternal importance of temple work with enthusiasm and thanksgiving. He will open up the way for us to be instruments of devotion in guiding our families to participate in the program of temple blessings that will secure for them their promised inheritance in the halls of glory. President Ezra Taft Benson has invoked upon us the Lord's blessing in this sacred duty: "God bless Israel! God bless those of our forebears who constructed this holy edifice. God bless us to teach our children and our grandchildren what great blessings await them by going to the temple. God bless us to receive all the blessings revealed by Elijah the prophet so that our callings and election will be made sure" (*Ensign,* Aug. 1985, 10).

It is sometimes the little things that have great impact for good. A good word shared with family members about the spiritual atmosphere of the Lord's house, a witness of the tender feelings we have in being part of an eternal family, a picture of the temple displayed in the home—all these things take little effort but can have great leveraging power to expand the harvest of positive outcomes for our families. In this regard, President Howard W. Hunter said: "Let us share with our children the spiritual feelings we have in the temple. And let us teach them more earnestly and more comfortably the things we can appropriately say about the purposes of the house of the Lord. Keep a picture of a temple in your home that your children may see it. Teach them about the purposes of the house of the Lord. Have them plan from their earliest years to go there and to remain worthy of that blessing" (*Ensign,* Feb. 1995, 6).

9. Extend the covenant blessings to your forebears. As a concept, temple work is a rational confirmation of God's universal design for bringing about the immortality and eternal life of His children. As an activity, temple work is proof of the force for good that this divine program can bring into our lives, enriching our relationships, edifying our character, and strengthening our hope and faith in the future. We find joy in transforming the concept of temple work into deeds of action. To this end, we need to return often to the temple, bringing before the altars of the Lord the names of all those special people who constitute our family tree, that they, too, can have the eternal blessings prepared for the obedient and righteous children of our Father in Heaven. President Ezra Taft Benson reminds us of this obligation:

> Do we periodically participate in all of the temple ordinances and thus receive the full blessings of vicarious work for our ancestors? Also, have we identified and received the ordinances for at least one of our ancestors? All members of the Church should be actively engaged in working on their family histories and receiving the help they need from trained stake and ward temple and family history consultants" (*TETB,* 179).

In the spirit of this counsel, Carol B. Thomas, former first counselor in the Young Women general presidency, provided a moving illustration of the commitment to carry the blessings of the temple to our ancestors:

The Spirit of Elijah is brooding in the land. As we work with youth of the Church, we see they are being drawn to their temples.

In Nicaragua, Central America, a group of 49 young women and their leaders took 2,000 names to the Guatemala City Temple. It took each girl a year to save enough money to go. These faithful young women rode a bus almost two days' journey through three country borders and spent two or three days at the temple before returning home.

In another ward, young people have located the names of 10,000 ancestors as they have turned their hearts to their families. Where temples are available, we see youth doing baptisms for the dead, sometimes on an individual weekly basis. (*Ensign,* May 1999, 12)

10. Be a "good ancestor" in all respects. Finally, enduring to the end means becoming what President Harold B. Lee called "a good ancestor" (*THBL,* 584). A good ancestor is one who lives an exemplary life of obedience and righteousness, who honors his or her covenants with persistence and care, who galvanizes and inspires descendants in pursuit of worthy family history objectives, who marks the trail toward the temple for the rising generations, and who leaves behind a legacy of being a stalwart savior on Mount Zion.

Concluding Wisdom

When we follow a course defined by obedience and fidelity to covenants such as those outlined in the preceding pages, then the likelihood of enduring to the end is greatly enhanced. Momentum builds. Faith increases. The blessings of the Spirit are poured out without measure. Confidence grows. Vision and discernment improve. The grand destination of all temple work—to ultimately return to the presence of the Father and the Son, along with our eternal families—is brought into clear focus. Hope abounds. Our lives have more meaning. Joy and happiness emerge through the clouds of adversity and tribulation. We accomplish all that is asked of us—in the strength of the Lord.

Temple work will bring into our lives great blessings—blessings that will help us to endure to the end in all diligence as we savor the continual joy of the house of the Lord: more loving relationships in our family circle, greater understanding of the nature of God and the grand purposes of the plan of happiness, and greater comfort and peace in completing the mission to bless the generations of mankind in keeping with the Spirit of Elijah to bind together the hearts of our Father's children. President Ezra Taft Benson assured us, in this respect, that great blessings flow from faithful temple service:

> Now let me say something to all who can worthily go to the house of the Lord. When you attend the temple and perform the ordinances that pertain to the house of the Lord, certain blessings will come to you: You will receive the spirit of Elijah, which will turn your hearts to your spouse, to your children, and to your forebears. You will love your family with a deeper love than you have loved before. You will be endowed with power from on high as the Lord has promised.
>
> You will receive the key of the knowledge of God (see D&C 84:19). You will learn how you can be like Him. Even the power of godliness will be manifest to you (see D&C 84:20). You will be doing a great service to those who have passed to the other side of the veil in order that they might be "judged according to men in the flesh, but live according to God in the spirit" (D&C 138:34; 1 Pet. 4:6). Such are the blessings of the temple and the blessings of frequently attending the temple. (*Ensign,* Aug. 1985, 10)

By looking to the temple, we can enjoy the vision of hope for the future. In the final chapter we will review the nature of hope that is engendered by temple attendance, and we will recall the magnificent blessings that await the faithful who respond to the invitation of the Lord to come to His house in humility and pure devotion.

Time to Meditate and Ponder

1. According to Elder Dallin H. Oaks, we can truly say that we are "saved"—in the sense that we receive our promised blessing of exaltation in the celestial kingdom—only after "the final judgment of Him who is the Great Judge of the living and the dead" (*Ensign,* May 1998, 55). How does this fact infuse the process of enduring to the end with added significance and urgency?

2. The Psalmist inquired: "Who shall ascend into the hill of the Lord? or who shall stand in his holy place?" (Ps. 24:3). Do you recall the answer given in this passage? How does this relate to the process of enduring to the end?

3. The scriptures on gratitude and related terms reveal an interesting pattern showing five main causes or reasons for us to be grateful: God (His greatness and mercy), the gospel (the Atonement and plan of salvation), the goodness of people (prophets, our forebears, our families), the gathering (into the kingdom of God where temples abound), and gifts (the gifts of the Spirit). How do you feel the temple relates to each of these five categories of blessings?

4. What are the blessings of returning to the temple regularly?

5. What are some ways we can include the temple and temple work in our regular prayers?

6. How can daily scripture study enhance our testimony of the temple?

7. How does each of the qualities of the divine nature—faith, virtue, knowledge, temperance, patience, brotherly kindness, godliness, charity, humility, and diligence—relate to the process of enduring to the end by looking to the temple for truth and light?

8. What are some ways to make our homes more like the temple in spirit and peace?

9. How can we follow President Harold B. Lee's advice to become "a good ancestor"(*THBL*, 584)?

CHAPTER 20
LOOKING FORWARD WITH HOPE—THE GLORY AND BLESSINGS OF THE FULLNESS OF THE GOSPEL

Guiding Principle: The Lord, in His loving-kindness and mercy, has given to His children the key to eternal peace and joy. It is the unfolding miracle of what is imparted to us in His holy house—pure knowledge of salvation and exaltation, sealing powers that transcend the boundaries of mortality and extend into the eternities, and the promise of receiving the kind of life that God lives, even eternal life and never-ending rest, "which rest is the fulness of His glory" (D&C 84:24).

> *Personal blessings come from temple attendance. And we again emphasize the personal blessings of temple worship and the sanctity and safety that are provided within those hallowed walls. It is the house of the Lord, a place of revelation and of peace. As we attend the temple, we learn more richly and deeply the purpose of life and the significance of the atoning sacrifice of the Lord Jesus Christ. Let us make the temple, with temple worship and temple covenants and temple marriage, our ultimate earthly goal and the supreme mortal experience.*
> —HOWARD W. HUNTER, *THE TEACHINGS OF HOWARD W. HUNTER*, 238.

Through the temple we are granted access to the glory and blessings of the fullness of the gospel. The seeds of hope for the blessings of salvation and exaltation are planted securely within our hearts in the house of the Lord. Such hope is based upon the atoning mission of the Lord Jesus Christ and upon the plan of happiness and eternal life that God provided for His children before the world began. Hope is the spiritual empowerment for our quest to become like the Savior. The feelings of hope that unfold within us in the temple provide us with a sense of confidence in looking forward in life as we strive to acquire and maintain a pattern of righteousness and obedience. When we lose hope, life becomes difficult in every sense. We fail then to enjoy life or look to do anything to build a better future. The temple is a check against the fading of hope, a safeguard against the loss of confidence in the future. A life without hope is empty, but a life filled with hope is a life filled with light and meaning. The temple is the symbol of hope and the institution of faith in the future.

We read in Proverbs, "The hope of the righteous shall be gladness: but the expectation of the wicked shall perish" (Prov. 10:28). Jeremiah declared, "Blessed is the man that trusteth in the Lord, and whose hope the Lord is" (Jer. 17:7). Authentic hope and genuine faith are centered in Jesus Christ and anchored in a commitment to become more like Him. Neal A. Maxwell shares with us his thoughts about this perspective:

> Real hope, said Paul, is a hope for things that are not seen that are true. (See Romans 8:24.) Paul accurately linked hopelessness and godlessness as he wrote of those "having no hope, and without God in the world." (Ephesians 2:12.) Christ-centered hope, however, is a very specific and particularized hope. It is focused on the great realities of the resurrection, eternal life, a better world, and Christ's triumphant second coming—"things as they really will be." (Jacob 4:13.) (*Notwithstanding My Weakness*, 40–41)

In a way, the essence of the preparatory qualities of the divine nature we have discussed in this book is captured in the quality of hope. The spiritual attributes that belong to the divine nature all become aligned and focused in our hope for oneness with the Lord through the temple and the assurance of receiving a place in the mansions of heaven in the presence of the great Elohim and His Son. What can we do each day to magnify our hope in the Lord as we look to the temple and enjoy the blessings of eternity provided there? Here are a few ideas:

Understand that hope is power. Hope, like faith, is a self-fulfilling prophecy, for it brings about the very conditions necessary to realize the vision that it sees for the future. Therefore, hope is an indispensable ally, especially as it is centered in Jesus Christ and connected to faith. Hope is a guide for life. Through the eyes of hope engendered in the temple, we see opportunities that would otherwise be invisible (see 2 Ne. 31:20).

Identify and do those key actions that generate hope. Count your blessings regularly; spend time with the hopeful; plan your agenda around hope; be a problem solver; work on long-range goals; visit the temple regularly; look to God and pray for hope and comfort each day; live positively and righteously (see 1 Ne. 3:7; Alma 26:12; D&C 123:17).

Give hope to others, and it will expand in your own life. Hope is a gift you give to others who depend on you. Be a leader of hope. Be a teacher of hope. Inspire others with the vision and blessings of the temple. Reach out to your forebears in vicarious service to fulfill their hope for salvation and exaltation. Hope truly empowers people to go forward, because it is always centered in Christ, the rock of our salvation.

Our hope for the future is sustained, confirmed, reinforced, and magnified by the Lord as He pours out blessing after blessing upon us and our families through the instruction and ordinance work of the temples. Let us conclude by reviewing these extraordinary blessings as viewed through the eyes of the prophets and other inspired Church leaders. In the pages that follow we will outline ten kinds of blessings that flow to us through the temple. May we always be grateful for the mercy, kindness, and eternal compassion of our Heavenly Father and

His Only Begotten Son for such unspeakable blessings as are accorded us in the holy temples.

Blessings of the Temple

1. The power of the priesthood. The temple is the house of God, a place of binding covenants sealed by the Holy Spirit of Promise by virtue of our obedience and commitment to enduring spiritual values. In the temple we are empowered by priesthood ordinances with the capacity to enter the presence of the Father and the Son as the ultimate realization of our deepest hopes and desires. In the temple we learn of the sanctity of our relationship with our Father in Heaven—that we are His children and that He loves us so deeply that He has made it His work and glory to bring us home again through the plan of salvation and exaltation. That return journey takes power—priesthood power brought to bear in behalf of mankind through the Restoration and activated through the keys of the ministry in the temples of God. In his inspired dedicatory prayer for the Kirtland Temple on March 27, 1836, the Prophet Joseph Smith invoked the following blessing on the Saints associated with the temple: "And we ask thee, Holy Father, that thy servants may go forth from this house armed with thy power, and that thy name may be upon them, and thy glory be round about them, and thine angels have charge over them; . . . We ask thee, Holy Father, to establish the people that shall worship, and honorably hold a name and standing in this thy house, to all generations and for eternity; . . . That no combination of wickedness shall have power to rise up and prevail over thy people upon whom thy name shall be put in this house" (D&C 109:22, 24, 26).

The sealing powers of the priesthood have been restored as an essential aspect of the "marvellous work and a wonder" (Isa. 29:14) and the "new covenant with the house of Israel" (Jer. 31:31) foretold by prophets of old as the means for bringing blessings of glory to the children of God. President Gordon B. Hinckley explained the everlasting nature of the power of the priesthood exercised for the blessing of the faithful in the temples of God:

While upon the earth the Lord conferred upon His chosen disciples the eternal priesthood, saying:

"And I will give unto thee the keys of the kingdom of heaven: and whatsoever thou shalt bind on earth shall be bound in heaven: and whatsoever thou shalt loose on earth shall be loosed in heaven." (Matt. 16:19.)

This same authority was bestowed in this generation under the hands of Peter, James, and John, who had received it directly from the Lord. This power, to seal in the heavens that which is sealed upon the earth is exercised in these holy houses. Every one of us is subject to mortal death. But through the eternal plan made possible by the sacrifice of the Redeemer, all may go on to glories infinitely greater than any of the wondrous things of this life. (*Ensign,* May 1993, 72)

2. Eternal perpetuation of loving relationships. One of the most grand and munificent blessings afforded the Saints in the temples of God is the assurance that their loving relationships in mortality will be preserved and sustained in the life hereafter. Of all the yearnings of the human soul, by far the greatest is the hope that family relationships—founded in love and secured in lasting devotion—will be perpetuated beyond the boundaries of the grave. We cannot conceive of these transcending bonds of familial belonging and unity ever being dissolved. If so, life would lose its meaning. And so it is that the Lord, in His eternal righteousness, has prepared the way for the family to remain together forever through obedience to the principles of the gospel and through the sealing powers administered in the temples of God. President Gordon B. Hinckley spoke of this reassuring promise as follows:

> Was there ever a man who truly loved a woman, or a woman who truly loved a man, who did not pray that their relationship might continue beyond the grave? Has a child ever been buried by parents who did not long for the assurance that their loved one would again be theirs in a world to come? Can anyone believing in eternal life doubt

that the God of heaven would grant his sons and daughters that most precious attribute of life, the love that finds its most meaningful expression in family relationships? No, reason demands that the family relationship shall continue after death. The human heart longs for it. The God of heaven has revealed a way whereby it may be secured. The sacred ordinances of the house of the Lord provide for it. . . .

But there are uncounted millions who have walked the earth and who have never had the opportunity to hear the gospel. Shall they be denied such blessings as are offered in the temples of the Church?

Through living proxies who stand in behalf of the dead, the same ordinances are available to those who have passed from mortality. In the spirit world they then are free to accept or reject those earthly ordinances performed for them, including baptism, marriage, and the sealing of family relationships. There must be no compulsion in the work of the Lord, but there must be opportunity. (*Ensign*, Aug. 1974, 39–40)

The nobility of the eternal family is the hallmark of the gospel of Jesus Christ. Each member thereof—husband and wife united in an everlasting partnership, children as the gifts of God unto the family, grandchildren and all further manifestation of the harvest of Zion—is of consummate value in the design of heaven to perfect the Saints and elevate them, as individuals and in family units, to their station as heirs of the glories of their celestial life. Elder Robert L. Simpson, former member of the First Quorum of the Seventy, declared these reassuring words concerning such temple blessings:

The temple is a house of eternal relationships, a place where families can come for the purpose of transforming their family circle into an eternal family unit, where all of a sudden "together forever" becomes far more important than the next trivial family difference.

The ultimate blessings of the temple are centered in the love and devotion between husband and wife. They must set the example—they are the core. The scriptures say it best of all: "Nevertheless neither is the man without the woman, neither the woman without the man, in the Lord" (1 Cor. 11:11). Everything in this world that is counter to a tender and loyal husband-wife relationship is a tool of the adversary. Everything that promotes and perpetuates family unity—mother, father, and children properly endowed with and motivated by the light and truth of Christ—is in harmony with the Lord's plan for mortal man. (*Ensign*, Nov. 1980, 10)

No more edifying and uplifting experience awaits the faithful in this life than the experience of seeing loved ones finally enter the circle of temple sealings as an answer to long-standing prayers and supplication. President Harold B. Lee related the following experience as a confirmation of sacred temple blessings:

I was down in a husbands-and-wives meeting in Provo years ago when a lovely sister bore her testimony as to the joy that had come into her home since her husband had become active in the Church. She told about going through the temple with her husband. She told how he had been inactive, how he had smoked and hadn't been advanced in the priesthood, and how someone took hold of him and finally helped him to become worthy and ready to receive the priesthood; and the bishop had finally given him a recommend to go to the temple. After she had described that wonderful evening, she said, Here, five little girls came in to be sealed to their father and mother. This man of God pronounced us a family for the eternities. And as she finished this story and bore her testimony, she looked over the pulpit and down in front of her where her husband was seated. She seemed to forget for that moment that there was anybody there but just the two of them, and she said to him, Daddy, I can't tell you how happy the girls now are and how grateful we are for what you have done for us, because, you see, Daddy, except for you who holds the priesthood, neither the children nor I could be together as a family in the hereafter. Thank God for our daddy who holds the key and unlocks the door to an eternal family home. (*Ensign,* Dec. 1971, 112)

President John Taylor assured us that our sons and daughters will be saved and exalted through our service as "saviors" to our God:

> God has fulfilled His promises to us, and our prospects are grand and glorious. Yes, in the next life we will have . . . our sons and daughters. If we do not get them all at once, we will have them some time. . . . You that are mourning about your children straying away will have your sons and your daughters. If you succeed in passing through these trials and afflictions and receive a resurrection, you will, by the power of the Priesthood, work and labor, as the Son of God has, until you get all your sons and daughters in the path of exaltation and glory. This is just as sure as that the sun rose this morning over yonder mountains. Therefore, mourn not because all your sons and daughters do not follow in the path that you have marked out to them, or give heed to your counsels. Inasmuch as we succeed in securing eternal glory, and stand as saviors, and as kings and priests to our God, we will save our posterity. (John Taylor, *Millennial Star,* 22 Jan. 1894, 51–52)

For a season, we mortals are exposed to the litany of worldly allurements that would draw us away from the straight and narrow pathway. Some may stumble; some may lose their grip on the iron rod. But above and beyond all that we can do as parents and guardians, the Lord in His infinite wisdom extends His arm of guidance and mercy over all, including those who slide into the byways of life where, for a time, the mists of darkness obscure the way. However, the pattern of hope in ourselves and our posterity, plus unshakeable faith in the strength of the Lord, will in due time carry the day so that our family circles, made whole and complete through the blessings of repentance and grace, sealed by the binding promises of the temple ordinances, will endure the tests of time. Elder Boyd K. Packer has emphasized the need to hold fast to our faith and hope in behalf of loved ones who might have strayed from the pathway of truth:

> It is a great challenge to raise a family in the darkening mists of our moral environment. . . .
>
> The measure of our success as parents, however, will not rest solely on how our children turn out. That judgment would be just only if we could raise our families in a perfectly moral environment, and that now is not possible.
>
> It is not uncommon for responsible parents to lose one of their children, for a time, to influences over which they have no control. They agonize over rebellious sons or daughters. They are puzzled over why they are so helpless when they have tried so hard to do what they should.
>
> It is my conviction that those wicked influences one day will be overruled.
>
> "The Prophet Joseph Smith declared—and he never taught a more comforting doctrine—that the eternal sealings of faithful parents and the divine promises made to them for valiant service in the Cause of Truth, would save not only themselves, but likewise their posterity. Though some of the sheep may wander, the eye of the Shepherd is upon them, and sooner or later they will feel the tentacles of Divine Providence reaching out after them and drawing them back to the fold. Either in this life or the life to come, they will return. They will have to pay their debt to justice; they will suffer for their sins; and may tread a thorny path; but if it leads them at last, like the penitent Prodigal, to a loving and forgiving father's heart and home, the painful experience will not have been in vain. Pray for your careless and disobedient children; hold on to them with your faith. Hope on, trust on, till you see the salvation of God."
>
> We cannot overemphasize the value of temple marriage, the binding ties of the sealing ordinance, and the standards of worthiness required of them. When parents keep the covenants they have made at the altar of the temple, their children will be forever bound to them. (*Ensign,* May 1992, 66)

3. Peace, comfort, and joy. The temple is the sanctuary of peace, comfort, joy, and happiness—beyond anything that can be experienced in any other way by mortals. In the house of the Lord we find peace that overcomes any despair, comfort in the face of all adversity, confidence in our selfless service to the Lord, joy in the power of the Atonement, and happiness in the circle of our loved ones.

These treasured rewards are illustrated in two experiences recounted by Elder Franklin D. Richards, while he served as a member of the First Quorum of the Seventy:

> I have witnessed the joy and satisfaction that come to those who serve in the temple. I recall on one occasion a sister coming through the temple door, her face bright with anticipation and her step quickened. She was a temple worker who had been back home for a visit. She grasped my hand and said, "It's so good to be back. I love my service in the temple, and know I cannot be happy, really happy, away from it. It brings me a joy and satisfaction that is found in no other place. I feel a sense of accomplishment in doing something of eternal value. It's a little like the work of the Savior, who did for mankind what they could not do for themselves. This work brings peace to my soul—yes, the peace that passeth understanding."
>
> One day, Sister Richards and I walked into the baptistry about noon and noticed a young girl sitting on one of the benches. As we talked with her, she told us she was from West Virginia and it was her twelfth birthday. Her mother had asked her what she wanted for a birthday present, and she had asked that her mother bring her to the temple so that she could perform baptisms for the dead.
>
> What an opportunity temple workers have to touch the hearts of our brothers and sisters of all ages! (*Ensign*, Nov. 1986, 70)

Often the temple provides succor to the bereaved and solace to the lonely. The sure knowledge of the eternal nature of the family robs death of its sting and lifts surviving loved ones beyond the vale of anguish and sorrow. The joy and comfort in the assurance of a celestial union transcends the heartache of temporary separation. Elder Russell M. Nelson has stated:

> The blessings of the temple become most meaningful when our loved ones are taken in death from our family circles. To know that our period of separation is but temporary provides peace that passes ordinary understanding. President Joseph Fielding Smith (1876–1972) wrote, "Through the power of this priesthood which Elijah bestowed, husband and wife may be sealed, or married for eternity; children may be sealed to their parents for eternity; thus the family is made eternal, and death does not separate the members." Blessed with eternal sealings, we can face death as a necessary component of God's great plan of happiness. (*Ensign*, Mar. 2002, 17)

The temple is our rock because it rests upon the foundation of the gospel of Jesus Christ; it is our fortress amid the stress and strain of worldly influences; it is our bastion of consolation when tribulation and trauma descend upon our souls. The temple is our triumph over mortal fears and our victory over vice and depression. Carol B. Thomas, former first counselor in the Young Women general presidency, related a story of how the Lord provides comfort and peace in the temple, especially during times of despair: "Recently I met a 35-year-old woman in the temple. As we visited, I asked if her husband was with her. With a look of tenderness in her eyes, she shared with me that he had died of a brain tumor three months ago. The temple is her anchor; the Spirit found in the temple gives her comfort and peace, and perhaps her husband was there" (*Ensign*, May 1999, 12).

4. Safety and protection. The temple provides to the Saints a comforting measure of sanctity and safety in the midst of the turmoil and ephemerality characteristic of worldly institutions. The temple offers refuge and protection from the onslaught of temptation and moral decadence so common in the culture of today. In the temple, one has a sense of the protecting hand of God extended in love and compassion. This shield of protection continues outside the temple in the form of the temple garment, which serves as a safeguard for the faithful against the influences of evil and destruction in the world. Thus fortified with the Spirit, one can remember in gratitude the promise of the Lord for those engaged in His errand: "There I will be also, for I will go before your face. I will be on your right hand and on your left, and my Spirit shall be in your hearts, and mine angels round about you, to bear you up" (D&C 84:88).

Why does peace prevail in the house of the Lord? Because the temple is the emblem of Christ's victory over death and the icon of His protecting hand extended in power over the people of Zion. No force of evil can forestall the inexorable advance of the kingdom of God in this, the last of all dispensations of time; no worldly influence can penetrate the covenant armor of God received and deployed by the faithful in sacred temple rites as a means of securing the ultimate safety of their families in the eternities. This kind of refuge, this "covert from storm and from rain" (Isa. 4:6), is a gift from heaven renewed each time we step foot in the temple of God.

Said Elder David B. Haight:

> The moment we step into the house of the Lord, the atmosphere changes from the worldly to the heavenly, where respite from the normal activities of life is found, and where peace of mind and spirit is received. It is a refuge from the ills of life and a protection from the temptations that are contrary to our spiritual well-being. We are told that "he who doeth the works of righteousness shall receive his reward, even peace in this world, and eternal life in the world to come" (D&C 59:23). (*Ensign*, Nov. 1990, 59)

5. Instruction and revelation. In the temples of God we learn pure knowledge concerning our purpose in life; we are granted access to a higher perspective from which to view the human condition—from the premortal realm to mortality and into the afterlife. The temple is a house of inspiration and revelation unlike any other place on earth. Prayers are answered there; guidance is given. Windows of wisdom are opened up. Often patriarchal blessings are fulfilled through experiences within the temple.

The temple is truly a place where the living waters of revelation flow unto the meek and lowly of heart, the humble and the receptive. Elder Robert L. Simpson taught this sacred principle on one occasion:

> The temple is a house of prayer, for Heavenly Father is glorified by every ordinance performed therein. He who enters for the first time receives a pronouncement of special blessings that are not available outside the temple.
>
> The temple is a house of instruction—yes, even divine instruction—about God's eternal plan for his children. In the temple one gains a superior perspective about his personal relationship with his Maker and with the Savior—yes, special knowledge about God and Jesus Christ, which is essential to the obtaining of life eternal. "And this is life eternal, that they might know thee the only true God, and Jesus Christ, whom thou hast sent" (John 17:3).
>
> The temple is a house of revelation—yes, continuing revelation. Whether that revelation be to a prophet or a member who seeks after truth, all who come to the temple seeking are continually taught and edified. (*Ensign,* Nov. 1980, 10)

Stories abound concerning the flow of inspiration that comes from temple activity. Here are two examples:

> Michelle Desputeau, who reared her two daughters alone as a single mother, has always found much of her spiritual strength in family history and temple service. "When I come to the temple with a problem," she says, "I find the answer here. When I pray, I feel his Spirit. I know the gospel is true. I have so many evidences of God's love for me."
>
> David Turley, a member of the Willow Canyon Eighth Ward, Sandy Utah East Stake, feels that because he was in

the temple one evening, he received inspiration and understanding concerning an experience that had happened to him earlier that day. He had been driving home from work that afternoon in light traffic. As he neared a normally busy intersection, he felt a strong impression to stop at the green light. Almost immediately, a vehicle whose driver had ignored the opposite red light entered the intersection and swerved to avoid hitting David's pickup truck.

Grateful but shaken, David continued home. That evening, he and his wife, Sheri, attended the Jordan River Temple. While in the temple, David received an overwhelming impression that his life had been spared as an answer to his son's prayer that morning. "I thought back to the morning," says David. "As usual, we had gotten our three children out of bed early enough to have morning prayers together before I left for work. Our six-year-old son had offered the prayer and said, 'Bless Daddy as he drives to work and back.' I feel that I received this insight because I was in the temple. The next day, I told my children about the experience. For them, it was a testimony of the power of prayer and the blessings of temple attendance." (*Ensign,* Oct. 1994, 6)

6. Opportunities for service. Where in the entire world—other than in the temples of God—can one find the sacred opportunity to be engaged in a work that reaches beyond the veil of mortality and into the eternities? The house of the Lord is the employment agency for the Lord's most spiritually transcendent enterprise—that of accomplishing vicarious service for our departed brothers and sisters. Temple work is also missionary work—missionary work that extends into the realm of the spirit world where numberless souls await the precious opportunity to "be judged according to men in the flesh, but live according to God in the spirit" (1 Pet. 4:6). From the gateways of the sacred temples, patrons and temple workers go forth with the commitment and training to improve this world and make it a better place—even as they regularly open up opportunities for countless concourses of the departed to improve their lot in the life to come.

How grateful we should be for the blessings of service in the temple, for the sacrifice of the Saints in building such structures unto God in all generations, and for the opportunity to pay our tithes and offerings today in support of erecting and operating the temples of God throughout the world. It is from such sacrifice that character is built and hearts and minds prepared to receive those blessings that "eye hath not seen, nor ear heard, neither have entered into the heart of man" (1 Cor. 2:9). But in the temples of God we catch the vision of the magnitude of the heavenly plan to enrich the lives of the faithful Saints and elevate them to a station of being the sons and daughters of the Almighty. Such incomparable blessings come to light through inspiration and revelation founded on sacrifice and valiant service: "But God hath revealed them unto us by his Spirit: for the Spirit searcheth all things, yea, the deep things of God" (1 Cor. 2:10).

Elder Robert L. Simpson confirmed the relationship between temple work and sacrifice: "The temple is a house of commitment and sacrifice, for it is truly stated that there can be no true worship without sacrifice; indeed, as the Saints sing, sacrifice brings forth the blessings of heaven" (*Ensign,* Nov. 1980, 10). Sacrifice, particularly sacrifice in support of the eternal cause of temple work, is the essence of faith, as Joseph Smith taught:

> Let us here observe, that a religion that does not require the sacrifice of all things never has power sufficient to produce the faith necessary unto life and salvation; for, from the first existence of man, the faith necessary unto the enjoyment of life and salvation never could be obtained without the sacrifice of all earthly things. It was through this sacrifice, and this only, that God has ordained that men should enjoy eternal life; and it is through the medium of the sacrifice of all earthly things that men do actually know that they are doing the things that are well pleasing in the sight of God. When a man has offered in sacrifice all that he has for the truth's sake, not even withholding his life, and believing

before God that he has been called to make this sacrifice because he seeks to do his will, he does know, most assuredly, that God does and will accept his sacrifice and offering, and that he has not, nor will not seek his face in vain. Under these circumstances, then, he can obtain the faith necessary for him to lay hold on eternal life. (*Lectures on Faith* [Salt Lake City: Deseret Book, 1985], 6:7)

The temple is the Missionary Training Center of the eternities. It is the ultimate venue for gathering in the dispersed of Israel and assembling the hosts of those without anchor and compass. Through temple work the sanctioning hand of grace and mercy is extended to the spirit children of the Almighty languishing in the spirit realm, awaiting the dawning of a brighter day. Who are the armies of workers in the temples of God but missionaries on the Lord's errand opening the floodgates of salvation through vicarious service administered by the priesthood of God! Elder J. Richard Clarke, formerly a counselor in the Presiding Bishopric and a member of the Presidency of the Seventy, observed the following concerning the synergy of temple work and missionary service:

> For you who are still preparing for your endowment and sealings, may I remind you of a very important opportunity. The most successful mission where more investigators are converted than all the missions in the world combined cannot perform a single baptism. This missionary labor is performed in the spirit world. All the great missionaries who have previously lived in mortality are, we are told, preaching the gospel but they must rely on worthy youth and young adults to be baptized for those who accept the gospel.
>
> When we presided over the temple in Hawaii we were thrilled to see the students of BYU—Hawaii organize into weekly ward groups to perform baptisms in the temple. We estimated that they had performed enough baptisms one year to equal the membership of 10 stakes. . . .
>
> Brothers and sisters, the work of the temple is the culmination of all missionary work, whether for the living

or the deceased. Though its magnitude of vicarious ordinances may seem overwhelming, it will be done in the due time of the Lord. I testify of that. Let us all live our lives so we can always have the privilege of serving in the house of the Lord (Brigham Young University—Idaho Devotional, Sept. 23, 2003).

The opportunity of serving in the temple augments and stimulates our level and commitment of service in the outside world. This point was emphasized by Elder Neal A. Maxwell:

> While the temple is a place of service, work done there is not a substitute for Christian service in the outside world. It can be a powerful spur thereto, however, by reminding us of the need for sacrifice—not the giving of just our means but also of ourselves. Temple attendance is not a guarantee that we will become better, but it provides a powerful and pointed invitation to become better. The ways of the world receive constant reinforcement—should not the ways of heaven?
>
> Temple work is not an escape from the world but a reinforcing of our need to better the world while preparing ourselves for another and far better world. Thus, being in the Lord's house can help us to be different from the world in order to make more difference in the world. (*Not My Will, But Thine* [Salt Lake City: Bookcraft, 1998], 133)

Thousands of faithful Latter-day Saints avail themselves of the opportunity to serve in the temples of God around the world. This number increases every year as new temples are brought into service. The sacred temples are staffed by a magnificent army of God—people from all walks of life and from every conceivable background and nationality, all united in the cause of helping the Lord to bring to pass the immortality and eternal life of man. The work of the temple brings together representatives of every profession—teachers, doctors, lawyers, farmers, police officers, government officials, custodians, business operators, craftspersons, salespersons, and those from the ranks of the retired—all engaged in the fulfilling and ennobling commission to serve God and help establish the cause of Zion. The temple is a haven of peace for singles and a venue of rejuvenation for seniors.

Many faithful Saints are able to fill regular assignments in the temple as ordinance workers and officiators. The blessings of this kind of service are unique and all encompassing. Devoted industry of a spiritual nature, as in temple service, builds fiber and strengthens character. The temple is a place of peace, but also of performance; of holiness but also of hard work. Elder David E. Sorensen articulates this point with candor:

> President Hinckley has suggested we not focus so much on the personal benefits of attending the temple but rather focus on temple work as "work." While the personal blessings resulting from temple attendance are numerous, we must not lose sight of the fact that it is work and requires commitment and duty. . . .
>
> When working in the temple, an ordinance worker finds it really is work; from memorization to procedure, there is much to do. The result of this effort is that ordinance workers gain familiarity with the ordinances and have an opportunity to learn and grow even more. . . .
>
> While the temple is certainly a place of refuge, a retreat to learn and understand ourselves, there may be even more benefit in going to the temple to actually do exacting, weighty, rigorous, demanding work. One of the benefits of having numerous temples is not only that more members can attend but that more members can serve as ordinance workers. (*Liahona,* Aug. 2002, 30)

Enduring to the end may mean that you will have the opportunity to serve in capacities beyond those of a regular patron in the temple. You may, in addition, be called on to contribute time and effort serving the needs of thousands of others who may come to the house of the Lord seeking light and truth.

All those who are worthy are welcomed into these holy precincts as they consecrate their time and talents for the blessing of God's children. Some devote early morning hours to the service, some evening hours. Many arrange to take time off from their work during the day to be agents on the Lord's errand. All are edified and enriched by the experience. There is nothing like it in all the world. No blessing surpasses the gifts of mercy and benevolence bestowed by God upon those who come to His house.

7. Fellowship through temple attendance. The Prophet Joseph Smith taught this principle: "When the Savior shall appear we shall see him as he is. We shall see that he is a man like ourselves. And that same sociality which exists among us here will exist among us there, only it will be coupled with eternal glory, which glory we do not now enjoy" (D&C 130:1–2).

Looking at these verses of scripture as a unified principle, we can discern the celestial blessing of being with our loved ones in worthiness in the presence of the Lord, His presence being the epitome of glory and spiritual illumination. The pleasant sociality that defines our current relationships with loved ones and friends will then be enhanced through the element of divine glory—which surely will elevate immensely the joy and happiness deriving from our closeness as an eternal family. The temple offers us a glimpse of the sublime rewards of heavenly fellowship. Our edifying associations in the temple with family, relatives, friends—and strangers whose spirit of commitment and trust is akin to our own—provide a rehearsal of the grand unfolding of eternal blessings in the courts on high.

Our associations in the temples of God remind us that the angels of heaven are everywhere present among us. President Thomas S. Monson recounted an event in the temple that helps us understand the power of this kind of blessing:

> When we realize just how precious children are, we will not find it difficult to follow the pattern of the Master in our association with them. Not long ago, a sweet scene took place at the Salt Lake Temple. Children, who had been ever so tenderly cared for by faithful workers in the temple

nursery, were now leaving in the arms of their mothers and fathers. One child turned to the lovely women who had been so kind to them and, with a wave of her arm, spoke the feelings of her heart as she exclaimed, "Goodnight, angels." (*Ensign,* May 1990, 53)

In that same spirit, think of the bond that is generated when we reach out and invite others to come with us to the temple. Think of the spiritual fellowship that is engendered when Church members encourage one another to be about the Lord's business in magnifying the harvest of the work accomplished through the Spirit of Elijah. Elder Dallin H. Oaks stated, in this regard: "A person who invites another to come along to the temple helps perfect the Saints as well as redeem the dead. All who attend the temple will be strengthened by the personal associations and Spirit in the house of the Lord. Adult members should be encouraged to receive their temple ordinances and to keep the covenants they have made in the temples. And young people should be encouraged to prepare for missions and temple marriages" (*Ensign,* June 1989, 6).

Several years ago, LaRene Gaunt, associate editor of the *Ensign,* reported a touching illustration of the influence that temple associations can have on spiritual development:

> One young man, recently returned from the New Zealand Auckland Mission, remembers when he received his endowment. "For about a year, my dad and I had a tradition of going to the temple every week to do baptisms for the dead to help me get ready to go on a mission," says the elder. "When I finally went to the temple to receive my own endowment, I was ready. I attended the temple as much as I could before I left for my mission and participated in the ordinances. I'm amazed at how much I learned. Bits and pieces of knowledge started to come together, and I understood them in a new way.
>
> "I'm grateful that my dad and I took the opportunity to take refuge at least once a week in the house of the Lord. The blessings that I have received there are too numerous

to name. In the past, my dad and I could sit in the same room and be a thousand miles apart. Going to the temple together, we found a friendship we never knew was there." (*Ensign,* Oct. 1994, 6)

8. Spirituality—the ongoing process of taking upon ourselves the divine nature. In baptism we take upon ourselves the name of Christ; in temple service we take upon ourselves the role of Christ. The vicarious service rendered in the temple in behalf of others is an unsurpassed manifestation of how to become more like the Savior. We prepare for the temple by taking upon ourselves the divine nature of Christ; we display that nature by doing for others in the temple what they cannot do for themselves. That is one of the greatest blessings of temple work.

The temple is the learning laboratory of spirituality. Within its walls transpires the great cycle of spiritual development: we prepare by becoming more like Christ; we perform our service in the temple like unto Christ—thus enhancing and increasing our spirituality; then we prepare yet again by emulating the Savior and return to the temple to act as saviors on Mount Zion—with the reward of receiving even more spiritual vitality. The process of enlarging the ranks of those who achieve and maintain temple worthiness has a profound and miraculous influence on the sociality within the kingdom of God. The result is an increase in devotion and expansion of the vision of promised celestial blessings in our lives, and a grand suffusion of harmony and fellowship among the Saints of God. President Howard W. Hunter taught:

> Temple worthiness is the key to building the kingdom. Earlier this month I began my ministry by expressing a deep desire to have more and more Church members become temple worthy. As in Joseph's [Smith's] day, having worthy and endowed members is the key to building the kingdom in all the world. Temple worthiness ensures that our lives are in harmony with the will of the Lord, and we are attuned to receive his guidance in our lives. (*THWH,* 240)

We have seen that preparing for the temple includes the process of taking upon ourselves more fully the divine nature of the Lord by strengthening such qualities as faith, virtue, knowledge, temperance, patience, brotherly kindness, godliness, charity, humility, and diligence. This comes as a result of obedience and sanctification through the "merits, and mercy, and grace of the Holy Messiah" (2 Ne. 2:8). Said President James E. Faust: "In the temples of the Lord, we learn obedience. We learn sacrifice. We make the vows of chastity and have our lives consecrated to holy purposes. It is possible for us to be purged and purified and to have our sins washed away so that we may come before the Lord as clean, white, and spotless as the newly fallen snow" (*Ensign,* Aug. 2001, 2).

May we all humbly and prayerfully make the temple a centerpiece of our lives in order to enjoy the heavenly blessings of increased spirituality and righteousness.

9. Betterment of our current circumstances. Let us not forget that temple worthiness and temple participation bring a harvest of immediate and tangible blessings into our current circumstances and relationships. We will find that our lives on earth will improve, that harmony will displace any tendency toward rancor and disagreement, that honor and fidelity will dethrone any inclination toward disloyalty, that balance and perspective will mitigate against heartache and despondency.

President Gordon B. Hinckley stated the following promise:

> If every man in this church who has been ordained to the Melchizedek Priesthood were to qualify himself to hold a temple recommend, and then were to go to the house of the Lord and renew his covenants in solemnity before God and witnesses, we would be a better people. There would be little or no infidelity among us. Divorce would almost entirely disappear. So much of heartache and heartbreak would be avoided. There would be a greater measure of peace and love and happiness in our homes. There would be fewer weeping wives and weeping children. There would be a greater measure of appreciation and of mutual respect

among us. And I am confident the Lord would smile with greater favor upon us. (*Ensign,* Nov. 1995, 51)

At another time he added:

> I hope that everyone gets to the temple on a regular basis. I hope your children over twelve years of age have the opportunity of going to the temple to be baptized for the dead. If we are a temple-going people, we will be a better people, we will be better fathers and husbands, we will be better wives and mothers. I know your lives are busy. I know that you have much to do. But I make you a promise that if you will go to the house of the Lord, you will be blessed; life will be better for you. Now, please, please, my beloved brethren and sisters, avail yourselves of the great opportunity to go to the Lord's house and thereby partake of all of the marvelous blessings that are yours to be received there. (*TGBH,* 624)

10. Exaltation in the celestial kingdom of glory. Finally, the temple is the culminating zenith of the gospel of redemption and exaltation. The ultimate blessing deriving from temple service is the privilege of being able to return, in person, to the presence of the Father and the Son, having completed our journey with honor and worthiness. We recall that the Prophet Joseph Smith saw the vision of that celestial abode, describing it in these words: "The heavens were opened upon us, and I beheld the celestial kingdom of God, and the glory thereof, whether in the body or out I cannot tell. I saw the transcendent beauty of the gate through which the heirs of that kingdom will enter, which was like unto circling flames of fire; Also the blazing throne of God, whereon was seated the Father and the Son. I saw the beautiful streets of that kingdom, which had the appearance of being paved with gold" (D&C 137:1–4).

Contemplate the unimaginable joy of going to that place, having been accepted as worthy through the blessings of the plan of exaltation, having rendered an honorable accounting of talents and resources given and then magnified through obedient and faithful stewardship—thus finally being favored to hear the comforting words, "Well done, thou good and faithful servant: thou hast been faithful over a few things, I will make thee ruler over many things: enter thou into the joy of thy lord" (Matt. 25:21).

Through the grace of the Savior in effecting the infinite Atonement for the children of God, we all receive the blessing of the Resurrection unto immortality. By virtue of the same endowment of grace and mercy, we all have the opportunity to accept the solemn invitation, "Come unto the Lord with all your heart, and work out your own salvation with fear and trembling before him" (Morm. 9:27). When we come unto Christ with broken hearts and contrite spirits, availing ourselves of every needful blessing, including the endowment and sealing powers of the holy temples, we embark on the pathway leading to eternal life and exaltation. Elder Russell M. Nelson has assured us:

> If we are true and faithful in this life, we may obtain eternal life. Immortality is to live forever. Eternal life means more than simply being immortal. Eternal life is to gain exaltation in the highest heaven and live in the family unit. God declared that His grand mission statement—"my work and my glory"—is "to bring to pass the immortality and eternal life of man" [Moses 1:39]. His gift of immortality is unconditional—a free gift of salvation to all humankind. The possibility of eternal life—even exaltation—is available to us through our obedience to covenants made and ordinances received in holy temples of God. (*Ensign,* Mar. 2002, 17)

The greatest of all temple blessings is eternal life and exaltation in the celestial kingdom—in the presence of Deity. The gospel in its fullness prepares us for that very eventuality. There is no training in the Church that targets a lesser outcome than that. Elder J. Richard Clarke observed: "You are being trained and proven for residency in His Kingdom only. There are no ordinances required for the Telestial or Terrestrial Kingdoms. You are heirs for the Fullness of the Father.

To achieve this, we must strive for purity of heart and master our physical appetites as fully as possible. Our Father expects none of His children to default on his Celestial covenants, thus forfeiting our royal birthright blessings" (Brigham Young University—Idaho Devotional, Sept. 23, 2003).

The ultimate destiny of the faithful children of God is to dwell forever in His presence in a state of everlasting glory as an eternal family. The design for ascending to the summit of this consummate destination is communicated by revelation from God "which shall come hereafter by the gift and power of the Holy Ghost, the voice of God, or the ministering of angels" (D&C 20:35). Thus we are instructed how to fulfill our celestial mission, line upon line and precept upon precept. Such a curriculum in celestial learning and certification includes a succession of essential steps and ordinances that constitute, in the aggregate, our all-encompassing training and preparation for the eternities. Concerning this process, President Gordon B. Hinckley expressed his inspired views on the blessing of exaltation through the temple of the Lord:

> Truly, salvation has come to all mankind through the Son of God, who gave his life that all might live.
>
> But there is a goal beyond the Resurrection. That is exaltation in our Father's kingdom. It will be achieved by obedience to the commandments of God. It will begin with acceptance of him as our Eternal Father and of his son as our living Redeemer. It will involve participation in various ordinances, each one important and necessary. The first of these is baptism by immersion in water, without which, according to the Savior, a man cannot enter into the kingdom of God. There must follow the birth of the Spirit, the gift of the Holy Ghost. Then in succession through the years will come, for men, ordination to the priesthood, followed by the blessings of the temple for both men and women who are worthy to enter therein. These temple blessings include our washings and anointings that we may be clean before the Lord. They include the instruction service in which we are given an endowment of

obligations and blessings that motivate us to behavior compatible with the principles of the gospel. They include the sealing ordinances by which that which is bound on earth is bound in heaven, providing for the continuity of the family.

These are beautiful experiences for those who participate in them in behalf of their own welfare. But it is because their consequences are *eternal* that they are unique among all religious ordinances. (*Ensign,* Feb. 1982, 2)

Look to the Temple and Live

Building the kingdom of God in partnership with the Savior is the most fulfilling and compelling mission of the human experience. This process is one of spiritual horticulture, for we are in very deed helping the Lord to grow souls—sons and daughters of God aspiring to be "just men [and women] made perfect through Jesus the mediator of the new covenant, who wrought out this perfect atonement through the shedding of his own blood" (D&C 76:69). Becoming even as He is requires strict adherence to the law of the harvest, which embraces the indispensable steps of spiritual preparation (including faith, repentance, baptism, and receiving the gift of the Holy Ghost), acceptance and nurturing of the full array of the transformational seeds of spirituality that comprise the divine nature, tending and nursing the tender shoots of development by means of which new souls are born and mature in honor and valor before God, and harvesting the output of fruitful gospel labors within the temples of the Most High. "I am the vine, ye are the branches," said the Savior. "He that abideth in me, and I in him, the same bringeth forth much fruit: for without me ye can do nothing. . . . Herein is my Father glorified, that ye bear much fruit; so shall ye be my disciples" (John 15:5, 8).

The seeds of spirituality that contribute to the dynamic process of taking on the divine nature (see 2 Pet. 1:4) and culminate in temple ordinances include this magnificent array of heavenly qualities: ongoing and maturing faith, uncompromising virtue, knowledge of all saving principles, temperance and moderation in all things, enduring patience, uncompromising brotherly kindness, authentic godliness (with an eye single to the glory of God), boundless charity and love, humility (with its associated quality of reverence), diligence (serving with all your heart, might, mind, and strength)—all destined to transform our eternal hope into the eventual reality of exaltation and eternal life with our families in the presence of the Father and the Son.

What a superlative and daunting agenda that is! Yet we are assured that in the strength of the Lord we can do all things (see Alma 20:4). And so it is. Through steady and humble prayer, through the support and buttresses of the priesthood of God, through the loyal and faithful encouragement of family and associates, through the whisperings of the Spirit, and through enduring effort, we can make it. We can take upon ourselves the divine nature in preparation for visiting the house of the Lord regularly. We can look forward to that day when the work will be done and the harvest of joy will be upon us. What a transcendent vision to cultivate within the soul: that the hour of faith will one day evolve into the hour of knowledge, and the hour of hope into the reality of the joy of entering the presence of the Father and the Son, accompanied by our loved ones, never again to leave.

TIME TO MEDITATE AND PONDER

1. In what way is the temple the symbol of hope?

2. The sealing power of the priesthood administered in the temple transcends mortality and remains effectual in the hereafter. How does this fundamental truth help us to prepare more fully to enter the house of the Lord?

3. One of the most potent truths of the restored gospel is the comforting doctrine that loving relationships will be preserved in the eternities through the eternal family. How does this knowledge render our preparation for entering the temple more urgent and compelling?

4. What is it about the temple that generates the greatest sense of added joy, happiness, and comfort?

5. In what ways is the temple a source of protection and security?

6. Robert L. Simpson taught that "the temple is a house of revelation—yes, continuing revelation." As we prepare for the temple, what issues and challenges will we be taking before the Lord for His guidance and inspiration? How does the promise of personal revelation in the house of the Lord stimulate our desire to prepare thoroughly and with devotion?

7. Temple work is also work. How does the opportunity to sacrifice in support of the temple constitute a blessing?

8. In the scriptures we read: "And that same sociality which exists among us here will exist among us there, only it will be coupled with eternal glory, which glory we do not now enjoy" (D&C 130:1–2). How will our activity in the temple give us a glimpse of how our relationships in this life will be augmented in the hereafter when coupled with eternal glory?

9. How will returning often to the temple serve to enhance the process of our taking upon ourselves the divine nature as we strive to become more like the Savior?

10. President Gordon B. Hinckley has promised that our activity in the temple will make us a better people in this life. How have your temple experiences already started to confirm this truth?

11. The greatest of all temple blessings is eternal life and exaltation in the celestial kingdom—in the presence of Deity. How should this inspire us as we complete our preparations for entering the temple each time we visit?

12. Now that you have completed this book, what does the expression "look to the temple and live" truly mean to you?

ABOUT THE AUTHORS

ED J. PINEGAR is a retired dentist and long-time teacher of early-morning seminary and religion classes at Brigham Young University. He taught at the Joseph Smith Academy and has served as a mission president in England and at the Missionary Training Center in Provo, Utah. He has been a bishop twice and a stake president and is a temple sealer. Ed and his wife, Patricia, are the parents of eight children and reside in Orem, Utah.

RICHARD ALLEN is a husband, father, teacher, and writer. He has served on several high councils, in several stake presidencies, and as a bishop. Richard's teaching assignments in the Church have included service as a full-time missionary, instructor in various priesthood quorums, Gospel Doctrine teacher, and stake institute director. He has served as a faculty member at both Brigham Young University and The Johns Hopkins University. Richard has coauthored many articles, manuals, and books and has served on a number of national educational boards. He and his wife, Carol Lynn Hansen Allen, have four children and five grandchildren.